An Introduction to Chinese
Culture through the Family

SUNY Series in Asian Studies Development
Roger T. Ames and Peter D. Hershock, editors

An Introduction to Chinese Culture through the Family

edited by
Howard Giskin and Bettye S. Walsh

State University of New York Press

Published by
State University of New York Press, Albany

©2001 State University of New York

For information, address State University of New York Press,
90 State Street, Suite 700, Albany, NY 12207

Production by Dana Foote
Marketing by Fran Keneston

Library of Congress Cataloging-in-Publication Data

An introduction to Chinese culture through the family /
edited by Howard Giskin and Bettye S. Walsh
p. cm. — (SUNY series in Asian studies development)
Includes bibliographical references and index.
ISBN 0-7914-5047-3 (alk. paper)—ISBN 0-7914-5048-1 (pb. : alk paper)
1. China—Civilization. 2. Family—China. I. Giskin, Howard, 1956–
II. Walsh, Bettye S., 1952– III. Series

DS721 .I66 2001
951—dc21

2001020807

10 9 8 7 6 5 4 3 2 1

CONTENTS

ILLUSTRATIONS

ACKNOWLEDGMENTS

In the summer of 1996, the National Endowment for the Humanities funded a summer institute at St. Mary's College, St. Mary's City, Maryland, which brought together teaching faculty from across the United States to study the Chinese classics under the leadership of Roger T. Ames, University of Hawaii, and Henry Rosemont, Jr., St. Mary's College.

This book is a direct response to the enthusiasm and scholarship that occurred in that institute.

Visiting scholars such as Tu Wei-ming and Irene Bloom provided information and a spirit of mentorship that permeated the experience. Further, the participants—"our institute family"—should be acknowledged for their thoughtful comments, insightful connections, and focused bull sessions, which generated enthusiasm and ideas for this book. They are Roberta E. Adams, Marjorie C. B. Allison, Fay E. Beauchamp, Jesse Bohl, Lawrence E. Butler, Marthe Chandler, Stanzi Comstock, Vance Cope-Kasten, James R. Estey, Julien M. Farland, Mary F. Gallagher, Howard Giskin, S. Louise Hanes, Kathleen Marie Higgins, Shirlee A. McGuire, Joseph McKeon, Richard H. Miller, Elizabeth Hobgood Murphrey, Linda S. Pickle, Judy Schaaf, Courtney D. Schlosser, Andrew L. Thornton, Bettye S. Walsh, and Uthaiwan Wong-Opasi.

In addition, the editors gratefully acknowledge the following for their assistance with the illustrations in this volume: Addison-Wesley Longman, Inc., for permission to reprint figures 1.3 and 1.9 from C. Lindqvist, *China: Empire of Living Symbols*, © 1989 Cecilia Lindqvist. English language translation © 1991 Joan Tate (from pages 25 and 42); the British Museum Press for permission to reprint figures 1.6 and 1.7 from Jessica Rowson, *The British Museum Book of Chinese Art* (1992), © the Trustees of the British Museum, British Museum Press; Westview Press for permission to reprint figures 1.5 and 1.10 from Richard J. Smith, *China's Cultural Heritage: The Qing Dynasty, 1644–1912, Second Edition*, © 1994 by Westview Press; University of Hawaii Press for permission to reprint figure 1.8 from John De Francis, *The Chinese Language: Fact and Fantasy* (1984); China Institute in America for permission to reprint figures 8.1, 8.2, and 8.3 from N.S. Steinhardt, *Chinese Traditional Architecture* (1984); and finally Angela Daniel for providing the preliminary design concept for the cover of the book.

As with any major project, many share the credit and few the blame.

—Howard Giskin and Bettye S. Walsh, editors

PREFACE

The world is small.
— Confucius

Few newspapers can avoid the topic of China these days. It's trendy; it's news. And for the last ten years or so, the average man-on-the-street has actively tried to learn about this vast culture, or at least a facsimile, through documentaries, reportage, editorials, politically motivated soundbites, and the arts. The total effort, however, recalls Ricardo Piglia in a recent novel quoting T. S. Eliot when he writes, "We have had the experience but missed the meaning."

As general studies, liberal arts, or professional development students at the freshman and sophomore levels, we have had some experience of Chinese culture but may have missed the meaning. Real understanding of China can be found only through study of core issues, often mistakenly assumed to be *common* knowledge and thus ignored, or esoteric presentations, which quickly go beyond the beginning learner. This text, *An Introduction to Chinese Culture through the Family*, begins at the very heart of China and Chineseness—the family, *jia*.

Family as a construct in China is both enriched and complicated by social and historical practices such as rituals of ancestor worship (family as spiritual necessity) and the codes of heredity and responsibility within a clan group (family as financial and demographic necessity.) The concept of family is further enlivened by its extension to groups not connected by familial ties, such as a family of scholars or artists. China's notion of family includes communal loyalty, respect and responsibility, love, trust, and maintenance of life essence, as well as harmony and balance, through relational living. Family is, then, complex because it interweaves place, pleasure, politics, spirituality, commerce, and health in ways that other cultures may not experience.

Using *jia*, or family, as a core issue through which to approach Chinese culture, the chapter authors treat this dense concept variously. Some chapters access the material using family as metaphor while others use the authenticity of family as presented in various cultural media as a snapshot of contemporary or traditional China. In so doing, the authors provide an introduction to some ways of knowing the culture and invite the learner to delve into this fascinating world of study.

There is much yet to know about China, and even more to comprehend. But T. S. Eliot's comment about experience without the meaning wisely advises us that as we strive to comprehend that vast and powerful culture known as the Middle Kingdom, we recreate our own understanding through a combination of humility, open-mindedness, and curiosity. There is an optimism in this text that comes from the enthusiasm of the chapter authors for a topic most came to out of the sheer joy of learning new materials, and it is our hope that this volume brings the study of China alive. We invite you to enter the dialogue.

—H. G. and B. W.

Introduction

Roger T. Ames

A glance at the table of contents of this anthology tells us that the editors, Bettye Walsh and Howard Giskin, have assembled a whole range of different perspectives on Chinese culture, from the evolution of the language to folk literature to contemporary film. But there is unity in this difference. In the *Analects of Confucius*, arguably the most influential little book in human history, Confucius himself claims that his "way (*dao* 道)" is "bound together with one continuous strand."[1] The "one continuous strand" that binds this anthology together is the continuing reference to the grounding and most pervasive metaphor for "order" in the Chinese world: the family (*jia* 家).

Stephen Pepper in his *World Hypotheses* advanced a set of "root metaphors" around which Western philosophy has posited its several alternative hypotheses regarding the definition of world order: "formism" (Plato), "organicism" (Hegel), "mechanism" (Hobbes), and "contextualism" (Dewey).[2] The Chinese variation on this notion of "root metaphor" is the family.

The Chinese character for family is *jia* 家, constituted by combining the radical for "roof (*mian* 宀)" and "pig or hog (*shi* 豕)." Anyone who has traveled through Shandong province in northern China even in modern times will recall the circular homes with the smaller circular structure in the front that houses the family pig.

It is not an exaggeration to say that in the Chinese world, all relationships are familial.[3] The ruler, referred to as *tianzi* 天子, "the son of Heaven," is *fumu* 父母, "father and mother" to the people, who are the minzi 民子, "people-children." Classmates are "older brother classmates *xuexiong* 學兄," and neighbors and friends constitute a community of "aunties and uncles." To say "everybody" in Chinese, one says "big family *dajia* 大家 or "the family of people *renjia* 人家." Academic "schools" are called *jia:* "families" or "lineages" of scholars. The familial roles and relationships are projected outward from the human world onto the cosmos, dominating the imagery of the first among the Chinese classics, the *Book of Changes*, which purports to give definition to cosmic order.

1

Linda Pickle begins her chapter on the Chinese language from this cosmic sensibility. She traces Chinese orthography back to the patterns that contextualized the proto-Chinese in their natural surroundings, and the attempts of these peoples to decipher their world. Out of this early experience emerges different scripts and signs. There are the fluid trigrams and hexagrams of the *Book of Changes* that provide its reader with a vocabulary of images for reflecting on and making sense of specific situations; there are the early yet very sophisticated markings on the oracle bones used to communicate with the ancestors, investing this early written language with its religious aura. Even in this earliest form, the Chinese script is sacred: a moving line that is relied upon diachronically to connect the present generation with those who have come before, and to pass on their wisdom and values to those yet to come. As it evolved, this script became the medium in which the scholar-apprentices were educated and trained for office, in which they reported to their ruler, and in which they exercised the power of government over what is literally called the "state-family (*guojia* 國家)."

The moving line, in the form of the standardized Chinese script, also served to unite the sinitic peoples synchronically through the use of a single, mutually understandable, written language. The word "sinitic" is appropriate because the language joined not only the ethnically diverse Chinese into a single population, but also drew in the border peoples of Korea, Japan, and Vietnam.

The role of the written language, parsed phonetically into "families" of cognate characters, and again semantically into terms that share a common classifier, has not been without controversy in modern times. Some scholars attribute the enormous accomplishments of Chinese civilization to the persistence of this medium, while others argue that China has succeeded as a culture not because of the written script, but in spite of it.

In Pickle's introduction to the nature and function of the Chinese language, she concentrates on the associative, analogical, and correlative character of both the spoken and written languages, illustrating how these features not only reflect but further reinforce the culture's commitment to the centrality of "family" as its governing metaphor.

Turning to the culture itself, Vance Cope-Kasten attempts to provide a general definition of philosophy and to argue for the inclusion of the classical tradition within these parameters. Given that important philosophical assumptions are sedimented into natural languages, Cope-Kasten mines a sampling of character clusters to assay their cultural implications. At the center of the Chinese world view—those assumptions about how one ought to live one's life—is the inordinate emphasis on the family, the relationships that constitute it, and the way in which it functions to get the most out of those who participate fully in it. All of the institutions of community, from religion to education to polity, are constructed around and function on the model of the family. Government, for better and for worse, has been largely patriarchal, appealing mostly to those virtues which, when adequately cultivated, make families work: credibility and trust, obligation and deference, contribution and privilege.

In the *Book of Changes* and the Daoist tradition, we find that the cosmos itself operates according to the interdependent and productive images of the human family, and pursues at the broadest level its highest goal: a productive harmony. There is a wonderful symmetry to the cyclical processes in which nurturing parents nurse their infants, only in the evening of life to be nursed and cared for by their grown children.

In living the philosophical life, the process of learning and transmitting the tradition occurs within philosophical lineages called "*jia* 家." Methodologically as well, Chinese philosophy is synthetic and associative. Thinking effectively means tracing out relationships and mapping out patterns, thereby making one's way in the world while avoiding obstacles to one's progress. "Reasoning" in Chinese is "tracing out contiguous patterns (heli 合理)," and "coming to know" is "unraveling patterns (lijie 理解)." Living harmoniously is nurturing those relationships which locate one within the matrix of a particular family and community.

Cope-Kasten then allows the canonical texts of classical Chinese philosophy, both Confucian and Daoist, to speak for themselves. This direct engagement with the philosophical text reveals how they present their wisdom by prompting the reader to pursue relevant associations in this literature, thereby deepening and extending one's understanding in the process of making the text one's own.

Laurence E. Butler's treatment of the visual arts in the Chinese tradition reminds the reader of some of the presuppositions of Chinese medicine. Chinese medicine is primarily physiological, and only derivatively anatomical. That is, health is to found and encouraged relationally in the way in which the various "orbes" of the body interact. The question is not *what* is the "heart," but *how* does it function systemically in the most productive way.

Butler is interested in artifacts as they functioned *in situ* to establish and encourage certain values. His primary question is: how were they used? Going back to the beginnings of Chinese civilization, much of the extant artifacts are associated with funeral ceremonies, sacrifices for the dead, and various forms of ancestor worship—practices directed deliberately at reinforcing a sense of family continuity within the living community. In context, their sacred function of perpetuating the ancestral lineage and its cultural values was even more important than their status and value as articles of exquisite workmanship.

As we learned in the chapter by Cope-Kasten, kingship and cosmos were ordered on familial lines, and ritual practices and their objects were necessary to sustain equilibrium at every level. Disparities in both quality and amount of grave goods is fair evidence of the society's hierarchical organization, and inscriptions on these objects are a record of the achievements bequeathed to posterity by its forbearers. In a cultural tradition that is defined by the observance of ritualized roles and relationships, the artifacts are themselves a documentary history of the ways of thinking and living that occasioned their production. Even though, in the course of time, clay surrogates came to replace human companions and earthly goods in the tombs, the original function of buried artifacts to stabilize and sustain the family-based social structure within the cosmos still continued in richly different expression across the dynasties. Just as the funerary objects are a material remnant of early attempts to cultivate a social and political order based on the model of family life, so the calligraphy and painting of later dynasties is a lingering expression of the personal cultivation of the literatus who did so to serve this same project. Throughout the tradition, the highest art is the presentation of the character of the literatus which, when aggregated, constitutes a narrative of Chinese communal order over time.

Mary Gallagher brings the conversation to the issues of women and gender in both traditional and modern China. She begins this study by reconstructing the image of a woman who, because of her gender and the institutionalized prejudice that denigrated it, suffered unremitting oppression from classical times down to the present day. Availing herself of a range of resources that have told this unhappy story, from folk beliefs to the orthodox literature of Confucianism, Gallagher paints a portrait that is unrelenting in its misery and misfortune.But this familiar picture might not be the entire story, and in fact, might nullify the heroic struggle that Chinese woman has waged within these constraints to find her own realization. There might be, suggests Gallagher, behavioral evidence available only for recent times that requires us to qualify our understanding of the experience of Chinese women earlier in the tradition. Without in any way justifying a repressive tradition, Gallagher provides a more complex and nuanced picture in which woman is ready to take advantage of her circumstances to turn misery into strength. There is clear evidence that down to the post-Mao era, woman in China has been unwilling to accept her institutionally defined inferiority, and continues to use whatever flexibility obtains within the social structure to assert her own worth.

Going back to the *Book of Rites* (*Liji*), Kathleen Higgins focuses her discussion of Chinese music on the early association between musical notes in the pentatonic scale, and the five family relations. In fact, this kind of relational association—defining the world in terms of a numbered pattern of correlations—is distinctive of Chinese cosmology broadly. What might seem at first to modern students of Chinese culture to be rather random and tentative associations are not only revealing of how the Chinese thought generally about order in the world but, more concretely, once one has been able to find a perspective within the world of classical China, these correlations make a great deal of sense.

In the Chinese world in which all things, including human beings, are constituted as a matrix of relationships, it is the perceived function of music to encourage productive harmony in these relationships. Thus, as Higgins points out, music has traditionally had a central place in Chinese ethics, social, and political philosophy, the full range of resolutely familial relationships extending outward as concentric circles from one's own personal center. Importantly, the character for "music (*yue* 樂)" actually means "to play music." The *performers* of music both shape and are shaped by the music that they make.

Higgins appeals to classical Chinese literature to draw the rather direct line between the capacity of music to foster harmonious relationships and the flourishing and communicating community. In fact, she sees music as a resource for cultivating personal equanimity, encouraging interpersonal harmony, and at an even more profound depth, effecting an appropriate relationship within the natural world itself. It is at this more profound cosmic level that Higgins turns from Confucianism to associate music with the "nonassertive activity (*wuwei* 無 爲)" and the "spontaneity (*ziran* 自然)" that are defining of the Daoist sensibility. It is the "free and easy wandering (*xiaoyaoyou* 逍遙遊)" of the dancing Daoist that is perhaps most instructive in teaching us to live harmonious and productive lives.

In Mary Gallagher's chapter on women and gender we learned that, beyond the orthodox literary canons, folk beliefs too can be an important window on cultural values. Howard Giskin uses specific selections from his own published collection of Chinese folktales as a demonstration of how this oral tradition of stories reveals attitudes about community identity and family values.

His first story, "Dragon Pond," is a rather straightforward account of how a particular community came to possess a local aquarian resource—a source of both food and water—by exhibiting public virtue. Such a story not only fosters a sense of local identity but serves to encourage community values in the population. Telling of the Chinese world is the appeal to the *long* 龍(translated as "dragon"), a totemic icon that can be traced back into the earliest material evidence of the culture, representing as it does an emerging harmony through the accommodation of ethnic diversity.

But symbols are seldom simple. The second story brings into question the often positive image of the "dragon" in recounting its destructive force in a particular village, and the self-sacrifice of a young couple in ridding their community of this evil.

Other selections are only deceptively transparent and really require context and interpretation. "River Snail Girl," for example, is a tale of a poor fisherman who, through empathy with other living creatures, is able to enrich his own life when the snail transforms into a beautiful young woman. Complexity arises when we reflect on the limited possibilities that those who are poor and without status have in a resolutely hierarchical society, with the unlikely intervention of "magic" being the only possibility for their escape. Further, the gender prejudice of this patriarchal tradition surfaces in the observation that this story could only be told of a young man. That is, even in folktales, the culture is unforgiving: the plight of disadvantaged young women, as we discover in other selections, is almost always resolved in their untimely death.

Giskin's point is made: folktales no less than elite culture provide ready access to often distinctive cultural assumptions.

Fay Beauchamp introduces the reader to the complexities entailed in attempting to interpret Chinese literature. David McCraw, an expert in Chinese premodern poetry, has used the many voices in conversation within a Bachian fugue as an analogy for the many perspectives nested within the language of the Chinese poem. Beauchamp, comparing two translations of a selection from the *Book of*

Odes, demonstrates how translation compounds this layering, bringing both historical commentary and the "prejudices" of the never-innocent translator into the swim. The translator's selection of terms, often reflecting real ambiguities within the original language, can conjure forth a radically different experience in the reader—in this particular instance, the difference between a disgruntled military officer, a long-suffering, neglected wife, and a chaste widow.

One important point that Beauchamp underscores is the way in which classical Chinese philosophical literature echoes through the tradition, made present in poetry and prose by oblique allusions that test the memory and acuity of the reader. She also uses the poetry of Du Fu and the short stories of Lu Xun to argue emphatically that these are pieces of a human narrative, where the personal response of the author to traumatic and sometimes overwhelming historical circumstances is implicated within the literary work itself.

Throughout her essay, Beauchamp challenges what are often wise cautions about reductionism that would set limits on the project of interpretation. While appreciating the degree of difference that situates Tang poetry and the British Romantics in radically different worlds, there is also much to be gained in living dangerously, creating new possibilities for understanding by following likely and sometimes less likely correlations where they might lead.

If there is any remaining question about the vagaries of interpretation, they are laid to rest by the divided and conflicted assessments of Ding Ling's genius, one of this century's most enigmatic, irrepressible literary heroes. A glimpse at the struggle of this one woman against the tyrannies of history, embedded in a swirling world of Gogol and the Guomindang, Ibsen and thought reform, May Fourth and Guo Moro, evokes the image of the solitary figure defying the tanks at Tiananmen.

In Chinese, the character for "house" and "family" is one and the same: *jia* 家. This observation opens Judy Schaaf's exploration of Chinese architecture and how it has been influenced by those ways of thinking and living that are distinctively Chinese. Said another way, from cave dwellings to *fengshui* to tamped earth walls, the construction of the varied structures in which the Chinese have lived their lives, in both classical and modern China, are both functional and unique to their place, revealing both the continuities and the diversity that make up the Chinese landscape. The houses and their sitings reflect the traditional "Confucian" sensibility, *yi* 義, the value of construing the locally available elements, both human and material, to maximize their fit. It is for this reason that one way the story of contemporary China can be told is through the changing face of the architecture.

Schaaf begins her discussion by identifying three Confucian sensibilities that make Chinese architecture one among a range of "Chinese" discourses. It is continuous with using names properly (*zhengming* 正名), observing ritual propriety (*li* 禮), playing music (*yue* 樂), and embodying culture (*ti* 體). That is, Chinese architecture strives to effect *proper order*, it is *performative*, and it is *adaptive*. We can borrow a passage from the *Analects of Confucius* that might suggest how constructing an appropriate house would be productive of a robust and vital home:

"Were the Lord of Wey to turn the administration of his state over to you, what would be your first priority?" asked Zilu.

"Without question it would be to insure that names are used properly (*zhengming*正名)," replied the Master.

"Would you be as impractical as that?" responded Zilu. "What is it for names to be used properly anyway?"

"How can you be so dense!" replied Confucius. "An exemplary person (*junzi* 君子) defers on things he does not understand. When names are not used properly, language will not be used effectively; when language is not used effectively, matters will not be taken care of; when matters are not taken care of, the observance of ritual propriety (*li* 禮) and the playing of music (*yue* 樂) will not flourish; when the observance of ritual propriety and the playing of music do not flourish, the application of laws and punishments will not be on the mark; when the application of laws and punishments is not on the mark, the people will not know what to do with themselves. Thus, when the exemplary person puts a name to something, it can certainly be spoken, and when spoken it can certainly be acted upon. There is nothing careless in the attitude of the exemplary person toward what is said."[4]

Siting houses appropriate to the topography and environment, constructing them to accommodate seasonal changes, furnishing and decorating them according to local religious values and customs, and living in them in a way that reflects proper family hierarchies is surely an extension of Confucius's message to Zilu.

Having located architecture within a cultural landscape, Schaaf introduces a sampling of the many kinds of buildings that give China its color and tradition, taking us on a trip across time and geography. An interesting observation she makes is that in spite of the diverse ways in which the Chinese have housed and continue to house themselves, there is almost always an immediately discernable continuity among the structures in any particular local. This notion of localized "harmony (*he* 和)" is again a central cultural value. Schaaf's conclusion recounts how recent it is that through contemporary technologies such as film, this place called China has at last arisen on our academic horizon, providing access to a truly wonderful world. This provides an easy segue for the final chapter in this volume: Bettye Walsh's analysis of contemporary Chinese film as a medium for portraying and critiquing traditional Chinese family values.

Philosophically, neither "change" nor "context" will be denied in the Chinese world. It is for this reason that "narrative" has been a privileged approach in understanding this tradition and its values. Bettye Walsh uses an exploration of Chinese cinema, a contemporary technology with enormous pedagogical power, to tell the Chinese story.

Selecting several of the internationally acclaimed "fifth-generation" films, Walsh identifies techniques that bring the tradition of the Chinese family dramatically (and often traumatically) to life. The directors avail themselves of the existential transparency of film to resist any uncritical romanticization of an institution that reflects perhaps the best and the worst that Chinese culture has to offer. There is the patient strength of Jiazhen as she endures the madness of modern China in "To Live" (much better translated "To Endure"), the faceless institutionalized decadence of concubinage in "Raise the Red Lantern," and the sometimes comic, often violent, and always poignant story of the narrator's grandparents in "Red Sorghum." What these films share in common is the tension between circumstances and persistent traditional values in the holocaust of twentieth-century China (we forget that Mao's Great Leap Forward cost as many if not more lives as either one of the World Wars).

Walsh's chapter is an appropriate end to this anthology because, like the narrative of Chinese culture itself, it is episodic and inconclusive: just a moment, just a taste. The complexities of this world will not resolve to common categories, and where language will always let us down, an image and a feeling is perhaps our best hope for understanding.

Notes

1. Roger T. Ames and Henry Rosemont, Jr., *The Analects of Confucius: A Philosophical Translation*. New York: Ballantine, 1998. 4.15.

2. See Stephen Pepper, *Work Hypotheses*. Berkeley: University of California Press, 1942. See also *Concept and Quality: A World Hypothesis*. La Salle, Ill: Open Court, 1967.

3. Ambrose King, "The Individual and the Group in Confucianism: A Relational Perspective." In *Individualism and Holism: Studies in Confucian and Taoist Values*, Donald Munro (ed.). Ann Arbor: University of Michigan Press, 1985.

4. Ames and Rosemont (1998), 3.3.

1

Written and Spoken Chinese: Expression of Culture and Heritage

Linda S. Pickle

Few languages reflect the cultural heritage to which they belong to the extent that Chinese does, particularly in its oral nature and the traditions associated with its script. Moreover, this is only partly the result of the language and the script having received the imprint of cultural forces. To an extent difficult to·assess, the written characters that non-Chinese find so enigmatic both shaped and were shaped by the linguistic qualities of the language they represent. And probably no other tradition of written language has influenced a people's culture as profoundly. Chinese language and culture are so closely intertwined as to make it difficult to say which has influenced the other more. As will be seen in the following pages, the primary quality they share is that of the central role of proximity and relationship, of "family" in the broadest sense. This chapter explores the many parallels between the linguistic qualities of the language that reveal this focus and various cultural expressions of the emphasis on proximity and relationship. How the script came to influence the development of Chinese history and culture through its identification with political power, religious potency, and aesthetic ideals is the other primary focus of this chapter.

Legendary Origins and Philosophical Implications of the Script

Fuxi[1] 伏羲 (trad. 2852–2738 B.C.E.) is a good departure point for a discussion of the significance of language and writing in the Chinese cultural tradition. This first of the legendary three sage-kings and ancestral founders of China is credited with some of the most fundamental accomplishments necessary for the establishment of society as the Chinese came to know it. Fuxi taught people how to hunt and domesticate animals and how to cook. He invented the first calendar and the first musical instruments, as well as the fishing net and the fish cage (Bodde 130; Williams 200–202, 281). The latter inventions established one of the four basic callings necessary to early society in the proto-Middle Kingdom, that of the fisherman (the others being peasant, woodcutter, and scholar). Within the overarching framework of the present collection of essays, it is also noteworthy that Fuxi is supposed to have instituted marriage:

> Flying in the face of Chinese morality as it was to develop later, he married his sister Nü-gua; and reliefs dating from Han times show the two in close embrace like intertwined snakes, with Fu-xi himself holding in one hand the protractor which is the symbol of building and architecture. The protractor also serves as the symbol of the magic and curative forces in nature. (Eberhard 121)

So Fuxi made it possible for the Chinese to feed and house themselves, he showed them how to understand, accommodate, and impose order on the natural world, he enabled them to develop the ritual use of music, and he founded the most central Chinese social and cultural unit, the family. But as if these accomplishments were not enough, Fuxi is said to have been the originator of the Chinese writing system:

> History relates that, at the moment Fu Hsi [Fuxi] was seeking to combine the characters proper to express the various forms of matter, and the relation between things physical and intellectual, a wonderful horse came out of the river, bearing on his back certain signs, of which the philosophic legislator formed the eight diagrams which have preserved his name. (Williams 441, 443)[2]

These signs were the eight trigrams of the *Yijing* (*Book of Changes*), the classic work of divination. (See figure 1.1) Within the Chinese tradition, the trigrams are considered to be the forms from which the script developed. A closer examination of the myth of their invention will elucidate the central significance of written Chinese within this ancient culture.

An important version of the story of Fuxi's creation of the trigrams is contained at the beginning of chapter 2 "History of Civilization," in part 2 of the *Dajuan* (*The Great Treatise*), the commentary on the *Yijing* said to have been written by Confucius (551–479 B.C.E.). It helps us understand the reverence with which the Chinese have regarded their script:

> When in early antiquity Pao Hsi [Baoxi, another name for Fuxi] ruled the world, he looked upward and contemplated the images in the heavens; he looked downward and contemplated the patterns on earth. He contemplated the markings of birds and beasts and the adaptations to the regions. He proceeded directly from himself and indirectly from objects. Thus he invented the eight trigrams in order to enter into connection with virtues of

the light of the gods and to regulate the conditions of all beings. (Wilhelm 328–329)

This passage makes clear that the trigrams are inscriptions that represent and are part of the pattern of existence. They connect humankind with the divine order of things and with nature, and therefore have a moral and philosophical dimension. They grant the power to regulate existence within the human sphere.

The *Yijing* contains the exegesis of the sixty-four hexagrams that result from the various combinations of the trigrams devised by Fuxi. This ancient text, the earliest versions of which probably date from the Xia dynasty (trad. 2205–1766 B.C.E.), has fuelled philosophical discussion and thought for thousands of years in China. The trigrams reflect and explain the most fundamental quality of life in the Chinese view of things: that all things are related because they are interdependent, constantly changing into something else. The connection between this cultural premise and the trigrams and hexagrams of the *Yijing* and the written characters that, it is said, evolved from them may be the most fundamental reason why the script attained its lasting cultural potency.[3]

To understand this, we have to appreciate the sense the Chinese have that the visual and symbolic qualities of the trigrams and hexagrams, like those of Chinese calligraphy, incorporate both movement and quiescence simultaneously. The solid and the broken lines that comprise the trigrams are constantly on the verge of changing into their opposite, related form, as are the configurations of the hexagrams. Similarly, it is the communication of the tension in calligraphy between the moving line of the hand and the static line laid down by the brush that the Chinese prize in this art form. The dynamic line of calligraphy represents the energy (*qi* 氣) that permeates and animates the cosmos. Attaining skill in calligraphy is therefore more than "learning how to write" or developing an artistic talent.

Figure 1.1 The *yinyang* symbol with the eight trigrams of the *Yijing*.

It is an exercise in expressing the underlying patterns of existence, in channeling the shared energy of self and place, and in developing an understanding of these forces and of how to regulate them within oneself.[4]

For more than two thousand years, learning to write in China has been undertaken for moral and social purposes rather than merely for the utilitarian goal of communication. Children learn to shape written characters in order to shape their character in appropriate ways. Certainly the exercise of memorizing thousands of characters and drawing them innumerable times in the unforgiving medium of ink painted on paper demands powers of concentration, determination, and perseverance that few Westerners ask of their children in quite the same way. Understandably, then, the Chinese believe that this process results in a script that reveals the most fundamental qualities of the calligrapher. A common saying states: *Jian zi ru jian ren* 見字如見人 ("Seeing the written character is just like seeing the person"). Still today, Chinese with aspirations for their children's future emphasize good calligraphy and often arrange extra lessons for them. Many prospective employers ask for a handwritten essay and judge the applicant not only by the content of the essay, but also by the quality of the personal character the script reveals.[5]

The family of words associated with *wen* 文, the term that means "inscription" or "to inscribe, articulate," illuminates the central position of calligraphy in Chinese culture and aesthetics. *Wen* or *wenzi* 文字 is the term for "Chinese character," that is, the individual cipher. *Wen* also appears as part of other terms related to writing and to the attainment of the high cultivation that literacy traditionally implied: *wenxue* 文學 ("literature"), *wenyi* 文藝 ("literature and art"), *wenwu* 文物 ("cultural or historical relic"), and *wenren* 文人 ("man of letters, scholar, literatus"). Significantly, it forms part of the words for "culture" itself (*wenhua* 文化) and for "civilization" (*wenming* 文明). In a characteristically allusive fashion, *wen* also appears in *tianwen* 天文 ("astronomy"). This combination of the words for "heaven" and "inscription" suggests the continuity between nature and culture and the interrelationships between the configurations of the natural realm and human scholarly and intellectual endeavors that guided Fuxi in his creation of the trigrams and the script. The Chinese conviction that persistent patterns permeate and unify all of existence resonates in this complex of related terms.

The interconnectedness of the many aspects of nature, life, and experience noted here at the core of the complex of ideas connected to *wen* is like that of the interrelatedness within a family. The eight trigrams of the *Yijing*, with which the written script is so closely associated, are also visualized as a family. The two lines of which they are composed stand for the basic concepts of the cosmos: *yin* 陰, the broken line, represents the female (or receptive, yielding) principle, and *yang* 陽, the solid line, represents the masculine (or dynamic, creative) principle. This is the most fundamental example of what is the pervasive Chinese way of viewing the world and existence: in terms of related, complementary opposites. This *yinyang* conceptualization of existence permeates every aspect of the *Yijing* and of the ever-changing world it explicates. Everything is related and, animated by *qi*, is in flux, just as in personal relationships within the family.[6] The family metaphor lends itself well to the representation of this world view. Thus the trigram composed of three solid lines is Qian 乾, the creative principle and the father. The trigram composed of three broken lines is Kun 坤, the receptive principle and the mother. The other six signs, various combinations of the broken and unbroken lines, are the three sons and three daughters. Taken together, this metaphorical family encompasses all "tendencies of movement" (Wilhelm *l*) of which existence is possible. The sixty-four hexagrams of the *Yijing*, comprised of all possible pairings of the eight trigrams, serve as expressions of the great principle of change that, in the Chinese view, can be deciphered and understood. The written script as well, if properly executed, can mirror the cosmic energy and patterns that underlie that principle of change and aid in communicating and understanding it.

Religious, Political, and Cultural Power of the Script

In addition to the ancient philosophical legacy of the *Yijing* that, by association, also permeates the traditional calligraphic script, writing and the characters used in the script came to be endowed with other potent cultural meanings. This evolved through the association of the script and of the ability to write with religious authority, political power, and high art. The connection to religious authority and political power was made through the earliest extant uses of writing during the Shang dynasty (1766–1122 B.C.E.), the calligraphic figures (*jiaguwen* 甲骨文) inscribed on the shells of tortoises and on the scapular bones of ox. The kings and shamans at the royal courts used these shells and bones for the purposes of divination. They drilled small depressions at regular intervals into them and inserted heated sticks or rods into the hollows in order to induce cracks that could be "read" as messages from the royal ancestors, who had access to their great ancestral god, Shangdi 上帝. The shamans then made predictions and decisions on matters as diverse as harvests, births, battles, and weather conditions and inscribed the results of the divinations on the oracle bones. The earliest answers from the ancestral gods were probably the unbroken line (for "yes") and the broken line (for "no") that became the trigrams of the *Yijing* (Wilhelm xlix). As time went on, the ceremonies of divination came to be performed daily during the Shang era and the following Zhou dynasty (1122–256 B.C.E.) for matters great and small. The recording of the answers and the commentary on them became correspondingly more complex, demanding a sophisticated record keeping that by the Zhou era resulted in the evolution of thousands of early characters (probably 5000, according to Gernet, *A History* 47). The first "books" were mat-like rolls of bamboo strips (*pian* 篇) on which the characters were painted with ink and brush, which may account for the traditional Chinese custom of writing in vertical columns from top to bottom and from right to left. Rolls of silk (*juan* 卷) were also used in these early times, until they were supplanted by rolls of the paper that the Chinese invented in the first century B.C.E. (Farrer 85–87).

The high cost of silk for the scrolls enhanced the value placed on writing, and the quasi-religious oracle bone inscriptions gave the script a sacred aura. The veneration for writing also grew because the characters were used within and upon the precious bronze sacrificial vessels and ritual objects that were so closely associated with the authority of the Shang and Zhou rulers. These inscriptions (*jinwen* 金文) often had to do with social status and family identity. For example, inscriptions in Shang and Zhou bronze ritual vessels on display at the Chicago Art Institute usually indicate the clan that used them. Some typical examples include *Zi Fu Geng* (made for Father Geng of the Zi family), *Ya Bing Fu Ji* (made for Father Ji of the [Ya] Bing family), and *Ja Qi Fu Yi* (made for Father Yi of the [Ya] Qi family).[7]

Given the mythical and concrete origins of the written script through its associations with Fuxi and with the revelations of the divine ancestors on the Shang and Zhou oracle bones and shells, it is perhaps not surprising that the characters were so highly revered and considered to have magical properties. As representations of patterns visible in nature, they not only communicated ideas but also assumed the force of the powers that ordered the cosmos. Richard J. Smith has written of the positive and negative potency attributed to writing in the Qing dynasty (1644–1911 C.E.):

> On the one hand, prayers were often written and then burned as the most efficacious way of communicating with the gods. Protective charms, designed to be hung inside the home or work place, often consisted only of a single character (or group of characters) with positive associations, such as "peace," "wealth," or "blessings." Auspicious "spring couplets" (*chunlian*), printed on red paper and displayed outside of virtually all Chinese households and businesses during the lunar New Year, had the same basic purpose. On the other hand, many Chinese believed that a piece of paper with the character "to kill" on it, or one that bore the word for a disease, a destructive animal, or an evil spirit, actually had the capacity to harm another person. (*China's* 106)

Educated Chinese have largely abandoned the negative superstitions described here, but they still hang *chunlian* 春聯 and four-character expressions conveying messages like *pan tao ji qing* ("long life and happiness galore"). They also display characters like that for *shou* 壽 ("longevity"—see figure 1.2) in their homes and communities for the sake of the positive connotations they incorporate.

The reverence accorded religious writing also contributed to the respect and power accorded the written word in Chinese cultural history. Both Buddhism (introduced into China from India ca. 150 C.E.) and Daoism stressed the copying of religious scripture as a meritorious deed, with "merit being judged both by the quantity of texts copied and the quality of the calligraphy" (Farrer 95). The reverence for the content of the text was transferred to the medium in which it was transmitted, with emphasis placed on the faithful transmission of calligraphic strokes so as not to lose any of the text's spiritual effectiveness. The same stress on exact knowl-

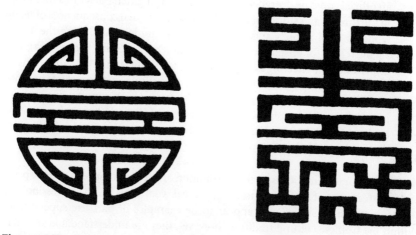

Figure 1.2 Two decorative versions of the *shou* character ("longevity").

edge and imitation of master texts as a basis for self-expression came to typify the Chinese state examination system and the traditions of painting and poetry.[8]

The close association of the characters to the tools of political decision making and authority during the Shang and Zhou dynasties also helps explain the power ascribed to them. This association was strengthened and eventually institutionalized when, during the Han dynasty (206 B.C.E.–220 C.E.), writing was put in the service of government and the scholar-official class came into being. By the end of the Song dynasty (1127–1279 C.E.), the Chinese system of government by officials was firmly established, as was the qualifying state examination system, based on the close study, memorization, and internalization of the Confucian classic texts.

Various stories show the extent to which the uses of writing by a privileged elite and the traditions associated with written texts and the script endowed them with potency. Farrer cites the following example:

> One of the most remarkable enterprises in the history of the Buddhist faith in China was the carving of the canon on stone slabs at Yunjusi, a monastery at Fangshan near Beijing. A monk called Jingwan conceived the project during the Sui dynasty (589–618 C.E.), because he thought the end of the world was near and he wished to ensure that the Buddhist texts would survive the ensuing catastrophes. He and his successors were responsible for engraving more than 14,620 slabs, which were then buried in caves in the mountainside and in pits in the ground. (95–96)

Smith offers interesting evidence of the care that had to be taken with the script. During the Qing, the last imperial dynasty, an official could be degraded for miswriting a single character in a memorial to the throne, and stories of the political and personal consequences of using taboo or even vaguely suggestive characters are legion. During the Yong-zheng reign, for instance, an official named Zha Siting (1664–1727) was imprisoned for selecting a classical phrase for the provincial examinations in Jianxi province that contained two characters similar in appearance to those of the emperor's reign title if the top portions had been cut off. Qing author-ities interpreted this phrase as an expression of Zha's wish that the emperor be decapitated. Zha died in prison, and orders were given for his body to be dismembered. (*China's* 105–106)

For contemporary Americans, with our tradition of freedom of speech and the press and our treatment of language and writing as everyday tools of self-expression and self-assertion, such stories may appear to be examples of barbaric superstition. Within the Chinese cultural tradition, however, they are understandable articula-tions of ancient patterns of thought.

The reverence with which the Chinese traditionally regarded the script was based most fundamentally on the assumption that it reflects and communicates the primeval patterns of the universe. In addition, its political function and its in-timate association with political and religious authority bolstered the respect given the written language. The almost exclusive possession of literacy by a powerful elite for thousands of years also did its part in conferring value on it. In addition to these historical, social, and cultural reasons, we may attribute part of the Chinese veneration of their written script to a natural attachment that any people might feel toward one of its most fundamental means of communication. Some might also take a more negative view and assert that the pride in and preference for their script that the Chinese exhibit are aspects of the isolationist arrogance and sense of cultural superiority that so long typified the literate elite of the Middle Kingdom. Whatever our opinion of the latter assertion, it is certain, however, that a decisive element in Chinese attitudes toward their traditional script is the aesthetic aura that came to surround the characters. Even today, of the "three perfections" (*san-jue* 三 絕—calligraphy, painting, and poetry), calligraphy is considered the highest and the most fundamental of all the art forms.

As mentioned above, the mastery of this art, like all valued knowledge and ability in China, began from imitation of the masters and from intimate familiarity with the great texts that had been written with the script. Writing, already imbued with political and religious authority, came to be equated with culture. It was the mark of the "family" of scholar-officials. The exemplary literate man (*wenren*), who invested many years of his life in memorizing the classic texts, in practicing calligraphy, and in developing subtle skills of literary expression and artistic taste, also then was the man "qualified to exercise political functions" (Gernet, *A History* 33). This helps explain why the written word in the Chinese world possesses the value and power which is the prerogative of the spoken word in other parts of the

world that developed writing much later and that do not have the strong bureaucratic tradition of China.[9]

The ancient legacy that associates political and social power, aesthetic ideals,
divination, moral development, and fundamental conceptualizations of the cosmos with the script helps us understand why the centrality of the written word is
one of the most distinctive features of the Chinese cultural tradition. As Derk
Bodde has said, "It is perhaps no accident that three of China's greatest inventions—paper, block printing, and movable type—are all closely associated with
writing" (27). As late as the nineteenth century, Pagodas for Cherishing the Written Word (*xizi ta*), dedicated to the ritual burning of waste paper, existed in many
cities (Smith, *China's* 105). Bodde writes further of the Chinese reverence for written artifacts:

> So great was the mystique of the written word that in imperial times papers
> bearing writing could not be indiscriminately discarded in the streets. This
> was not so much because they polluted the streets as that such an act would
> show disrespect to the written word. The author, as a student in Peking in the
> 1930s, remembers still occasionally seeing trash receptacles in public places
> inscribed with the traditional exhortation: *Ching hsi tzu chih* [*Jing xi zi chi* 敬
> 惜字紙], "Respect and care for written paper." (27)

From the above discussion, it is clear that the most fundamental reason for the special prominence given the written word in traditional Chinese culture is its close
relationship from its very beginnings to religious and political potency and to the
establishment of precedents by which to guide all political, social, and personal
activity. Although not the oldest extant written language (Sumerian is older by
about 1500 years), the Chinese writing system is, among the scripts in use today,
the one with the longest history of continuous use.[10]

The Evolution of the Script

A look at the development of this ancient script may help us better understand the
allegiance that the Chinese exhibit toward it. Let us begin with the earliest known
examples. Some of the Shang oracle bone characters were relatively simple pictographs, or representations of concrete things. Most of these characters are still in
use today. One of the most fundamental is that for "person, human being" (*ren*
人). Figure 1.3 shows that the character has not changed markedly during the millennia of its use.

Closely related to pictographs is what Chinese scholars have called "indicative characters," characters that by their shape indicate abstract concepts. Such a
character would be that for *li* 禮, meaning "ritual" and by extension "propriety;
decorum; ethos." In its traditional form, *li* is represented by a ritual bronze cooking

Linda S. Pickle

man, mankind, person

Figure 1.3 The evolution of the character *ren*. (Courtesy of C. Lindqvist, *China: Empire of Living Symbols*, Copyright 1989 Cecilia Lindqvist, English language translation copyright 1991 John Tate. Reprinted by permission of Addison-Wesley Longman, Inc., 24.)

pot on a tripod filled with pieces of meat sacrificed to the ancestral gods. (See figure 1.4.)

Grouped characters, or ideographs, combine two or more pictographs in order to form another character, usually of a more abstract nature. Some characters were "borrowed" or "loaned" to signify a new meaning, if the sound of the word was the same. And other characters were "transformed" by extension of their

Figure 1.4 Traditional (l.) and simplified (r.) forms of the character *li* "propriety," "ceremony."

Types of Characters:

1. Representations of objects (*xiangxing*): 人 ("person") 口 ("mouth") 日 ("sun") 月 ("moon") 子 ("child")
2. Indicative characters (*zhishi*): 上 ("up") ("down") 下 ("arrive"; an arrow hitting a target) 高 ("tall"; the picture of a building)
3. Grouped characters (*buiyi*): 木 ("wood"), together with 斤 ("axe"), becomes 析 ("to split"; "to analyze")
4. Semantic-phonetic combinations (*xingsheng*): 言 ("words," the semantic element), together with 公 ("public," used here only for its phonetic value, pronounced *gong*), becomes 訟 ("litigation," pronounced *song*)
5. "Borrowed" words (*jiajie*): 萬 ("scorpion," used for the word "ten thousand" because it had the same sound, *wan*)
6. "Transformed" characters (*zhuanzhu*): 布 ("cloth," used by extension to mean "money" since it was a unit of exchange)

Figure 1.5 Types of Chinese characters. (*China's Cultural Heritage: The Qing Dynasty, 1644–1912*, second edition. Richard Smith, 107. Copyright 1994 by Westview Press. Reprinted by permission of Westview Press.)

meanings through the associations (concrete or metaphorical) that they had acquired. (See figure 1.5.)

The historical development of the script is thus often directly revealed in the characters, which adds to their potential for allusion, intellectual appeal, and aesthetic beauty, as well as to the general charm they hold for the Chinese.[11]

By far the largest class of contemporary Chinese characters (about 90 percent) is that which combines characters that have a semantic and a phonetic significance. These combinations, sometimes called phonograms, are composed of a radical (that usually appears on the left or on the top of the combination) indicating the meaning of the character and a phonetic element indicating the pronunciation of the character. The 186 radicals now in use were "often originally the representation of an object"; they "provide fairly reliable and sometimes quite revealing clues" as to "the category of phenomena to which the word belongs" (Smith, *China's* 107). All of these methods of surmounting the limitations of an ideographic script were already in use during the Shang dynasty, indicating the strong possibility that the origins of Chinese writing lie even farther back in prehistoric times. The very antiquity of the script makes strong claims on Chinese loyalty.[12]

Other concrete aspects of the written tradition unique to China also help explain its people's lasting attachment to it. Classical Chinese, the script and writing style used as the model for all literate learning in the past two millennia (until the middle of the present century), became the *lingua franca* of Chinese administration. Literacy, defined as the ability to understand and use written Classical Chinese, therefore became a tool and a manifestation of central power. This was especially true as this authority came to be codified in the state examinations based on the texts of antiquity written in Classical Chinese. Like Latin in medieval Europe, Classical Chinese was used long after the oral language that it represented

Linda S. Pickle

Figure 1.6 The *yong* character ("eternity"), show-ing the direction of the brush strokes. (*The British Museum Book of Chinese Art,* ed. Jessica Rawson [1992], 89. Copyright the Trustees of the British Museum, British Museum Press.)

had gradually, but dramatically, changed.[13] For more than 2,000 years, the written language remained comprehensible in spite of regional language differences throughout the vast empire. After the Japanese, Koreans, and other border peoples adopted it as the basis for their writing system, it was also a means of communication beyond the empire's borders. The present-day characters are equally useful for communication within vast and ethnically diverse China, since they have the same meaning in every language and dialect, no matter how the words associated with them may be pronounced. Thus the written script has served as a powerful unifying force throughout Chinese history and as a symbol and transmitter of the grand imperial and centralized bureaucratic traditions that molded China's social and political structures. Bodde has expressed the political and cultural implications of the Chinese writing tradition in a particularly trenchant manner: "The script and its accompanying literary language gave China a cultural continuity in time and unity in space so powerful that without it one may seriously wonder whether the Qin-Han creation of the bureaucratic state could ever have happened" (28).[14]

Nonetheless, in the course of the past century, under the influence of pressures to modernize, the Chinese themselves have debated the merits of their written script. Foreign scholars of Chinese language and culture have joined in the debate. The latter have differed in their assessments of the degree to which written Chinese has impeded "progress" in China. Such discussions are, of course, laden with cultural pitfalls.[15] But in order to gain a more complete picture of the basis for these discussions, we must look at certain difficulties that the Chinese script poses in the context of a modern, literate society.

Not the least of these difficulties is the complexity of the written language. A modern unabridged Chinese dictionary contains nearly 50,000 characters, of which 5,000 to 8,000 are in common usage (Farrer 89–90). Learning to write the characters is therefore a long and arduous proposition for the individual Chinese. It begins in the third year of school and continues throughout the rest of elementary and secondary education. In the fourth year, a child writes the characters in ink and also begins to learn how to use the brush. The methods of learning the

Figure 1.7 *Xie* ("to draw, write") written in the six scripts: (a) small seal script, (b) clerical script, (c) draft script, (d) running script, (e) standard script, (f) simplified characters. (*The British Museum Book of Chinese Art*, ed. Jessica Rawson [1992], 89. Copyright the Trustees of the British Museum, British Museum Press.)

characters are the same as they have always been: memorization and repeated practice. Not only the shape of each character must be learned, but also the direction and sequence of the brush strokes used. (See figure 1.6)

Well-educated Chinese are also able to recognize and, perhaps, write the six calligraphic styles that have evolved over the millennia. (See figure 1.7)

As part of the language reforms of the 1950s, the government mandated a reduction in the total number of characters and a reduction in the number of strokes in individual characters in order to make this task somewhat easier. (See the examples in figures 1.4 and 1.7) John De Francis has summarized the results in this way:

> There has been little reduction in number of characters—of the ten thousand characters in the Chinese Telegraphic Code, a reduction of only 7 percent has been achieved, of which 4 percent comprised variants and a mere 3 percent nonvariants ... Reduction in the number of strokes in complex characters has been more extensively carried out ... [affecting] 2,238 out of the approximately 7,000 characters in general use. This progress has resulted in a reduction of 12.5 percent in the average number of strokes in the 2,000 most frequently used characters (11.2 before simplification, 9.8 after). A count of a quarter of a million characters of running text showed that simplification had resulted in a reduction from 9.15 to 7.67, or 16.1 percent, in the average number of strokes per character. (*The Chinese* 260)[16]

In addition, the 214 radicals were recently reduced to 186. All of this is progress of some degree. Nevertheless, when one considers that basic literacy in Chinese involves the mastery of at least 3,000 characters (enough to read the daily newspapers with the aid of a dictionary), the task is daunting. It is perhaps understandable that as many as 18.5 percent of the present adult population are still functionally illiterate.[17]

The lack of alphabetization in a character-based system such as Chinese leads to other language-associated difficulties. For example, a Chinese dictionary is arranged by radicals. (Here, by the way, we note the Chinese tendency to seek relatedness as an organizing principle. "Families" of calligraphy characters people the pages of their dictionaries.) Within the 186 radical groupings, characters are ordered according to the number of strokes required to write them, from one to seventeen.

Within each grouping by number of strokes, however, the arrangement of characters follows no particular pattern, which can make finding the particular character
one seeks difficult, particularly if it contains one of the more heavily used radicals.
In the dictionary listing for the "hand" radical (no. 64), for example, one must
search through eighty-five characters in the five-stroke subcategory to find the one
sought. Such a system is based on the presupposition that after years of practicing
the characters, one knows the number of strokes in each, something that is not always self-evident to the eye of a foreigner. And as if this were not challenging
enough, "we should note that numbering [of the radicals] is a device used only in
Chinese-Western dictionaries. The Chinese themselves learn the 214 [now 186] radicals by unnumbered sequence only, just as we learn the letters of the alphabet"
(Bodde 68).

Related to this is what appear to the Westerner as other difficulties in
classification. The problems posed by the cumbersome and often nonexistent system of classification in written Chinese texts before this century have compro-
mised their accessibility to scholars from other traditions and may have impeded
Chinese scholarly development in the natural sciences, where clarity of classification is so fundamental. Derk Bodde's discussion (68–73) of related matters, such as
the absence of punctuation and pagination and the lack of useful methods for
numbering and dividing text in traditional Chinese texts, is also enlightening. As
Bodde points out, much of the reason for the laborious quality of scholarly activity
in the Chinese tradition had to do with the expectations attached to the literate,
cultivated man:

> If a pre-modern Chinese scholar could have been asked why all these cum-
> brous procedures had not been simplified long ago, he no doubt would have
> answered that the real scholar would never dream of avoiding them because,
> by definition, he would have a photographic memory, encyclopedic knowl-
> edge, and ample time at his disposal. (71)

Within this context of the Chinese scholarly tradition, it makes sense that an educated elite would have seen little reason to make the writing system and the
related apparatuses for gaining knowledge more readily accessible. But in the
modern world, and given the contemporary resolve on the part of the Chinese to
educate their people in order to interact with that world, this no longer is self-
evident. As mentioned above, the language reforms of the 1950s attempted to
make progress on this front, while retaining culturally important aspects of the
written language.

Perhaps the most radical of these reforms was the creation of *pinyin* 拼音
(which means "linked sounds"). *Pinyin*, instituted in 1958 in the People's Republic
of China, is a carefully devised phonetic system depicting Chinese sounds through
the Latin alphabet. It has made the possibility of acquiring proficiency in reading
Chinese as an adult foreign learner much more likely. The problem is that it has

not penetrated broadly or deeply into Chinese society. It is not used at all in Taiwan presently. In the People's Republic, children learn *pinyin* in the first two years of school, but after that concentrate on learning the traditional characters that are used almost exclusively in China. De Francis lists the following limited areas where *pinyin* is used:

> Some dictionaries and textbooks requiring character annotation; some library catalogues and other situations involving alphabetic sequence; special education for the blind; transmission of international news by the New China News Agency; labeling of industrial and commercial products; names of streets, post offices, and railway stations; flag signaling between ships; and transcription of Chinese terms in United Nations usage [as well as] the official way of transcribing Chinese personal and place names. (*The Chinese* 265)

Pinyin is used relatively little even though the traditional characters pose, in the contemporary world of mass communication and computer-transmitted information, a seemingly unsolvable problem for easy, widely accessible technological transmission. Presently, in order to produce the characters by computer, one must either know a special, separate computer language or use a word-processing system that requires one to type in the *pinyin* word and then choose the correct character from the homonyms that appear on the computer screen. In spite of the awkwardness and labor-intensive qualities of either alternative, at this time no more efficient systems exist.[18] The relatively shallow penetration of *pinyin* into contemporary Chinese usage indicates an aversion to it as an alien script.

Hostility to foreign writing systems, as part of the general skepticism about and animosity toward outside influence, has a long history in China. Certainly some aspects of the traditional script argue against its continued use in modern Chinese society. These include the following: the laborious rote learning required to master it; the emphasis on matters like elegance of calligraphic style that seem (to a Westerner, at least) peripheral to useful applications of the script for learning and scholarship; the difficulties it poses to foreigners as a means of communication with and understanding of the Chinese people; and the impediments to the application of modern means of technology for recording, duplicating, and processing written materials rapidly, easily, and inexpensively. But we must remind ourselves of the script's history, traditional significance, and cultural power. These help explain why the Chinese have clung to a writing system that causes such difficulties in their communication with the outside world and, perhaps, in their attempts to educate their own people. In addition, the very shape and form of this writing system reflect the associative, relational manner of thought at the core of Chinese culture. Families of words related by common components and associations evoked by the pairing of pictographs and the use of phonograms mirror in both concrete and abstract ways this "correlative" way of thinking. For a people to whom relationship is so fundamental, this script is eminently well suited.

Linda S. Pickle

The Linguistic Characteristics of Chinese

Let us now turn to an outline of the general linguistic aspects of the language. For the purposes of this chapter, I will consider only that dialect spoken by approximately 70 percent of the citizens of present-day China, primarily in its north and southwest regions, and more specifically, the version of this dialect that shapes the speech of educated natives of Beijing. This "Mandarin" Chinese, or *putonghua* ("ordinary" or "standard speech"), as it is now called, is the official norm in the People's Republic of China. It is a Sino-Tibetan language, related to Tibetan, Burmese, Siamese, and Laotian, among other tongues. The other 30 percent of the residents of China speak dialects that are as different from *putonghua* as French is from Italian, as well as languages that are as different in origin as English is from Native American tongues.[19]

Chinese (the term I will use in this chapter to refer to *putonghua* 普通話) is a tonal language. The four tones of Chinese, like those of other tonal languages in Asia, Africa, and Latin America, "are not fixed notes on a scale but relative sounds or contours that vary according to the normal voice range of individual speakers" (De Francis, *The Chinese* 45). They may be represented as in figure 1.8.

The effect of the tones is to give a single sound four possible meanings (and often more than this). The classic example is *ma*. Pronounced with the first (high level) tone, *ma* 媽 means "mother." The second (high rising) tone used with this syllable results in the words for "hemp 麻" or "numb 痲" (among others). *Ma* 馬 pronounced with tone 3 (low dipping) means "horse," and with tone 4 (high falling) "to curse, scold 罵." Although each of these words is clearly distinguishable to the eye because of the distinctive written characters that represent them, the tonal distinctions may, in some circumstances, be difficult even for a native speaker to distinguish by ear. This has sometimes been given as the reason why the Chinese tend to speak loudly.

A long, lively scholarly debate exists over the extent to which Chinese is a monosyllabic language. To a large degree, this debate has its origins in related discussions about the nature of the classical language of more than two millennia ago, upon which the written tradition was based and which remained the primary means of

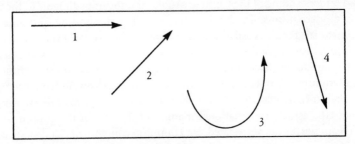

Figure 1.8 The four tones in spoken standard Chinese. (Courtesy University of Hawaii Press, J. De Francis, *The Chinese Language* [1984], 45.)

educated communication throughout the vast Chinese empire until recently. Reviewing that debate lies outside of the scope of this study. Suffice it to say that there is general agreement that the fundamental unit of meaning of the present spoken language is the single syllable. The single syllable is, however, often combined with others to create polysyllabic morphemes. Whether these are actually "words" or "compounds made up of two words" we can leave to linguists.[20] In contemporary Chinese there are somewhere between 398 and 418 different syllables. When the variations on the syllables induced by the four tones are added together, the end result is 1277 syllables. (By way of contrast, English has more than 8000 different syllables.)[21] The result of this combination of large numbers of monosyllabic words and paucity of individual syllables is a language extremely rich in homonyms (analogous to "to," "too," "two" in English). It is possible that this has had interesting implications for the Chinese world view, particularly for the propensity to see proximity and relatedness in everything, as we have mentioned earlier and will discuss further below.

The final important quality of the Chinese language is that it lacks inflection. Words undergo no morphological change, regardless of whether used in the singular or plural, whether they designate masculine or feminine, past, present, or future. Many words can, depending on their position in a sentence, function as nouns, verbs, or adjectives without any modification. This means that context and word order are of central importance (Bodde 16).[22] In this regard, Chinese resembles English, which has shed most of the inflections of its Indo-European origins during its development. John De Francis has written:

> Overall, for a native speaker of English, learning to speak Chinese is not much more difficult than learning to speak French. It is in the traditional writing system that the greatest difficulty is encountered. The blanket designation of "Chinese" as a hard language is a myth generated by the failure to distinguish between speech and writing. Perhaps we can put things in perspective by suggesting, to make a rough guesstimate, that learning to speak Chinese is about 5 percent more difficult than learning to speak French, whereas learning to read Chinese is about five times as hard as learning to read French. (*The Chinese* 52)

The adult language learners among us will have to make up our own minds whether De Francis's estimate of the difficulty of learning to speak Chinese is accurate. But it is certain that the written characters pose the greatest problem for Westerners seeking to gain some proficiency in the language.

Aesthetic Qualities of Chinese

Other general qualities of the language as it was and is both written and spoken also have cultural implications. Chinese has merits in which the Chinese people take pride and that nonnative speakers can also appreciate, among these, its "ambiguity . . . , its musical rhythm and tone, and its marvelous capacity for rhymes and puns" (Smith, *China's* 103). These qualities stem to no small extent from the already-mentioned fact that Chinese is a language particularly rich in homonyms. This has facilitated the development and refinement of a special allusive and ambiguous quality that literary texts cultivate in particular, but that is evident as well in everyday usage and culture. Puns abound in Chinese. For example, the spoken phrase *xiang qian kan* means both "look toward future 向 前看" and "look toward money 向 錢看." The phrase *yanjiu* 研究 (second tone in the first syllable) means "Think it over." *Yanjiu* 煙 酒 (first tone in the first syllable) means "cigarette, wine," the implication being "You'd better bring me a gift."

The lack of inflection (that is, of varying forms that indicate tense, number, gender) in the language also contributes to the possibility of a word or phrase having more than one meaning in any particular context. This potential for allusion enables the Chinese writer to create texts that are remarkable both for their terseness and for their ability to communicate multiple meanings and feelings. Joseph Needham has said of Classical Chinese in this regard: "this old language, in spite of its ambiguity, has a concentrated, laconic, lapidary quality, making an impression of austere elegance, pith and virility, unequalled in any other invented instrument of human communication" (*Science* 41). The lack of punctuation intensified the epigrammatic brevity and potential for multiple interpretations of texts written in Classical Chinese. This made it necessary for state examination candidates to memorize the texts, impressing the succinct and allusion-rich style upon the minds of this cultural elite and by extension influencing the official and unofficial language in general. Literary texts and even popular proverbs also exhibit the same preference for pithiness, balance, and rhythm that the classic Confucian texts display.

The preparation for the state examinations also established the tradition of reference to ancient texts, including the canon of commentary on masters and their paradigmatic masterpieces. This, too, has enhanced the allusive quality of many commonly used Chinese words and phrases. It is "the height of culture" and "the mark of good breeding" to quote famous texts, especially if the quotation contains "a metaphor with a history" (Karlgren, *Sound* 83–84). Sometimes the metaphor has become so elliptical that it is in itself unintelligible without knowing its literary source. Karlgren offers the following example:

> The phrase "to have the shadow for third man" is equivalent to "being happy in solitude," and is derived from the following little poem by China's greatest poet, Li T'ai-po [Li Taibo or Li Bo] (eighth cent. C.E.):
>
> *hua kien i ku tsiu* [*hua jian yi hu jiu*]
> Flower middle one kettle wine
> *tu cho we siang-ts'in* [*du zhuo wu xiang qin*]

alone pour-out not-have comrade.
ku pei yao ming yue [*ju bei yao ming yue*]
lift cup invite bright moon,
tuei ying ch'eng san jen [*dui ying cheng san ren*]
corresponding shadow form third man.

(*ts'in* and *jen* were anciently rhyming words: *ts'ien: njien*)
"Among flowers, with a kettle of wine, I fill my cup in solitude and have no
companion. If I lift the cup and invite the bright moon, my shadow becomes
the third man of the company." (Karlgren, *Sound* 86–87)

Historical allusions are also common. Symptomatic of the Chinese cultural tradition, it was often trifling matters that became the stuff of citations, for familiarity
with these showed the depth and breadth of scholarly knowledge. Karlgren gives the
example of the expression *tao si* [*dao si*], "slippers turned the wrong way," which
signifies "a courteous reception," because the famous scholar Ts'ai Yung [Cai Yong]
was in such a hurry to run out and welcome a visitor that he put his slippers on back-
wards (*Sound* 90). This referential richness of the Chinese vernacular contributes to
the esteem in which Westerners as well as the Chinese hold it.[23]

One further prominent quality of Chinese language usage is closely linked to
the central position of relatedness and of family in the Chinese world view. Chinese
abounds in analogies and paired concepts that indicate correlation, proximity, and
relationship. We can think of this as reflecting the *yinyang* belief system we noted earlier. In the opinion of many scholars, this has structural, linguistic, and cultural roots:

Given that Chinese is an uninflected language, all that helps to guide one
through a phrase, with the aid of a very limited number of particles, are the
links between terms of similar meaning, the oppositions between terms of
opposite meaning, the rhythms and parallelisms, the position of "words" or
semantic unities and the types of relationship between them; and yet the
infinite possible combinations of two semantic units are the source of an
inexhaustible fund of meanings. At every level, meaning stems from the way
terms are combined. No doubt this is what accounts for the predominant
role played by complementary pairs of opposites and correspondences in
Chinese thought and above all for its fundamental relativism. Nothing has
meaning except through opposition to its contrary. Everything depends
upon position (*wei* 位)and timing (*shi* 時). (Gernet, *China* 242)[24]

As Richard Smith has written, "many if not most of these polarities can be correlated directly with *yin* and *yang*—an expression of the central Chinese notion that
ideas are complemented and completed by their opposites" (*China's* 112). Many
individual words reflect this quality. For example, as Smith has pointed out, the
phrase meaning "distance is *yuanjin* 遠近 ('far-near'); quantity, *duoshao* 多少

('much-little'); weight, *qingzhong* 輕重 ('light-heavy'); length, *changduan* 長短 ('long-short'); and so forth" (*China's* 112). Other prominent juxtapositions are *nannü* 男女 (man and woman), *riyue* 日月 (sun and moon), *tiandi* 天地 (heaven and earth), *dongjing* 動靜 (activity and quiescence), *guijian* 貴賤 (high and humble), and *huofu* 後福 (misfortune and fortune). These examples illustrate the peculiarly Chinese nature of this prevalent polarity. It usually implies "either complementary opposition or cyclical alternation" (Smith, *China's* 113). "Contraries which succeed, combine with and complement one another . . . potentialities and tendencies, phases of flowering or decline" are preferred to logical articulations in the Chinese language, as in Chinese thought (Gernet, *China* 242). Again we are reminded of the *yinyang* dynamics of the *Yijing*.[25]

The reciprocal balance of meaning between pairs of words and phrases may, then, have encouraged the Chinese inclination to think in terms of relatedness. Visually, the fact that characters signifying complementary opposites occupy more or less the same space on the page contributes to the sense of equilibrium and symmetry that the pair communicates. The aural rhythmic balance possible in a language dominated by monosyllabic word-syllables also encourages thought patterns marked by proximity and relationship. As one linguist has written:

> It might seem that the monosyllabism in the word-syllable would tend to interfere with flexibility in expression. But in some ways it actually gives more flexibility. I even suspect that this flexibility in the medium has had its influence on the style of Chinese thinking. The brevity and regularity of meaningful units in the language tend to make structural words and phrases fall into convenient patterns of two, three, four, five, and sometimes larger numbers of syllables . . . Although larger numbers than two do not play such all-inclusive parts as the polarity of two, they also form convenient units that can easily be grasped in one mental span. I seriously believe that one important reason why conceptions like those of *chin* [*jin*], *mu, shui, huo, t'u* [*tu*] 金木水火土 "metal, wood, water, fire, earth" have played a much greater part in Chinese thought than have the corresponding conceptions of *fire, air, water, earth,* or *pyr, aer, hydro, ge* in the Occident is that *chin-mu-shui-huo-t'u* makes a more convenient rhythmic unit, and thus can be much more easily handled. (Chao, *Aspects* 289)

The same scholar asserts that this linguistically based tendency to think in terms of phrases comprised of related ideas rather than in terms of single words and their isolated meanings also explains why Chinese dictionaries include proverbs and metaphors in the form of complete sentences (Chao, *Aspects* 290). Utterances related through meaning and usage form word and conceptual families, a linguistic mirroring of the Chinese cultural preference for relatedness rather than separateness (see the discussion of *wen* above). This is why polarities are frequently used as subject headings in traditional Chinese encyclopedias. The organization of these encyclopedias is that of the same allusiveness and assumption of relationship that is so fundamental to Chinese thought patterns.

The sense of relatedness evident in Chinese thought patterns may then have its roots in the structure and usage of the language itself. At the very least, the readiness with which Chinese as a language lends itself to such dichotomous and yet analogous, integrative thinking has reinforced these patterns. Bodde has evaluated this mutual cause and effect in this way:

> It is my belief that the linguistically generated principle of stylistic balance, as exemplified in parallelism, served to stimulate, or at least reinforce, the Chinese tendency to look at the world in terms of symmetrically paired analogies. And I also believe that there is a further link between this and the broader Chinese search for cosmic order and harmony—especially as exemplified in the concept of the "harmony of man and nature." (46)

As proof of the prevalence of the Chinese taste for such symmetrical, mutually dependent polarities, Chao has pointed to the scrolls "hanging in every home and in every public building" on which are written *duizi* 對子 (lit. "juxtaposed things"), "exact antitheses between words or phrases according to definite tonal and grammatical rules" (*Aspects* 290). But in these texts, as in the other examples cited above, relatedness and integration of opposites, not antithesis, contradiction, or dichotomy, are primary.

The Chinese Language and Family Relationships

We might think of the previously discussed linguistic and organizational aspects of the Chinese language and thought in terms of family. The complementary relationships among words and concepts are like the reciprocal relationships among members of families. We know that the family is the most fundamental social and cultural unit of traditional Chinese culture, the "other" into which the individual is inextricably integrated.[26] Just as selfhood is understood in China primarily as a matter of relationships, rather than as individualism in isolation, so the language reflects a preference for analogy, correlation, and reference to relationship in the ways discussed above. Isolated words or concepts have no meaning without the complex of related words and concepts to which they belong.[27]

The importance of family-based relationships manifests itself concretely in a variety of ways in the language. In the *Erya*, a lexicon dated over 2000 years ago, more than one hundred specialized kinship terms occur. In contemporary times, the Chinese make clear distinctions among maternal and paternal relatives and among older and younger relatives. For example, "a male cousin on the father's side older than oneself would be referred to as *tangxiong* 堂兄, a male cousin on the father's side younger than oneself as *tangdi* 堂第, a male cousin on the mother's side older than oneself as *biaoxiong* 表兄, and so on for five other types of cousins" (Smith, *China's* 116).

Words and written characters related to the family and the ideas associated with them also tell us much about Chinese culture. *Fu* 父, the word meaning "father," has many positive homonyms. Among them are bat (an animal signifying good fortune), riches, fisherman (one of the four basic occupations), and good luck. Similarly positive connotations have accrued to *zi* 子, the word for "son." The connection between father and son is one of the central human relationships in the Chinese tradition. As Eberhard has put it: "Implicitly, if not explicitly, for the Chinese, 'children' means 'sons.' Before 1949 only a male heir could inherit the parental estate and perform the ancestral sacrifices for father and forefathers" (61). Already in the Shang dynasty, the oracle bones tell us that the birth of a son was considered "good," or *jia* 嘉, and the birth of a daughter "not good," or *bujia* 不嘉 (Smith, *Fortune-tellers* 15). We see this attitude in the evolution of usage of the term and written character for "son." In connection with a family name, "*zi*" came to designate "master." Eberhard tells us that "a cultured young man of outstanding gifts is often called a *cai-zi* 才子" (270). The character for *zi* appears to the right of the radical for "woman 女" resulting in the meaning "good, well 好." The character for "peace 安" is made up of those for "woman 女" under the radical for "roof 宀."

This positive association of the character for woman, *nü*, with "good" and "peace" is, on the other hand, the exception rather than the rule. Woman's subordinate position within traditional Chinese society is indicated visually by the origins of the written character, which, most scholars agree, was an ideograph depicting a woman kneeling with her hands either bound in front of her or extended in a gesture of service.[28] Figure 1.9 shows the evolution of the ancient character into the one now in use.

In this context, Richard J. Smith has noted

the relatively large number of Chinese characters with the "female" radical (*nü*) that have decidedly pejorative connotations, including *jian* 奸 ("villain-

woman

Figure 1.9 The evolution of the *nü* radical. (Courtesy of C. Lindqvist, *China: Empire of Living Symbols,* Copyright 1989 Cecilia Lindqvist, English language translation copyright 1991 John Tate. Reprinted by permission of Addison-Wesley Longman, Inc., 42.)

ous"), *fang* 妨 ("to hinder"), *du* 妒 ("to be jealous"), *nu* 奴 ("slave"), *mei* 媚 ("to flatter"), and *jian* 姦 ("licentious"). Of course, a number of very positive terms in Chinese also contain the *nü* radical, but most of these have to do with traditional female physical attributes, roles, and relationships. In speech these associations would not be apparent, as they are with, say, the English sound "sissy"; but as I have tried to indicate, Chinese culture as a whole paid far greater attention to the constituent elements of written words than did Western culture. Thus, such associations, both positive and negative, were never far from consciousness—at least not for the more literate members of Qing society. (*China's* 117)[29]

What was true of literate Qing society was no doubt equally true in earlier eras. The influence, for good and ill, of the visual representations of gender and family relationships in the written characters was not accidental, but rather the result and reflection of ancient cultural attitudes. And on the other hand, the written language, invested as it was with the force of religious, political, and cultural power, helped institutionalize and perpetuate attitudes and behavior in personal relationships.

The Chinese characters have retained the capacity to trigger associations and analyses of their meaning, even as literacy has spread to the less highly educated. The Chinese break them down into their component parts, "either for their own amusement or in order to better commit them to memory," and archaeologists and historians continue to use them as a source of information about the culture of ancient China (Niederer 8). Here, too, the *nü*-radical is instructive. In the modern era, numerous Chinese brought the misogynist associations caused by the appearance of the *nü*-radical in negative word contexts to the attention of the Committee for Character Reform and the journal *Language(s) in China (Zhongguo yuwen)*, both created in 1949. They suggested the "thorough eradication of the phenomenon of inequality between men and women in Chinese script." In an article published in 1952, the editor of *Zhongguo yuwen* rejected the suggestions, saying that altering the offending characters would lead to having to respond to endless complaints about others. The article also referred to the comment of a member of the Committee for Character Reform, indicating that women "have

女 *nü* (woman; female)
奸 *jian* (villainous)
妨 *fang* (to hinder)
妒 *du* (to be jealous)
奴 *nu* (slave)
媚 *mei* (to flatter)
姦 *jian* (licentious)

Figure 1.10 Negative associations of the *nü* radical. (*China's Cultural Heritage: The Qing Dynasty, 1644–1912*, Second Edition, Richard Smith, 117. Copyright 1994 by Westview Press. Reprinted by permission of Westview Press.)

understood that the question of equality does not lie in the written language, but elsewhere" (cited by Niederer 11).

Another example of the encoding of interpersonal and familial relationships in Chinese characters is the expression *fumu* 父母. This term, however, points to the equality of the sexes within the family and to the broader social role of the family. Taken by itself, *fumu* means "parent" (literally, father-mother). It is one of the words that illustrates the *yinyang* balance of correlated opposites discussed earlier as fundamental to the Chinese world view. The word also appears in the expression *fumu guan* 父母官 that refers to judicial officials at the county or local level. Family is the training ground for the appropriate behavior and morality that such officials seek to regulate, often by drawing on the resources of the erring individual's personal relationships. At the same time, these officials are, as the term indicates, public "parents," exercising the kind of influence and authority with which biological parents are naturally endowed because they represent the great complementary duality of existence.

If we think of kinship in the broadest sense, as relatedness and proximity, the metaphor of the family permeates Chinese culture. Indeed, the family is the foundation of all that is proper and moral in the Chinese cosmos. Consider hexagram 37 of the *Yijing, jiaren* 家人 (the Family [the Clan]). The commentary on the judgment for this hexagram reads:

> THE FAMILY. The correct place of the woman is within; the correct place of the man is without. That man and woman have their proper places is the greatest concept in nature.
>
> Among the members of the family there are strict rulers; these are the parents. When the father is in truth a father and the son a son, when the elder brother is an elder brother and the younger brother a younger brother, the husband a husband and the wife a wife, then the house is on the right way.
>
> When the house is set in order, the world is established in a firm course. (Wilhelm 570)

The family relationships mentioned here are those fundamental to pre-Confucian society: between husband and wife, father and son, and older brother and younger brother. Interestingly, the hexagram *jiaren* is comprised of none of the trigrams representing the family members mentioned in this judgment, but rather of the first daughter in her proper place, above that of the second daughter. Here again, as always in Chinese culture, the balance of appropriate reciprocal and complementary concepts is sought.

Summary

We have returned to our point of departure, the *Yijing*, for the final example in our discussion of Chinese language as an expression of cultural heritage. This is appropriate, for such circulatory or spiraling reasoning is more congenial to the associative manner of thought of the Chinese than the development of a linear argument. Indeed, the interweaving of Chinese language and culture is so dense that it is often difficult to separate out the threads in order to describe it in a linear fashion. Nonetheless, in conclusion let me summarize the associations I have attempted to identify between the history and nature of written and spoken Chinese and the centrality of family as a cultural concept.

The mythical origins and metaphorical world of the most ancient Chinese cultural text, the *Yijing*, point to a connection between the script and the fundamental ordering principle of human society, the family. Fuxi as the founder of marriage and the trigrams as representative of family relationships and of the ordering patterns of the universe cause the legend of the creation of the script from the trigrams to resonate with references to the family. The restriction of the script to privileged groups within religious, political, and artistic circles led to its identification with culture and civilization (seen in the *wen* family of words) and to its contributing to the formation of "families" of scholars who shared common knowledge, skills, prerogatives, and history. These groups and the elliptical language used in the classical texts influenced the development of Chinese culture through their connection to religion, politics, and art. We might even say that literacy and the classical texts and master practitioners associated with them therefore came to be regarded with a reverence parallel to that the Chinese accord their ancestors. This, along with the aesthetic and cultural value placed in calligraphy, helps us understand the lasting veneration accorded the Chinese characters.

The linguistic qualities of both written and spoken Chinese have also fostered the emphasis on relationship that is at the center of Chinese culture. In their structure and appearance, the characters themselves often express the consanguinity of thought and the historical development behind their evolution. In other words, they have a "family history." The many characters formed with two or more components also create a visual association of objects and ideas in relation to each other. They thus reinforce the Chinese tendency to think first of the kinship among all things in the world. The possibility for ambiguity because of the many homonyms and the lack of inflection makes it particularly easy for the language to imply interrelationships and correlation among things and concepts. Such ambiguities are exploited to express the embracing of complementary opposites so fundamental to Chinese thought.

Just as selfhood in Chinese culture is relational at base, so too are association and affinity paramount in the Chinese language. This ancient tongue and its writing system incorporate and express the *yinyang* mentality that accords all members of the personal, social, natural, and cosmic family their appropriate place within the complex network of relationship.

Glossary

Canon A group of written texts given high status by a society.
Confucian Society A society based on the teachings of Confucius (Kongfuzi), a teacher,

philosopher, and political theorist (551–479 B.C.E.) from the state of Lu. Confucius's teachings formed the basis of Chinese education for 2,000 years, and have influenced all civilizations of East Asia.

Pinyin To combine (*pin*) sounds (*yin*). Refers to the transliteration of Chinese ideograms into the roman alphabet. The system was developed in Soviet East Asia in the early 1930s and, with modification, was introduced by the Chinese in the 1950s. The official romanization of the People's Republic of China, pinyin has largely replaced the older Wade-Giles system.

Putonghua The general language or vernacular language of China, taught and promoted since the beginning of this century. Usually the standards of pronunciation are those of an educated speaker from Beijing.

Qi Configured energy; the fundamental stuff that composes everything in the natural world.

Shaman A priest or medium able to commune with the spirit world while in an induced trance state. Shamans played a major role in the neolithic and bronze-age rituals of rule, ancestral sacrifice, and interpretation of oracles.

World view A unified understanding of the nature of reality and our place in it, including an understanding of what is important or significant and so of how we should live, act, feel, and so on.

Yijing *The Book of Changes*, sometimes written as *I Ching*.

Notes

1. I have used *pinyin* transliteration for Chinese names and words throughout this paper, except in those instances when citing from sources that use the older Wade-Giles system. In those instances, I have inserted the *pinyin* equivalent in brackets. I have also retained other minor spelling variations in citations, such as the hyphenation of "Fu-xi" and "Nü-gua" in the following paragraph.

2. In some versions of the tale, it is on the back of a turtle that Fuxi sees the trigrams (Williams 201). In view of the role of the turtle in some Chinese creation legends and of the use of turtle shells for divination and the inscribing of early texts (see below), it is perhaps fitting that this animal should have come to be associated with Fuxi's creation of writing. Horses also have strong positive connotations within the Chinese cultural tradition, of course.

3. Richard Wilhelm's succinct introduction to the *Yijing* as a book of wisdom, as well as his summary of its history, are much to be recommended (*livlxi*). Contemporary Western scholars agree on the significance of the *Yijing* within the development of Chinese language and culture. As Richard J. Smith has put it: "Like Chinese characters, these hexagrams were a distinctly visual medium of communication, concrete but ambiguous, with several possible levels of meaning as well as a great many accumulated allusions and associations" (Smith, *China's* 120). Jacques Gernet has called the hexagrams "a superior and refined form

of the language itself" (Gernet, *China* 242). Smith bases his fascinating study *Fortune-tellers and Philosophers: Divination in Traditional Chinese Society* (1991) on an exploration of the cultural power of this classic work.

4. John Hay discusses the articulation of the "pulse" of the energy arteries of the forces of nature in calligraphy and the appreciation of this among connoisseurs of the art: "One of the most highly regarded forms of script is the least legible cursive style, in which the energy pulse may be drawn out to dramatic lengths and can be physically sensed through moments when it becomes invisible" ("The Persistent" 143). See also Hay's related analysis of the relationship of calligraphy to the Chinese world view in "The Human Body as a Microcosmic Source of Macrocosmic Values in Calligraphy" (1993). Driscoll and Toda write of the "organized movement" of a well-written character: "The ideal seems to be an equilibrium so delicately adjusted that repose is only temporary . . . a feeling of rhythmic continuity of uneven interval, an equilibrium achieved, lost, regained - a 'way of giving life'" (1). Li also discusses calligraphy as an art of the dynamic line (33–38).

5. I am grateful to my colleague Liu Yingqin of Xi'an Foreign Languages University for pointing this out to me and for other valuable advice in the writing of this chapter. In his discussion of the principles fundamental to Chinese painting, Wucius Wong points out the insistence on the identity of the self with the work of painting or calligraphy (22). Rawson (26) and Farrer (90–94) also comment on the connection the Chinese have traditionally made between calligraphy and the expression of character and social standing. I have listed further readings on Chinese calligraphy at the conclusion of this chapter.

6. See Vance Cope-Kasten's discussion of the Chinese world view in his chapter on Chinese philosophy in this volume. Kathleen Higgins makes a similar point in her discussion of the analogic *yinyang* thinking that underlies the conceptualization of musical tones in the Chinese tradition.

7. Chicago Art Institute, Lucy Maude Buckingham Collection, numbers 1927.602, 1926.1827, 1938.1115. On the oracle-bone inscriptions, see Needham (*Introductory* 83–84; *History* 347), Smith (*Fortune-tellers* 14–18); Keightley (28–90). The reader is also referred to Allen's intriguing discussion of the relationship of the Shang *divination* writings and associated practices to the intersections of art, culture, and religion in ancient China (1, 4, 112–123 passim*)*. See also Lawrence E. Butler's discussion of the ancient bronzes in this volume.

8. Gernet asserts that the Shang oracle-bone inscriptions were "the oldest form of historiography in China," and that they already exhibited the essential characteristics of that branch of scholarship, "its close link with political activity and the aspect which made it a sort of science of precedents" (*A History* 46). In this volume, Lawrence E. Butler, Vance Cope-Kasten, and Fay E. Beauchamp discuss the imitation of master texts in art, philosophy, and literature, respectively.

9. Gernet, *A History* 29, 33. Vance Cope-Kasten notes the use of the word *jia* ("family") to refer to a school of philosophy in his chapter in the present volume. *Jia*, of course, is also a homonym for "family." On the significance of calligraphy for Chinese art and aesthetics, see Li's discussion of "the art of line" (32–38, et al.) and Farrer's study "Calligraphy and Painting for Official Life" in *The British Museum Book of Chinese Art*.

10. See Gernet (*A History* 46) and De Francis (*The Chinese* 40).

11. Smith discusses the ancient technique of word analysis known as "dissecting characters" (*chaizi*) engaged in by philologists, literary scholars, fortunetellers, and ordinary people (*China's* 109-10; *Fortune-tellers* 202-204, 216-18, 226-29, 250-52).

12. Cecilia Lindqvist offers a lucid and attractive presentation of about one hundred of the most fundamental and ancient characters and their development in her 1991 monograph. See especially the overview of the various types of characters in her final chapter, "Meaning and Sound: From Pictographs to Phonetic Compounds" (349-60).

13. Again, the scholarly debates about whether or not Classical Chinese ever was a true, living, spoken language lie outside of the scope of this chapter. This writer tends to agree with those who claim that it is likely that Classical Chinese was an allusive, abbreviated representation of a much fuller spoken language, which explains why many of the conditions that linguists impose on it as a written record of speech do not work well. Those interested in a further discussion of this complex question should consult Rosemont ("On Representing" 80-83; "Gathering Evidence" 135, 146 n19), Hall and Ames (298-99), and Graham (392-97).

14. On the unifying effect of the written language, see also Smith (*China's* 101, 104, 127-28), Karlgren (*The Chinese* 57-58), and Gernet (*A History* 32).

15. This chapter is not the place to evaluate the respective merits of the arguments among Western scholars on this question. The interested reader may consult the summary of the various arguments and the views expressed by Derk Bodde (88-96) on the extent to which Classical Chinese influenced subsequent Chinese scholarship and thought.

16. De Francis (*The Chinese* 240-78) presents a lucid and very readable account of the debate sparked by the reform of the writing system. It should also be noted at this juncture that some Chinese and Sinologists have protested the aesthetic diminishment that, in their view, results from the simplification of ancient characters with deep significance in Chinese cultural history. See *li* (fig. 1.4) for an example.

17. Bodde (18) cites the nearly 50,000 characters in a modern unabridged Chinese dictionary and the 3,000 characters that enable one to read newspapers and similar material. The *1995 UNESCO Statistical Yearbook* estimates that 10.1percent of all Chinese males age fifteen or older are illiterate, while 27.3percent of the females are, resulting in an overall average illiteracy of 18.5percent ("Table on Selected Indicators, Adult Illiteracy Rates, Estimates" [Lanham, Maryland: UNESCO and Bernan Press, 1995], 1-6).

18. De Francis (*Visible Speech* 267) discusses the difficulties of transferring the Chinese characters into efficient word-processing programs in comparison to "alphanumeric systems."

19. De Francis (*The Chinese* 37-40) and Gernet (*A History* 1-13) offer visual depictions and more detailed examinations of the linguistic distribution in China.

20. For lucid and accessible discussions of this point, see Bodde (17) and De Francis (*The Chinese* 46-49). Chao decides not to decide on the basis that the concept "word" varies among cultures and scholars: "Since there is no word but there are word-conceptions of various types, we can say neither that Chinese is monosyllabic nor that it is polysyllabic" (*Aspects* 288-89). Karlgren (*Philology; The Chinese* 3-27; *Sound* 1-83) has written the classic descriptions of Chinese as a monosyllabic language. Whether he and others have been

unduly influenced in their views by the written Classical Chinese of 2000 years ago is also a question for others to decide.

21. De Francis (*Visible Speech* 55).

22. See also Bodde's more detailed discussion of Chinese morphology and grammar (31–42), as well as Karlgren's studies (*The Chinese; Sound* 74–83), Chao's monumental monograph (*A Grammar*), and the related discussions by De Francis (*The Chinese* 47–50) and Graham (398–97).

23. See Bodde (74–82) and Smith (*China's* 110–15) for insightful discussions of the connection among linguistic characteristics of the language, literary style, and patterns of thought.

24. See also Bodde (42–55), Chao (*Aspects* 289), and Granet (56–82).

25. This linguistic characteristic mirrors the fundamental assumption in Chinese thought that there are no absolutes and that everything is relational. Graham's Appendix 2: "The Relation of Chinese thought to Chinese Language" (389–428) contains a particularly rich discussion of this subject. The correlative thinking typical of the Chinese has had certain consequences for their interactions with Westerners. The lack of a belief in transcendency or in absolute concepts like "truth" has caused Christian missionaries great difficulties in their work among the Chinese. It has led some Western philosophers to assert that the Chinese are incapable of philosophical thought. See Gernet (*China* 239–47) on the relationship between Chinese language and thought and the implications for the Christianization of the Chinese. Graham (329–97 passim) also considers the relationship between language and thought in his study of classical Chinese philosophical works.

26. See Mary F. Gallagher's comments in this volume on this aspect of Chinese society and culture.

27. Roger Ames has referred to the allusive quality of the Chinese language and to its ability to define the world through associative references as "paronomesia" (keynote address, ASIANetwork Annual Conference, Manchester Center, Vermont, 26 April, 1997).

28. Niederer says that the representation of this physical position "may be interpreted as a gesture of humility, a serving posture, or simply a passive attitude typical of women" (8).

29. For a further discussion of the *nü*-radical, see Lindqvist (42–43).

Works Cited

Analects of Confucius. Trans. Arthur Waley. New York: Random, 1989.

Allan, Sarah. *The Shape of the Turtle: Myth, Art, and Cosmos in Ancient China.* Albany: State University of New York Press, 1991.

Bodde, Derk. *Chinese Thought, Society, and Science: The Intellectual and Social Background of Science and Technology in Premodern China.* Honolulu; University of Hawaii Press, 1991.

Chao Yuen Ren. *Aspects of Chinese Sociolinguistics.* Stanford, Calif.: Stanford University Press, 1976.

———. *A Grammar of Spoken Chinese.* Berkeley: University of California Press, 1968.

De Francis, John. *The Chinese Language: Fact and Fantasy.* Honolulu: University of Hawaii Press, 1984.

———. *Visible Speech: The Diverse Oneness of Writing Systems.* Honolulu: University of Hawaii Press, 1989.

Driscoll, Lucy, and Kenji Toda. *Chinese Calligraphy.* 2d ed. New York: Paragon, 1964.

Eberhard, Wolfram. *A Dictionary of Chinese Symbols: Hidden Symbols in Chinese Life and Thought.* Trans. G.L. Campbell. London and New York: Routledge, 1986.

Farrer, Anne. *The Brush Dances & the Ink Sinks: Chinese Paintings and Calligraphy from the British Museum.* London: Hayward Gallery, 1990

Gernet, Jacques. *China and the Christian Impact: A Conflict of Cultures.* Trans. Janet Lloyd.

———. *A History of Chinese Civilization.* Trans. J.R. Foster. Cambridge: Cambridge University Press, 1985.

Graham, A[ngus] C. *Disputers of the Tao: Philosophical Argument in Ancient China.* LaSalle, Ill.: Open Court, 1989.

Hall, David L., and Roger T. Ames. *Thinking Through Confucius.* Albany: State University of New York Press, 1987.

Hay, John. "The Human Body as Microcosmic Source of Macrocosmic Values in Calligraphy." *Self as Body in Asian Theory and Practice.* Ed. Thomas P. Kasulis, Roger T. Ames, and Wimal Dissanayake. SUNY Series, The Body in Culture, History, and Religion. Albany: State University of New York Press, 1993. 179–212.

———. "The Persistent Dragon (*Lung*)." *The Power of Culture: Studies in Chinese Cultural History.* Ed. Willard J. Peterson, Andrew Plaks, and Ying-Shih Yu. Chinese University Press, 19 XXX. 119–149.

Karlgren, Bernhard. *The Chinese Language: An Essay on Its Nature and History.* New York: Ronald, 1949.

———. *Philology and Ancient China.* Series A: Forelesninger 8, Instituttet for sammenlignende kulturforskning. Oslo: H. Aschehoug and Co; Cambridge Mass.: Harvard University Press, 1926.

———. *Sound and Symbol in Chinese.* Rev. ed. [Hong Kong]: Hong Kong University Press, 1962.

Keightley, David. *Sources of Shang History: The Oracle-Bone Inscriptions of Bronze-Age China.* Berkeley: University of California Press, 1978.

Li Zehou. *The Path of Beauty: A Study of Chinese Aesthetics.* Trans. Gong Lizeng. Hong Kong: Oxford University Press, 1994.

Lindqvist, Cecilia. *China: Empire of Living Symbols.* Trans. Joan Tate. Reading, Mass.: Addison-Wesley, 1991.

Needham, Joseph. *Science and Civilisation in China.* Vol. 1, *Introductory Orientations.* Cambridge: Cambridge University Press, 1954.

———. *Science and Civilisation in China.* Vol. 2, *History of Scientific Thought.* Cambridge: Cambridge University Press, 1956.

Niederer, Barbara. "Women in Chinese Script," in *China for Women.* New York: The Feminist Press at the City University of New York, 1995.

Rawson, Jessica, ed. *The British Museum Book of Chinese Art*. New York: Thames and Hudson, 1992.

Rosemont, Henry, Jr. "On Representing Abstractions in Archaic Chinese," *Philosophy East and West* 24. 1 (1974): 71–88.

———. "Gathering Evidence for Linguistic Innateness." *Synthese* 38 (1978): 127–148.

Silber, Cathy. "Women's Writing from Hunan," in *China for Women*. New York: Feminist Press at the City Univeristy of New York, 1995. 13–19.

Smith, Richard J. *China's Cultural Heritage. The Qing Dynasty, 1644–1912*. 2d ed. Boulder, Colo.: Westview, 1994.

———. *Fortune-tellers and Philosophers: Divination in Traditional Chinese Society*. Boulder, Colo.: Westview, 1991.

Wilhelm, Richard, trans. and commentator. *The I Ching or Book of Changes*. English Trans. Cary F. Baynes. 3d ed. Bollingen Series XIX. Princeton: Princeton University Press, 1967.

Williams, C. A. S. *Encyclopedia of Chinese Symbolism and Art Motives*. New York: Julian, 1960.

Wong, Wucius. *The Tao of Chinese Landscape Painting*. New York: Design, 1991.

2

Meeting Chinese Philosophy

Vance Cope-Kasten

Is Chinese "philosophy" really philosophy? That this question seems reasonable to many of us in the West indicates one of the main stumbling blocks for our ability to appreciate and learn from the Chinese traditions. Chinese thought at least seems very different in many ways from our modes of thinking, which derive philosophically and scientifically from the ancient Greeks. So considering the Chinese tradition, which begins about the same time as ours, we will have the opportunity to think about some things we might otherwise take for granted.

Nonetheless, this chapter will try to show that what is called "Chinese philosophy" certainly is philosophy in most of the major senses of that term as it is used in the West. And it will try to show how the differences between the two traditions can be incorporated into a richer, more complex sense of "philosophy" than the one we usually take for granted. Understanding this can increase our own options for getting more out of thinking philosophically, for succeeding at what human beings try to do when they philosophize. In doing these things, we will pay special attention to a notion that has been much more central to the Chinese philosophical outlook than it has been to ours: the family.

What Is Philosophy?

Philosophy can be described as the attempt to make rational sense of things once all the information is available. Thus understood, it is a basic human activity and not one confined to intellectuals, since almost everyone finds at times that things don't make complete sense. The following table may help you place some of the more famous ancient Greek and ancient Chinese philosophers.

Religion and science are two other basic ways in which we try to make sense of ourselves and our universe. It is characteristic of religion to rely on faith rather than rationality. Thus it differs from philosophy by its method, though the two

Ancient Chinese Philosophers	Ancient Greek Philosophers
Laozi—(legendary dates, 600–510)*	Milesians—c. 600–500
	Pythagoras—c. 550–496
Confucius—551–479	Heraclitus—c. 544–484
	Parmenides—c. 515–440
Mozi—c. 480–390	Socrates—470–399
Zhuangzi—c. 399–290	Plato—428/7–367
Mencius—c. 340–245	Aristotle—384–322
Xunzi—c. 340–245	Epicurus—341–270

*All dates B.C.E.

may or may not arrive at the same answers. Science shares the appeal to rationality with philosophy, but it uses reason essentially to gain more information, to find out more facts. Sometimes, however, things don't seem to make sense even when we have all the information we could get or could imagine getting. That is when philosophy comes into play, as, for example, in trying to think about the morality of abortion. And sometimes philosophy is needed when the issue does not seem to be one for which more information is relevant. "How shall I treat my parents?" is an example of this situation. Philosophy is a basic human activity: almost everyone finds that things don't make complete sense at all times.

Following Plato and, especially, Aristotle, we have come to think of philosophy as a kind of thinking in which reason or evidence is given in support of the truth of a statement: if this thinking meets certain criteria, we call it logical or reasonable or, even, a proof. As we shall see, it is certainly not appropriate to consider the bulk of Chinese philosophy as anything other than rational in just this sense, even if it sometimes looks that way at first glance. And we will also see that some of the characteristic patterns of Chinese thought might enrich our own self-understanding of what it means to be "rational" by enabling us to identify—and to label as rational—ways of thinking we already engage in and find quite acceptable but which do not fit the official philosophical patterns of "logical reasoning." These ways have an interesting, and perhaps even ironic, relationship to the theme of "family," as we shall see in the last section.

Language and Philosophy and the Family

Chinese writing does not use an alphabet like Western writing. Instead, it employs characters, representations in a single symbol for an entire word or concept. Written language has bound the Chinese civilization together for longer than we have had the Roman alphabet to work with. And even today, people from different parts of the vast country of China who cannot understand each other's speech can communicate by their shared written language.

More relevant for our purposes is the philosophical idea that language embodies (much of) a people's philosophy. It reflects some of the basic ways in which a people make sense of things. The categories of a language indicate the kinds of things that a person brought up in the language can consider to be real or important and how those things relate to one another.

For example, the Chinese character for a person is 人 (*ren*). By adding just one line to this character, the meaning changes to "big" or "great 大 (*da*)." Adding yet another line on the top, the meaning changes to "heaven 天 (*tian*)." When one realizes that the ancient Chinese expressed their understanding of the universe as consisting of *tian* and earth, with people in between, the fact that the characters for heaven and for humans have so much in common says some things about how they understood the relationships between us and the highest reality.

Instructive, too, is the character for "goodness, 仁 (*ren*)." This is made from the character for "person" in its so-called radical or joining form, 亻, and the character for "two," which is simply 二 . Thus the character for "goodness," 仁 (romanized also as "*ren*" and pronounced in the same tone as "人 (*ren*)" that means "a person") suggests that goodness is not something you can have or do alone; instead, it involves how you act toward and with others.

For now, we can conclude these examples by noting, first, that the character for "infant" or "son 子 (*zi*)," also means "master" as a title of respect for great wisdom (We find *zi* in Confucius's Chinese appellation, Kongfuzi 孔夫子, and also in that of the legendary founder of Daoism, Laozi 老子), suggesting that though one may have gone through a long period of learning to become a master, human relationships are nevertheless dynamic and changing; *zi* thus evokes the notion of relationality: you are a child to your parents but you may well become a parent to your children (and you may even have to "parent" your parents when they get very old).

Language, philosophy, and the family are connected in yet another way in Chinese thought. The Chinese term for a school or lineage of philosophy, 家 (*jia*), is the same character as that for home, a fact that is highly suggestive of the connections between family and philosophy in China. Though both ancient Chinese and Western thinkers thought a lot about language, the main concerns of the Chinese were with how to live and how to act. Those are, of course, the central concerns of a family, especially in its role of bringing up children. The basic Western philosophical concern, in contrast, is largely with whether something is real. Plato, for example, wonders whether names are natural (whether things have true names) or arbitrary. These two concerns—what is real and how to live—are not unrelated, but the difference in emphasis is important to bear in mind.

There is, to illustrate, a passage from the *Analects* in which Confucius, speaking of a ceremonial bronze wine cup called a *gu*, exclaims: "A *gu* that is not a *gu*! A *gu* indeed! A *gu* indeed!" (VI.23). While Westerners might think it a bit silly to worry about whether this cup really is a certain sort of cup, Confucius's words can be seen as a comment on pretending to be something you aren't. His point seems to be that we should be sure we are who we'd like to think we are, that we act in such a way that our lives are consistent with our ideals. Since we are daughters or sons, do we behave in appropriate ways toward our parents? If we are students, do we actually do what this term would indicate? Language is thus seen as of immense practical importance.

The Family in the Philosophical World View

Philosophy's attempt to make sense of reality and our place in it implies developing an understanding of what is important or significant. This understanding, in turn, fits together with understandings about how one should live and act, what one should feel under various circumstances, and so on. A shorthand term for all of these things is a "world view." Ordinarily, one is more or less given a world view by virtue of learning the language, as we have discussed, and also by learning the accepted practices and beliefs of those around one. In China, as in most but not all societies, these powerful influences are predominantly one's family. And in China, unlike in the West, the family itself has provided the main model or metaphor for understanding the rest of reality.

Of course, the family itself does not have the same shape in all societies. In China, as in modern Europe and America, the norm has been the nuclear family, consisting of a wife and husband and their children. But in China this norm has also involved the extended family, including grandparents and great-grandparents. This sense of family has dwindled away, for us, to very little. Grandparents are still a part of our thinking, to be sure, but it is thought ideal if they have "a life of their own." Such a thought would have been virtually unthinkable and certainly undesirable in China, at least until very recently. Even after death, one's parents, grandparents, and so on, were to be kept alive in memory by rituals and, more deeply, by how one lived. (Guiding how one lives is a main function of rituals.) It was thought ideal to live as one's ancestors would have wanted. Confucius provided the philosophical expression of this ideal when he said, "Observe what a man has in mind to do when his father is living, and then observe what he does when his father is dead. If, for three years, he makes no changes to his father's ways, he can be said to be a good son" (*Analects* I.11). This idea is repeated later (IV.20), which indicates its importance to Confucius. In real degree it is still operative in China, twenty-five hundred years after Confucius, despite enormous recent Western-based influences.

So the idea of the family was central to Chinese philosophical thinking about how to live. More unusual is that this idea served as a model for understanding the nature of reality itself. Key differences can be detected between the Chinese and Western world views by examining the different concepts of the individual, of the self. A basic Western model or image of the individual is that of an atom—a thing which is complete and independent by nature. Each "atom" might join with other atoms to form such molecules as family, society, or government, but it must always worry about the infringements that the other atoms and molecules pose to is own integrity, its own rights and independence.

To the Chinese way of thinking, this is highly artificial. There is no atomistic, independent self which may or may not be involved in relationships with others. Being related to others is necessary, beginning with the infant-caretaker (usually parent) relationship, and, in fact, individuals can be much better thought of as different centers of webs of relationships, with the webs themselves being as real and as important. Individuals are daughters (or sons), fathers (or mothers), wives or husbands, sisters or brothers—and by extension of these family relationships, subjects (or rulers) of so-and-so, friends of so-and-so; and so on. There just is no self (or soul or mind) there all by itself. As a consequence, for the Chinese to find the meaning of life is to find meaning in life, as one commentator has so nicely put it (Rosemont 92).

According to the Confucian tradition, which has dominated most of China's cultural history, there are five basic relationships: husband-wife, parent-child, older sibling-younger sibling, ruler-ruled, and friend-friend.[1] Sometimes the husband-wife relationship is considered the most basic, and sometimes the parent-child relationship has this status. The important philosophical significance is that these relationships were given much attention not only in themselves, but also as models for other relationships. Thus the teacher-student relationship is modeled after that of parent and child, and so is that between the ruler (prince, king, or emperor) and the ruled. *The Great Learning*, "*Daxue*,"[2] one of the Four Classics that shaped Chinese thought and education in ancient times and then again from about 1200 to 1900, refers to a still older work in making this modeling clear: "In the *Book of Poetry*, it is said, 'How much to be rejoiced in are these princes, parents of the people!' When *a prince* loves what the people love and hates what the people hate, then is he what is called the parent of the people" (X.3).

Much of early Chinese philosophical concern with reality is with social reality and especially with social order, in part because the period was one of great disorder and under the threat of complete chaos. The old unified order had collapsed a couple hundred years before the time of Confucius (551–479 B.C.E.). China then consisted of small nation-states in constant warfare with one another for nearly three hundred more years, until the Qin (pronounced like the English word "chin" and giving us the name "China") succeeded in conquering all the rest and reunifying China in 221 B.C.E. During this period—which is the period of ancient Chinese philosophy—survival itself was a major concern, with warfare intensifying what has always been at the back of the minds of Chinese thinkers: there might not be enough food to go around. The history of massive famines in China is connected to a different mindset from that which has been characteristic of Western social philosophy. In the West, the issue has more typically been how to distribute goods and resources, while in China it has been to worry about making sure there are enough resources so that people could survive.

Thus we find Chinese thinkers concerned with how to rule and often talking as if they were addressing rulers, for this seemed the only way to get their ideas accepted. The notion of a revolt of the people or of democracy made no more sense to the Chinese of this period than it did in the West from the time of the Roman Empire until about three hundred years ago. So philosophers of all sorts spoke about (and to) rulers in the hopes that they would act as an enlightened parent would. For example, in *Analects* we read: "Chi K'ang Tzu [Qi Kangzi] asked Confucius about government. Confucius answered, 'To govern is to correct. If you set an example by being correct, who would dare to remain incorrect?'" (XII.17).

From the same classic, *Analects*, we can also find this rather extreme statement of the ideal:

> Tzu-kung [Zigong] asked about government. The Master said, "Give them enough food, give them enough arms, and the common people will trust in you."
>
> Tzu-kung said, "If one had to give up one of these three, which should one give up first?"
>
> "Give up arms."
>
> Tzu-kung said, "If one had to give up one of the remaining two, which should one give up first?"
>
> "Give up food. Death has always been with us since the beginning of time, but when there is no trust, the common people will have nothing to stand on." (XII.7)

Surely trust, most notably the trust of children in their parents, is a key part of the idea of the family. In the passage cited, we see it forming a model for thinking about government.

By and large, the Confucians tended to base their conception of the ruler on the model of a father, which was reasonable in that virtually all Chinese rulers have been males. Interestingly enough, Daoist thought, the main competing-yet-complementary strain to Confucianism from the beginning, sometimes employed mother images for the ruler. For example, the *Daodejing* contains the following passage:

> A large state is the lower reaches of a river—
> The place where all the streams of the world unite.
> In the union of the world,
> The female always gets the better of the male by stillness.
> Being still, she takes the lower position.
> Hence the large state, by taking the lower position,
> annexes the small state . . .
> All that the large state wants is to take the other under its wing.
> (Lau sec. 61; see also sec. 28)

A less conservative translation of another portion of the same document—and there are many translations—makes things even bolder in this regard:

The Tao is called the Great Mother:
empty yet inexhaustible,
it gives birth to infinite worlds.
It is always present within you.
You can use it any way you want.
(Mitchell sec. 6)

We have seen that Chinese concern for how to live was basically a concern for how to live with others in a society, and that society itself was understood mainly on models derived from the family. But Chinese thinkers were aware that there was more to the universe than human society, a point the Daoists emphasized in contrast to the Confucian concentration on humanity. Both these traditions, influenced in part by the even older *Book of Changes*, the *Yijing*, thought of the entire universe itself on the model of the family, with *Qian* 乾, "the Creative," and *Kun* 坤, "the Receptive" (Wilhelm translation) being the basic sources from which all reality was thought to spring, including Heaven (*Tian* 天) and Earth (*Tu* 土).

Humanity is of course the child of *Tian* and *Tu*, with the responsibility of learning from them so as to integrate them and all that is between them into a harmony. That is, in fact, what it means to grow up—to help bring all things into a harmony so far as it is within our power or else to find serenity in realizing the harmony that is already present.

Tu, and the vaguer *Kun* force behind it, are thought of in terms of mother and other female imagery, while *Tian* and *Qian* are spoken of in terms appropriate to fatherhood and other male roles. For example, an ancient commentary, traditionally thought to be by Confucius, that has been incorporated into the *Yijing* exclaims, "How great is the fundamental nature of *Qian*! The myriad things are provided their beginnings by it and, as such, it controls Heaven" (Lynn 129). For the mother image, we find the same text saying about *Kun* that "*Kun* consists of fundamentality and prevalence, and its fittingness is that of the constancy of the mare" (142). An important commentator from the third century c.e., Wang Bi, noted about the quotation just given: "The horse is a creature that travels by staying down (on the ground), but even more important we have the female of it, so it is something that represents the acme of compliance" (cited in Lynn 142–43).

It is vitally important for understanding Chinese philosophy to realize that no matter which member of a pair appears dominant, these contrasting pairs are deeply dependent on one another: there is no "Creative" without a "Receptive," no heaven without earth, no father without mother, and vice versa. Not only are these notions interdependent, but they are dynamic, in that one of them is something of a snapshot taken of a process which is bound to be on its way to become the other, if it hasn't already started in that direction. This is symbolized in the famous *yin/ yang* image,[3] where not only does each part literally contain part of the other, and not only is the shape of the division flowing and moving, but the yin, the principle usually associated with the female (the mother, the earth, the receptive), is expressed first in the label for the symbol, *yinyang*.

Perhaps the clearest and most poignant instance of the dynamic nature of these relationships is in how elderly parents can become like children, needing parental-type care by their own children. And for us in our time, with our increasing sensitivity to environmental problems, it is clear that both the earth and at least part of the heavens need our care to maintain an order that would help us continue to live. We may indeed, then, have something to learn from the Chinese philosophical outlook, which tries to make sense of reality itself in terms of images and metaphors based in the family.

The Family and the Practice of Chinese Philosophy

While the family is a central topic for Chinese philosophy, both as an explicit concern and, as we have seen, as a metaphorical source of ideas about society, government, and the cosmos, it also plays a key role in how the Chinese have engaged in philosophical thinking. In this section, we shall consider three ways in which (the idea of) the family has shaped the character of how the Chinese actually do philosophical thinking: it has served as a model for what we might call "philosophical families"; it has functioned as the basis for a method of thinking that we don't usually make much use of in Western kinds of philosophizing, though this might make a valuable addition; and, thirdly, it has motivated the development in China of philosophical methods that are familiar to us in the West.

Philosophical Families: The Philosophical Schools

The Chinese understanding of the teaching-and-learning process was modeled on the parent-child relationship, as noted in the previous section. This was not limited to a way of understanding particular lessons. Far more ambitiously, the family served as a model for the notion of a philosophical "school" or a philosophical lineage. Indeed, as was observed earlier in the chapter, the same character, *jia* (家), that is used for a home was also used for a school of philosophy.

The notion of a philosophical school is not unknown in the West. There were famous Greek institutions, such as Plato's Academy and Aristotle's Lyceum, where people of various ages lived in a familylike social setting, learning a particular philosophical perspective. In China an important imperial academy, centered on the study of the Confucian classics, was founded in 124 B.C.E. (Fairbank 67). And while such institutions came and went over the next few centuries, the famous Hanlin Academy, founded in 745 C.E., lasted well into the nineteenth century as an educator and preserver of the official imperial, usually Confucian, philosophy (Goodrich 136). These official academies were understood to be under the stewardship of the emperor, who, like a parent, had control over what should be learned and even read. This familylike organization was also mirrored in the numerous monasteries that have characterized much of the history of Chinese Buddhism and Daoism for the last two thousand years.

Broader than these particular institutions is the notion of a philosophical school in which students are disciples of a master. A philosophical school of this sort includes not only certain beliefs about how to live, about the nature of reality, and other philosophical topics, but it actually involves a way of living. The ancient Chinese had schools for Confucians, Daoists, and so many others that people spoke of "the hundred schools" of philosophy. Later periods in China have rarely been without a considerable group of people who belonged to some sort of Confucian school, and there have been powerful schools of Buddhism, considered by many to be a philosophy as well as a religion.

Closely associated with the paternalistic nature of the Chinese schools of philosophy is a concern for lineage. Chinese thinkers often claimed that they were the true heirs of an important figure. While the Daoists have wanted little to do with this concern except perhaps to make fun of it, issues of lineage have been central to the Confucians (especially the neo-Confucians in the early centuries of this millennium) and to the Buddhists. For many Buddhists, this concern took the form of discovering (and perhaps even creating) alleged lineages, so that the founder of one's sect is seen as a member of a direct line of succession going all the way back to Buddha himself. This concern with true lineage, clearly based on the model of the patriarchal father, is still very much in evidence in Zen Buddhism as practiced in contemporary Japan and America. Zen itself is derived from Chan Buddhism, which the Chinese developed between 600 and 900 C.E.

Family as a Basis for a Philosophical Method

The idea of family as a system of relations had an important impact on what it meant to philosophize, on the method of philosophy. The way in which Confucius himself and his immediate disciples were shown to be thinking can be our starting point here (meaning is found in one's position and actions with regards to others, and not in a unique, "atomic" essence), as it is one of the oldest and yet most enduring features of Chinese philosophy. This relational way of thinking is something we often do when trying to make sense of things, and yet it has not received much attention or status from Western logicians—those philosophers concerned with what counts as "rational" thinking. The suggestion here is that this way of thinking really can help us make sense of things and that, therefore, it should be acknowledged as having a rationality of its own and as being perfectly appropriate to the practice of philosophy.

Ironically enough, it is an important recent Western philosopher who has provided an image and a name for this kind of thinking. Ludwig Wittgenstein

(1889–1951), an Austrian who spent most of his life in England, pointed out the importance of what he called in his telling phrase (one astonishingly relevant for our topic): "family resemblances." He felt that Western philosophy since Plato had been on a wild-goose chase of seeking to identify the essences of things, to discover what a thing absolutely had to have to be that sort of thing; only then, it was thought, could one use the same term for different individual things, and so on. Wittgenstein argued that there is no one necessary characteristic or set of characteristics that makes things what they are, but there are various ways in which games and different members of a family, for example, resemble one another. Some games are competitive, some are not; some use balls, some do not; some family members have hooked noses, and some might not; some use characteristic phrases, but others might not; and so on. These different but overlapping similarities are what Wittgenstein called "family resemblances," and his insight was that appealing to these similarities is a perfectly good way to make sense of things (Wittgenstein; especially secs. 66, 67).

Wittgenstein put forth these ideas in his consideration of philosophy after World War II, but this sort of thinking has been in the philosophical tool kit of the Chinese since Confucius, as can be seen most clearly by considering the central work attributed to him, the *Analects*. This work, most of which was probably written by Confucius's immediate followers, consists of twenty short chapters or "books." Each of these is divided into numbered sections, many of them only a paragraph or so in length. But most of these sections don't seem to have much to do with the sections that come before and after. This makes Confucius very difficult for us to understand at first, and it also gives the impression that he did not think very deeply or fully about anything—that, in other words, he wasn't much of a philosopher.

Still, the works of Confucius have been the main philosophical shaper of an entire culture for nearly twenty-five hundred years. And their influence on other East Asian cultures, especially Japan and Korea, has been enormous. This is no doubt partly due to many of the things already discussed in this chapter, but it seems likely that it is also due to their embodying a very fruitful method of thinking. This method is simply to seek connections, not so much through deductive arguments or scientific generalizations as through seeking associations, correlations, and resemblances—family resemblances. Chinese students memorized the works of Confucius (and other thinkers) and were then able to make such connections between, for example, scattered sections of the *Analects*, and deepen their understanding of Confucius's work.

That this way of understanding things makes good sense can be seen by noticing how common it seems to be for us. Many people have, in effect, memorized considerable portions of TV programs or movies, and they can use these characters, plots, actions, jokes, and so on to help them understand more richly some topic or issue in real life. Then, too, people who know something about history—and most everyone knows something about some aspect of history, such as their own life, that of their family, and so on—operate in much the same way when faced with a puzzling situation or crisis. They remember what was done before and whether or not it was helpful; and they examine how much the current situation resembles those they remember, in order to reach a more thoughtful judgment about what to do now. As these examples suggest, we do this thinking all the time. What's more, we believe it to be rational to think this way, and we are perfectly able to evaluate some proposed connections as being more or less reasonable than others. The suggestion, then, is that this way of thinking, so characteristic of much Chinese philosophy, could be added to our ways of philosophical thinking or, more accurately, could be acknowledged as already a part of it.

Let us use the *Analects* themselves to show how this way of thinking worked and how it can increase one's understanding of things, how it would thus be reasonable to think of the early Confucians as philosophers. The topic that binds the following selections together is itself that of the family. Notice that while questions like What is the family? or What is a good family? are not explicitly posed, one could begin to assemble an idea of how to answer them by thinking about these passages and interrelating them. (By the way, these passages were not selected by someone who has memorized the book, but by someone who has only recently thought of using it this way.)

Yu Tzu [Youzi] said, "It is rare for a man whose character is such that he is good as a son and obedient as a young man to have the inclination to transgress against his superiors; it is unheard of for one who has no such inclination to be inclined to start a rebellion. The gentleman devotes his efforts to the roots, for once the roots are established, the Way will grow therefrom. Being good as a son and obedient as a young man is, perhaps, the root of a man's character." (I.2)

The Master said, "Observe what a man has in mind to do when his father is living, and then observe what he does when his father is dead. If, for three years, he makes no changes to his father's ways, he can be said to be a good son." (I.11)

Meng Wu Po [Meng Wubo] asked about being filial. The Master said, "Give your father and mother no cause for anxiety other than illness." (II.6)

Someone said to Confucius, "Why do you not take part in government?" The Master said, "The *Book of History* says, 'Oh! Simply by being a good son and friendly to his brothers a man can exert an influence upon government.' In doing so a man is, in fact, taking part in government." (II.21)

The Master said, "In serving your father and mother you ought to dissuade them from doing wrong in the gentlest way. If you see your advice being ignored, you should not become disobedient but remain reverent. You should not complain even if in so doing you wear yourself out." (IV.18)

The Master said, "A man should not be ignorant of the age of his father and mother. It is a matter, on the one hand, for rejoicing and, on the other, for anxiety." (IV.21)

The Governor of She said to Confucius, "In our village there is a man nicknamed 'Straight Body.' When his father stole a sheep, he gave evidence against him." Confucius answered, "In our village those who are straight are quite different. Fathers cover up for their sons, and sons cover up for their fathers. Straightness is to be found in such behavior." (XIII.18)

Ch'en Kang [Chen Kang] asked Po-yu [Boyu], "Have you not been taught anything out of the ordinary?"
"No, I have not. Once my father was standing by himself. As I crossed the courtyard with quickened steps [a sign of respect], he said, 'Have you studied the *[Book of] Odes*?' I answered, 'No.' 'Unless you study the *Odes* you will be ill-equipped to speak.' I retired and studied the *Odes*.
"Another day, my father was again standing by himself. As I crossed the courtyard with quickened steps, he said, 'Have you studied the rites?' I answered, 'No.' 'Unless you study the rites you will be ill-equipped to take your stand.' I retired and studied the rites. I have been taught these two things."
Ch'en Kang retired and said, "I asked one question and got three answers. I learned about the *Odes*, I learned about the rites, and I learned that a gentleman keeps aloof from his son." (XVI.13)

While it is not obvious what Confucius thinks about family from these examples, it does seem that thinking about what each passage says helps illuminate what some of the other passages say. By looking for these "family resemblances" and thinking about them, one can come to a clearer understanding of the Confucian ideal of the family. Similar things can be done with many other topics. To be sure, this method requires some active thinking, some stretching of the mind on the part of the reader. But since philosophy is concerned to make people think, this seems a most appropriate tactic.

Family as a Motivator for Other Philosophical Methods

Having seen how an important and distinctive dimension of early Confucian philosophizing can be related to the idea of the family, we may conclude this discussion of the practice of Chinese philosophy by meeting two other ways in which it has been shaped by the idea of the family. These methods owe the most to the ancient competitors of the Confucians.

According to traditional accounts, the earliest rival to the Confucians was the Daoists. As noted earlier in the chapter, the Daoists were interested in the relationship between individuals and all the other parts of the universe, whereas the Confucians focused on human relationships. The Daoists thus thought that the Confucians were too narrow, while the Confucians thought that the Daoists did not have a real sense of order, such as a family-centered understanding would provide.

If one looks at the two great classical Daoist works, the already quoted *Daodejing* and the *Zhuangzi*, a fourth-century B.C.E. work, the Confucians seem to have a point. If the *Analects* of Confucius strike us as hard to understand, these Daoist works are even more difficult. The style of the *Daodejing* is often obscure or paradoxical:

> XLVII
> Without stirring abroad
> One can know the whole world;
> Without looking out of the window
> One can see the way of heaven.
> The further one goes
> The less one knows.
> Therefore the sage knows without having to stir,
> Identifies without having to see,
> Accomplishes without having to act. (Lau)

> XIX
> Exterminate the sage, discard the wise,
> And the people will benefit a hundredfold;
> Exterminate benevolence, discard rectitude,
> And the people will again be filial;
> Exterminate ingenuity, discard profit,
> And there will be no more thieves and bandits.
> These three, being false adornments, are not enough
> And the people must have something to which they can attach themselves:
> Exhibit the unadorned and embrace the uncarved block,
> Having little thought of self and as few desires as possible. (Lau)

Notice that for all the obscurity of these passages, the notion of family persists in the concern for what we might call genuine familyness (being "filial"), which is sought in more open and spontaneous ways than by following the rules and roles, something the Daoists accused the Confucians of overdoing.

In the *Zhuangzi* we find stories, often strange and extravagant, about monsters and giant birds or about extraordinary people, such as a butcher who never had to sharpen his knife for nineteen years! These stories are often humorous, and not just because they poke fun at the Confucians, though they do that at times. Yet the stories seem to be told to make a point, and it is in their extravagant style in poetry and especially in storytelling that the Daoists offer an additional method of philosophizing to the Confucian model sketched above. This Daoist approach to philosophy has made permanent contributions to the Chinese tradition, for one can see it also very much at work in the writings of Chinese Buddhism. In particular, Chan or Zen Buddhism is much given to telling stories that are apparently nonsensical, because they are pursuing a deeper truth than words can provide. By contrast with China, it is only within the last hundred years that similar storytelling has made a bid, still controversial, to be a part of the method of Western philosophy.

A very brief example illustrates both the flavor and the power of Zhuangzi's Daoist storytelling:

> Once Chuang Chou [Zhuang Zhou, that is, Zhuangzi] dreamt he was a butterfly, a butterfly flitting and fluttering around, happy with himself and doing as he pleased. He didn't know he was Chuang Chou. Suddenly he woke up and there he was, solid and unmistakable Chuang Chou. But he didn't know if he was Chuang Chou who had dreamt he was a butterfly, or a butterfly dreaming he was Chuang Chou. Between a butterfly and Chuang Chou there must be some distinction! (Watson 45)

Confucian storytelling gets better as time goes on, but it never reaches the brilliance of the Daoists. It is, however, better than that of the other main rival of the early Confucians, the Mohists. This school, founded by Mozi, who lived from c. 480–390 B.C.E., was given to preachy essays instead. With them the family can be seen to play yet another important role in the dynamic of Chinese philosophy, this time as the main issue which led to the birth of another philosophical tactic: providing what we would call rational arguments.

The Mohists believe in what we might call "universal love." By this they meant that one should care for all other people equally, without regard not only to their gender, race, creed, social status, and so on, but also, and most importantly, without regard to whether they were part of your family. It is apparently the need to defend this extraordinarily un-Chinese idea (and Mohism does not survive the ancient period in China) that these people developed the use of rational argumentation. As A. C. Graham puts it, in his *Disputers of the Tao*, one of the best overviews of ancient Chinese thought:

> It is in the *Mo-tzu* [*Mozi*], the classical Mohist text, that we first meet the word *pien* [*bian*] "argue out alternatives". . . which was to become the established term for rational discourse. It is the distinguishing of the right alternative, the one which "is this" . . . from the wrong alternative, the one which "is not." . . . We find also in Mo-tzu a recognition that the soundness of a thought has nothing to do with who thinks it. (36)

In other words, the Mohists introduce in an abiding way a method of philosophizing which is central to the Western tradition: looking for good definitions and defending one's proposals for them by what we would recognize without question as rational arguments.

As a consequence of the Mohist and Daoist alternative philosophical methods, one finds more developed stories and, in particular, explicit argumentation in the writings of subsequent ancient Confucians such as Mencius (c. 390–305 B.C.E.) and Xunzi (c. 340–245). These two defended Confucian ideas, and they also argued with each other over such topics as the natural goodness of human nature. By the time of Plato and Aristotle, then, the practice of Chinese philosophy included rational argumentation, as well as such features as one could find in the Greek tradition before Plato: poetry, storytelling, and "wise sayings."

If all these features are accepted as a legitimate part of philosophy in the West, so they should be in their Chinese garb. Therefore, to answer the question with which we began, Chinese philosophy is philosophy. Furthermore, we could well consider enriching our tradition by making more of the characteristic Confucian method of seeking "family resemblances" and by exploring more fully the model of family to help us understand our own situation. Chinese philosophy is different from Western philosophy, to be sure, but it is nevertheless understandable—with some effort at times—by Westerners. The effort seems well worth a try, given that our world often still doesn't make as much sense as we would like.

Glossary

Analects A collection of teachings attributed to Confucius (Kongfuzi), this classic text reflects Confucius's emphasis on the unique, the concrete and the particular and reports his deep distrust of metaphysical, universalist claims.

Book of Changes An ancient classic text, the *Yijing* is one of the Five Classics of Confucianism; believed to have originated in the twelfth century B.C.E., the *Yijing* contains a discussion of Zhou dynasty divination, and sets out a cosmology that involves humans and nature in a unified system.

Book of Poetry One of the Confucian classics, sometimes translated as *The Book of Songs* or the *Book of Odes*; written as *Shijing, Shi Jing,* or *She King.*

Chan Buddhism One of the distinctively Chinese forms of Buddhism, it is often thought to be the result of the interdependent influences of Buddhism and Daoism, the direct ancestor of what is known in Japan as Zen Buddhism.

Confucianism A philosophical world view in which the idea of the family is central to an understanding of the nature of reality and of how to live. Its origins are attributed to Confucius (551–479 B.C.E.), and it has survived in China, often very influentially, to the present day. Confucianism is centrally concerned with creating harmonious order, in ourselves and in society.

Daoism A philosophical world view roughly as ancient as Confucianism, in which the idea of nature is more central than the family (which is seen as part of nature) and which points to spontaneity as the key to harmony.

Family resemblances The ways in which some members of a family distinctively resemble other members, emphasizing the idea that, within one family, different resemblances are characteristic between any two members. This is taken as a metaphor in philosophical thinking to explain how different specific instances fit under a given general term.

Filial Behavior befitting a son or daughter. In traditional China, this meant being responsible, caring, and fulfilling the rituals for one's parents.

Jia The Chinese term for (a) "family," in the sense of husband and wife and their children, grandparents, aunts and uncles, and so on; (b) "school," in the sense of "school of philosophers," a group of people with not only similar ways of thinking and similar world views, but also with similar ways of living; (c) the physical structure one lives in or "house."

Mohism A philosophical world view which arose in response to Confucianism and which did not take the family to be central to its understanding of how to live, preferring instead to think of all others as equally worthy of our concern. This philosophical world view did not survive the ancient period in China.

Philosophy The attempt to make rational sense of things once you think you have all the relevant information.

Yijing See *Book of Changes*; sometimes written as *I Ching*.

Yin/Yang An important Chinese symbol expressing the interdependence of apparent opposites and the sense of how they dynamically include and lead to each other.

Notes

1. See *The Doctrine of the Mean*, section 20, in Legge, James, trans. *The Chinese Classics: Confucian Analects, The Great Learning, and the Doctrine of the Mean*. Vol. 1. Hong Kong: Hong Kong University Press, 1960.

2. See Legge.

3. See Linda Pickle, in this volume, figure 1.1.

Works Cited

Fairbank, John King. *China: A New History*. Cambridge: Belknap Press of Harvard University Press, 1992.

Goodrich, L. Carrington. *A Short History of the Chinese People*. New York: Harper, 1959.

Graham, A. C. *Disputers of the Tao*. LaSalle, Ill.: Open Court, 1989.

Lau, D. C., trans. *Confucius: The Analects*. New York: Penguin, 1979.

———, trans. *Tao Te Ching*. New York: Penguin, 1963.

Legge, James, trans. and ed. *The Chinese Classics: Confucian Analects, The Great Learning, and the Doctrine of the Mean*, Vol. 1. Hong Kong: Hong Kong University Press, 1960.

Lynn, Richard, trans. *The Classic of Changes (I Ching)*. New York: Columbia University Press, 1994.

Mitchell, Stephen, trans. *Tao Te Ching*. New York: Harper, 1988.

Rosemont, Henry, Jr. "Rights-Bearing Individuals and Role-Bearing Individuals." *Rules, Rituals, and Responsibility: Essays Dedicated to Herbert Fingarette*. Ed. Mary I. Bockover. La Salle, Ill.: Open Court, 1991.

Watson, Burton, trans. *Chuang Tzu: Basic Writings*. New York: Columbia University Press, 1964.

Wilhelm, Richard, trans., and Carey Baynes, trans. *The I Ching*. Princeton, N.J.: Princeton University Press, 1950.

Wittgenstein, Ludwig. *Philosophical Investigations*. New York: Macmillan, 1953.

3
The Role of the Visual Arts in Confucian Society

Lawrence E. Butler

Chinese art is a vast and rich topic that can be approached in many ways. Traditional descriptions of Chinese art have been organized chronologically by dynasty, or by medium, such as bronze vessels or landscape painting. More recent studies have organized this material by the various contexts of use, such as art of the tomb or art of the temple. But what exactly is art? Most of the objects displayed in museums of Chinese art were made for a specific, utilitarian function. We study them as "art" because they are often so very beautiful. In imperial China, "the fine arts" were understood to mean the "three treasures" of calligraphy, poetry, and painting, as practiced by the educated elite. Other kinds of objects could be admired and collected for their visual qualities—jades, porcelain, and bronzes, for example—but would be considered "craft," made by anonymous workers and lacking in intellectual value.

In this chapter, we will consider a broad range of visual material as "art," while leaving calligraphy and architecture aside for separate in-depth consideration in chapters of their own. Rather than attempting a survey of all five thousand years of the visual arts in China, we will concentrate on those aspects of premodern Chinese art that illuminate Chinese cultural concepts of *community, family, lineage,* and *the orderly Confucian cosmos.* We will consider the role the visual arts have played in a Confucian society, and some of the communities that have grown up around the visual arts of China.

Art and Family Use: The Archeological Evidence

One of the great continuities of Chinese culture, reaching far back into the archeological record, has been the desire to comprehend and apprehend the spiritual forces that surround daily life. The most ancient Chinese texts we have—the questions from animal divination, inscriptions on bronze vessels, the *Book of Songs*, and the innermost core of the *Yijing*—attest to the importance of setting questions, seeking answers, and establishing connections to the spirit world, particularly the ancestral spirits, during the Chinese Bronze Age. Decorated objects from the prehistoric Neolithic cannot be "read" so easily, and yet they contain images that seem to anticipate such well-known features of later Chinese art and material culture as shamanistic ritual, burial with goods for an afterlife, shrines for ancestor veneration, protective animals such as dragons and phoenixes, and orientation to the cardinal directions.[1]

Ancestor Worship and Jade Burial Art of Early China

Understanding religious beliefs through prehistoric archeology is difficult. However, archeology can provide evidence of rituals surrounding the cycle of life and death, particularly through burial practices. In burials as old as that of the "Peking Man" *(Sinanththropus pekinensis)*, dating to around 16,000 B.C.E., archeologists in China have found grave goods and red powder indicating special care was taken to give the dead body comforts or honor in death. This suggests a belief in an afterlife; perhaps the soul of the dead was expected in some way to linger in the human community (Lei 219–20).

Ancestor worship may well be an outgrowth of such beliefs. Oracle inscriptions and texts from the Bronze-age Shang dynasty refer to a deified great ancestor, as *di* or *shangdi* 上 帝. Further, at least among the upper classes, the dead were given posthumous or "temple" names, and were buried in ceremony. Jade, imported at great cost and fashioned with great difficulty, has been excavated from the Liangzhu culture where burial sites have produced dozens of jade objects per grave, occasionally over one hundred. The objects fall into several groups: zoomorphic figurines of birds, turtles, cicadas, and fish; small ornaments such as buckles, rings, and beads; and the ceremonial axes, plaques, disks, and tubes whose meaning is still largely mysterious (see *Freer* 15–20). *Bi* 璧 disks (perfectly round, flat, and pierced with a circular hole) and the *cong* 琮 tubes (square with round interiors) are found by the dozens in individual graves, stacked in heaps or carefully outlining bodies. The use of jade may have peaked in the Western Han Dynasty (206 B.C.E.–9 C.E.), judging from the astonishing amount of jade found in elite burials. The forms included the full range of ritual jades, as well as ornaments, apotropaic carved animals, body orifice plugs, and the famous jade suits, consisting of hundreds of jade plaques stitched together with gold or silver. Cosmological associations must account for the use of jade to protect the body, perhaps even to confer immortality, since jade plaques had been sewn onto burial suits since at least the eighth century B.C.E. (Rawson, *Mysteries* 27).

Ancestor worship required males in the lineage to make regular sacrifices in the ancestor halls erected over the tombs of illustrious family members. Possible female and male fertility imagery at Neolithic sites fuel speculation about the possible existence of matriarchal societies at Banpo and elsewhere; but by the Zhou Dynasty, a pattern of hereditary male rule was clear, and by the Eastern Zhou (770–256 B.C.E.) emperors claimed descent from a great ancestor, the Yellow Emperor, Huangdi. Sacrifices to the ancestors were extremely important duties of a ruler, at least as important as the duty to lead in war (Chen 270–271). Ritual texts from the *Book of Songs*, some of which must date from the early Zhou or perhaps even before, make clear the importance of the ritual sacrifices to the well-being of the clan:

> Very hallowed was this service of offering;
> Very mighty the forefathers.
> The Spirits and Protectors have accepted;
> The pious descendant shall have happiness,
> They will reward him with great blessings,
> With span of years unending.

The same ode goes on to describe the solemn festivities of the feast, during which a young male of the clan impersonates the Ancestor and is inhabited by his spirit who promises blessing after the appropriate rituals:

> "The Spirits," they say, "enjoyed their drink and food
> And will give our lord a long life.
> He will be very favoured and blessed,
> And because nothing was left undone,
> By son's sons and grandson's grandsons
> Shall his line for ever be continued."
>
> (no.199)

As Chen Lie puts it, "The ancestor cult was entirely dependent on procreation. If a person had no descendants, the continued existence of his soul would be endangered" (272). Having no descendants, then, was worse than neglecting the performance of ancestral sacrifices. Today, we look at the burial objects and the artifacts attendant to the rituals associated with ancestor worship as examples of Chinese art of exquisite workmanship and outstanding beauty.

Ritual Bronzes and Li 禮

Some of the most impressive artistic remains from ancient China are the bronze vessels and implements from the Shang and Zhou dynasties used in the ancestral rites (see *Freer* 1–6). Vast numbers of heavy, ornate bronzes have been found in a number of elite burials. This is especially remarkable considering the heaviness of the Chinese vessels, cast rather than hammered, using an enormous amount of bronze processed from copper and tin mined far from the capitals and transported as heavy bars—metal that might have gone into weapons (Rawson, *Mysteries* 250).[2]

Conspicuous display of disposable wealth seems to have been an important function of these bronze objects in their social context. Social hierarchy was reflected in the materials and ornaments used. Grave goods, then, are a reliable indicator of social status; common people were buried with ceramic vessels only, while just up the social scale people were buried with a few simple bronzes without elaborate decoration. In burials with many bronzes, the size, number, and splendor of the vessels indicate status; clearly these objects conferred great prestige on clan and on the deceased individual (Rawson, *British Museum* 33–34, 60). They also functioned as dynastic trophies:

> When a great state attacks a small one, and takes the spoils to make an article to furnish the ancestral temple, it engraves on it its successful achievement to show to posterity, at once to manifest its own bright virtue, and to hold up to condemnation the offenses of the other. (Legge trans. *Tso Chuen* 483)[3]

Ritual bronzes were produced from about 1700 B.C.E. and were used throughout the Shang Dynasty and through most of the Zhou, with forms and decoration changing over time, most notably in the early ninth century B.C.E.. The most common shapes of vessels indicate their functions: wine vases, wine cups, food cauldrons, and plates. These pieces served at functions presumably resembling the clan feast cited in the song above. Many are inscribed, making their ownership and clan connection clear, sometimes indicating the occasion for which they were cast. Changes in type over time, or by region, probably reflect differences in ritual practice and belief. In the Shang royal tombs, for example, one typically finds bronze axe heads, pierced with anthropomorphic masks. These were used for ritual killing, including the sacrificial beheading of servants to accompany the deceased royals. Human sacrifice was very much part of Shang and early Chou royal burials, but by the late Zhou the practice was abandoned; representations of people and possessions were buried instead. Even the bronzes were increasingly replaced by ceramic copies in burials in the Han, reflecting economic traditions, perhaps reflecting as well the decline of traditional ancestor worship as the sole mode of popular religion (Rawson, *Mysteries* 265). Many of the objects that we enjoy as Chinese art announced, to some degree, the wealth, social status, and power of the family and performed specific roles within the context of family rituals.

Bronzes reflected dynastic history in other ways. When the Zhou conquered the Shang, about 1050 B.C.E., they adopted the elaborate Shang ancestor rituals as part of their propaganda campaign to legitimize the dynasty, proclaiming their ability to make the all-important ancestral sacrifices. The bronze vessel types they had used now changed to imitate Shang models (see *Freer* 7–10). But more striking, the Zhou bronzes contained long inscriptions that communicate the dynastic achievements to the living and the dead. These inscriptions provide invaluable information about the Zhou state and its ideology, parallel to the ancient accounts in the *Book of History* (see *Freer* 29). Thus, some artifacts acted as family or dynastic diaries recording a family's history.

One of the later innovations of the Western Zhou dynasty in the ninth century "ritual revolution" was the addition of great sets of bronze bells to the ritual accoutrements, a change so sudden and so widespread that it must have been the result of a decision at court (Rawson, *Mysteries* 260–61). The music of the bronze bells became part of the observances of ritual and propriety, or *li* 禮, that came to govern all aspects of Zhou Dynasty aristocratic life.

Another bronze vessel shape, particularly important for its association with the notions of family, dynasty, and general cultural resonance, was the food cauldron, or *ding* 鼎 (see *Freer* diagram 182*)*. The *ding*, tripod or square, was central to the sacrificial rites for the entire Bronze Age.[4] The legendary heroes Yu and Qi, founders of the Xia Dynasty, were credited with casting nine *dings* that became symbols of dynastic legitimacy, possessed in turn by the Shang and the Zhou as clear symbols of the "mandate of Heaven." The *Tso Chuen* gives one version of the legend:

> Anciently, when the Xia was distinguished for its virtue, the distant regions sent pictures of the [remarkable] things in them. The nine pastors sent in the metal of their provinces, and the tripods were cast, with representations on them of those objects. All the things were represented, and [instructions were given] of the preparations to be made in reference to them, so that the people might know the sprites and evil things. Thus the people, when they went among the rivers, marshes, hills, and forests, did not meet with the injurious things . . . Hereby a harmony was secured between the high and the low, and all enjoyed the blessing of Heaven. When the virtue of [King] Jie [of Xia] was obscured, they were transferred to Shang, for 600 years. [King] Zhou of Shang proved cruel and oppressive, and they were transferred to [the kingdom of] Zhou. When virtue is commendable and brilliant, the tripods, though they were small, would be heavy; when [virtue] gives place to its reverse, to darkness and disorder, though they were large, they would be light. Heaven blesses intelligent virtue; on that its favor rests.[5]

Excavated *ding* sets from the Bronze Age are usually an odd number; traditional scholarship suggested that nine *dings* were used in royal sacrifices, seven by feudal lords, five by grandees and so on down through class ranks, though such rigid limitations broke down in the later Zhou (Yang Xiaoneng 25). In the *Yijing*, the *ding* is Hexagram 50, and contains associations of benefit to the whole nation through wise rule, good character, and appropriate behavior. The tripod *ding*, an object of art in a museum, developed from family and ritual needs and eventually became a metaphor for the harmonious unity of the heavens, earth, and humankind.

The passage above also gives a late Zhou Dynasty explanation for one of the most puzzling but striking features of the ancient Chinese bronzes, the pervasive use of an abstract monster mask in the incised decoration. Known by the later term *taotie* 饕餮 , this face often consists of a mouth, nose, eyes, and horns/antlers centered on the ritual vessels' sides, giving zoomorphic meaning to the pot. Tremendous speculation surrounds the origin and meaning of these masks: representations of dragons, sacrificial animals, the ancestor, a gluttonous demon, or perhaps the shaman himself?[6] The term *taotie* is first found in a late Zhou text but is not applied to the decoration of ritual bronzes until the Han Dynasty, a millennium after the motif appears in the Shang. The etymology of the word may have to do with "glutton," and the bronzes on which the *taotie* appears were used in ritual feasts. A tempting explanation characterizes the *taotie* as a supernatural force devouring the sacrifice, but the *taotie* takes so many variant forms that it may not represent a single idea at all. At this point, there is simply no scholarly consensus concerning this distinctive feature of antique Chinese ritual bronzes.

The Philosophy of Rulership and the
Arts of State Ritual Commemoration

Ancestor-oriented family rituals are key to Chinese culture, both at the level of individual families and of the state, embodied by the emperor. Beginning with Confucian writings of the late Zhou Dynasty, and especially in the books of ritual written in the Han Dynasty, we are better able to follow the exact procedures of family rituals and the meaning behind them.[7] Confucius (551–479 B.C.E.) was instrumental in revolutionizing the meaning of the ancestral ritual feasts. Conceived many centuries earlier as shamanistic communications with the spirits of the ancestors—celebrations of clan and dynastic power with implications of military conquest and human sacrifice—they were still practiced in his own turbulent times with elaborate ceremony, but with many of the original meanings obscured. Confucius, an antiquarian of early Zhou dynastic history and practice, deplored the way upstart states had usurped the practices of rituals once reserved for the high king. He closely studied the proper methods and attitudes for ritual observance, or *li*, and declared them to be central to the harmonious functioning of society.[8] Whether he believed in the presence of ancestral spirits, or in any particular heavenly forces, is unclear. According to the *Analects*, "He sacrificed *to the dead*, as if they were present. He sacrificed to the spirits, as if the spirits were present" (III.XII.1). He taught that the correct practice of *li* was essential, but for new reasons in troubled times: not just as a way of appeasing ancestors, but as a path of cultivation for the gentleman, a mirror of the correct filial relationships within society, and thus a guarantor of harmony in the state. To Confucius, the ancestral sacrifices using the ritual bronzes represented the hope of regaining an orderly civilization, such as he believed had existed in the early Zhou Dynasty, through shared rituals of filiality.

After the Zhou Dynasty and by the advent of Imperial China under the first emperor, Qin Shi Huangdi, the old Zhou rituals were no longer observed in the same ways, whatever their prestige. A number of tombs from the Han Dynasty have been excavated, and show us that ritual bronze shape of the Zhou period changed into more utilitarian forms. The grave goods show a substitution of ceramic vessels for the traditional bronze ones, and increasing use of clay models of earthly goods for the real things (see *Freer* 121) . Human and animal sacrifice no longer seem part of even the most aristocratic burials after the Qin; again, clay models are substituted for the real thing. Later Tang Dynasty burials are famous for their ceramic tomb figures of members of court, guardian figures, and even exotic foreign types made familiar through the Tang Dynasty's trade along the Silk Routes.

Late Zhou Dynasty family rituals were studied in detail for use in the Han Dynasty and later. Descriptions have come down to us via Han Dynasty authors in three fragments: the *Ritual of Zhou (Zhouli)*, *Etiquette and Ritual (Yili)*, and the *Record of Ritual (Liji)*. These texts give elaborate prescriptions for families at the level of lower officer or gentleman, though family rites were by no means restricted to the upper strata of society. Four great family ceremonies were observed: capping (or initiation and introduction to the ancestors), weddings, funerals, and sacrificing to the ancestors (Buckley 18–24). Of all these ceremonies, the greatest visual evidence belongs to funeral practices and beliefs, particularly from the Han Dynasty.

Three tombs at Mawangdui in the Southern state of Chu dating to the Western Han (206 B.C.E.–C.E. 9) preserve relics of these burial practices. Bodies were dressed, wrapped in shrouds, and placed in elaborate heavy coffins. Elsewhere bodies have even been found clothed in suits of jade, stitched together with gold. The Mawangdui tombs were found to contain an extraordinary array of preserved grave goods in materials that rarely survive: lacquer, wood, textiles, even texts on bamboo. Objects with probable cosmological purpose included mirrors, jade *bi* disks, and incense burners in the shape of the "fairy mountain," or Isle of the Immortals in the Eastern Sea.

While jade and bronze artifacts provide part of the historic story, so textile art plays an important role. Perhaps the most famous single object found at Mawangdui is the silk funerary banner found in Lady Dai's tomb, painted with striking images of the funerary rites and the ascent into the afterlife. One of two "flying banners" draped over the body to carry the *hun* 魂 soul aloft, the banner hangs vertically, and is divided into three zones. In the middle, one sees a portrait of the lady as in life, being served (by filial relatives?). Below, in a realm of *yin* tigers, fish, demons, and a *bi* disk, is a representation of the funeral feast; probably a depiction of the afterlife of the *po* 魄 in the underworld. At the top, amidst immortals riding flying dragons, singing birds, and the sun and moon, the lady's *hun* soul presumably is shown the way to enter the realm of the spirits. The banner may have been used in ritual procession to summon the soul into its new home. Although precise interpretations are controversial, the banner seems to represent the triad of *tian* (heaven), earth, and humankind according to early Han cosmology and further recalls funereal poetry from the *Songs of the Chu,* in which the soul is recalled to the safety of a ritualized setting, since the rest of the cosmos is inhabited by frightful forces.[9]

The Grand Union, Small Tranquillity, and the Great Plan

To understand the rhetoric of tomb and funeral imagery of the later Eastern Han (C.E. 25–220), we need to consider in more detail the Confucian ideology of kingship. What is an orderly cosmos? There is a nostalgia throughout the writings of traditional China for a Utopian time before dynasties, even before filiality, when people lived well without rules or rulers. The clearest statement of this is in the *Liji,* a Han dynasty *Book of Rites* here quoting conversation purported to be that of Confucius:

> When the Grand course was pursued, a public and common spirit ruled all under the sky [that time] we call the Grand Union.
>
> Now that the Grand course has fallen into disuse and obscurity, the kingdom is a family inheritance. Every one loves (above all others) his own parents and cherishes (as) children (only) his own sons. People accumulate articles and exert their strength for their own advantage. Great men imagine it is the rule that their states should descend in their own families.[10]

In short, kings, proprieties, even filiality are necessary evils in a selfish age. The good king is one who pays careful attention to these proprieties and rules with benevolence. As for his relationship to the larger forces of the cosmos, the *Book of History,* the *Shijing,* contains the "Great Plan," a systematic explanation of the moral order of the cosmos as understood in the Zhou Dynasty. The king's central role is maintaining cosmic harmony through his cultivation of virtue and good government.[11] This secures for him the Mandate of Heaven and keeps the people happy as contrasted to the fate of the last king of the previous Shang Dynasty, who lost the Mandate of Heaven through his wickedness.

Early Chinese political theorists were divided roughly into two camps. The Confucians never forgot the Utopian tradition of the Sage Kings, the legendary founders of the early dynasties, who transferred power voluntarily and ruled "all under heaven" by public-mindedness. The Legalists of the short-lived Qin Dynasty (221–206 B.C.E.) advocated an absolutist imperial state ruled through a centralized bureaucracy, transferring power "selfishly" through inheritance. Notions of cosmic rule and misrule—in harmony with the Great Plan or in tyrannical opposition to it—should be kept in mind as we examine tombs of the Qin and Han dynasties as examples of visual metaphors of orderly empire.

Tombs and Ancestral Shrines of the Qin and Han Dynasties

The most extraordinary tomb of the period, of course, is the vast funerary complex of the first emperor himself, Qin Shi Huangdi. The tomb mound has long been known, but in 1975 were discovered its most famous components, a series of burial pits containing an entire army of life-size terracotta (baked-clay) warriors, horses, and chariots, some six thousand figures in the first pit alone. All were originally painted, outfitted with appropriate details of function and rank, and individualized to a surprising degree. The terracotta army pits represent only the outlying elements of the tomb complex, the full extent of which is not yet clear.

The first emperor—who united China, standardized the writing, and created the unified Great Wall—clearly wanted to surround himself with his own realm in death as in life. But the tomb represents more than just wanting to enjoy it all in the afterlife. His more notorious actions included burning all copies of the Confucian classics (except one set buried with him) and slaughtering Confucian scholars who objected to his absolutist program. While the emperor hardly ignored the heavenly sphere—he sacrificed at Mount Tai, guarded his tomb, and was obsessed with achieving immortality—he clearly claimed "all under heaven" without regard to Confucian notions of humanistic rule. Clearly his vast tomb project is at one level an expression of Legalist ideas that the absolutist emperor and his centralized bureaucracy were the state, and were the best guarantee of order. Simply the scale of the vast project attests to his ability to mobilize all the resources of the empire. This tomb art then is clearly making a tremendous philosophical as well as sociopolitical statement.

Later imperial tombs of the succeeding Han Dynasty continued the use of large armies of inanimate figures. Han Dynasty aristocratic tombs recently excavated around Xi'an show courtly life in great mural frescoes, lining the walls of the multichambered stone funereal mansions. Spirit Ways lined with propitious sculpture were developed, leading to both tomb and shrine. Guardian and courtly figurines of terracotta, such as the famous Tang Dynasty tomb goods, were substituted for the once all-too-human companions of an emperor in death. Never again was the Legalist vision of the autocratic emperor expressed quite so vividly in the rhetorical language of tomb art.

In the Eastern Han Dynasty (c.e. 25–220) a number of funerary structures reflect more Confucian concepts of the harmonious cosmos in their art. Typically, great families would erect both underground tomb and above-ground public offering shrine. Stone or brick shrines were built above ground by court officials and aristocrats to hold memorial tablets and house the *hun*, while the body was buried underground with the *po*. A shrine inscription from c.e. 154 at Donga in Shandong makes the filial purpose clear:

[The second son,] Wuhuan, is carrying on the family line. He deeply bears in mind his parents' generosity and remembers constantly the mournfulness and grief [that he felt at his parents' death]. He and his younger brother worked in the open air in their parents' graveyard, even early in the morning and even in the heat of the summer. They transported soil on their backs to build the tumulus and planted pine and juniper trees in rows. They erected a stone shrine, hoping that the *hun* souls of their parents would have a place to abide. (Wu 221)

Such elaborate expressions of filiality remind us of the very public role these shrines played. The *Book of Rites* made clear that virtuous men should serve their deceased relatives as if they were alive. Important family rituals would be enacted here, in the public gaze; and court employment depended on an individual's reputation for filiality (Powers 11–13).

The best-preserved ensemble of Eastern Han funerary art to survive may be the bas-relief carvings on the stone walls of the Wu family shrines in Shandong, dated between c.e. 151 and 170.[12] The carvings, which may reflect wall-painting compositions of the same period, display the entire cosmos—heavenly forces, the earth, and humanity—in its idealized, harmonious form. On the ceiling vaults of the Wu Liang shrine are auspicious heavenly omens, while the walls record human history, starting with the mythological snake-humans Fu Xi and Nu Wa, proceeding through the standard historiography of virtuous and bad emperors, Confucian worthies, and ending with the deceased, Wu Liang. In this shrine, the relationship between *tian* and humankind is presented as ethical and political. Also, by this time, *tian* was viewed as heavenward—above—and the earth below, with the soul making the journey upward. Wu Liang was a retired Confucian scholar engaged in private learning and teaching, and the shrine seems infused with a specifically Confucian view of the cosmos. Groupings suggest three themes: cosmic order as an outcome of virtuous behavior, filiality (represented by paradigmatic bonds between ruler and ruled, husband and wife, parent and child), and the safe journey of the *hun* soul. All this presupposes a moral cosmos and hints at criticism of current events.

In Han art, the image of harmony, as represented by yin and yang emblems and paradigmatic historical figures, could be a veiled reference to its opposite, the corrupt court and the abuse of power (Powers 253–54). Portraits such as those used in the Wu Liang shrine have served as moral exemplars, and as evidence of connections through time and hierarchy, at least since the Han Dynasty.[13] The Han tombs use images of Confucius and his followers, of culture heroes such as Yu or the Duke of Zhou, and of virtuous emperors as paragons of virtue. Vilified historical figures, such as the last king of Xia or the first emperor of Qin, serve not only for contrast but also as warnings, for these are figures who lost the heavenly mandate. As interest in secular portraiture increased after the Han in the period of disunity (220–581), one also finds a growing interest in idiosyncratic Confucian personalities, such as the "Seven Sages of the Bamboo Grove," exemplars not of governing virtue but of cultured (not to say drunken) leisure.

Art at Court

Most of what we know about ancient Chinese palaces and their decoration comes from literary descriptions. The great palaces of the Qin, Han, and Tang Dynasty emperors around Chang'an (Xi'an) have long since disappeared. Archeology has discovered the foundations of Qin Shi Huangdi's palaces at Xianyang, but only bronze finial details and fragments of painted murals remain as hints of the original splendor. Poets have left descriptions of the Han palaces and allow us to imagine interiors rich in colors and hung with patterned silks such as are occasionally found in excavations. In later Chinese art, life-size and larger portraits of emperors were used in the rituals of court, hanging in palace halls or in dynastic shrines where they could be venerated as ancestor portraits by the living emperor as part of the dynastic cult (Vinograd 5–9). The Han palace itself, fabled for its luxury, became a popular subject in later Chinese art, particularly during times of foreign-born dynasties, when the native Han dynasty became a subject of nostalgia. Textual evidence confirms that didactic images of Confucian worthies and meritorious officials were commonly painted on the walls of palaces and houses in the Han Dynasty, though we have only the tomb images now as reflections of that practice.

Many accounts of womens' lives in the Han and Tang courts have been enshrined in literature and art, often as moral exemplars (Murray 27–53). These are the subjects of some of the earliest painted handscrolls that have come down to us in the original, or have been preserved in copies—it is not always clear which is which. The most famous of these are attributed to the painter Gu Kaizhi (c. 345–406) or his copyists. One, in the Beijing Palace Museum, records "Portraits of Exemplary Women Known for Their Kindnesses and Wisdom." Another, in the British Museum in London, records the "Admonitions of the Court Instructress" to palace ladies on proper courtly behavior. A painting in the Freer Gallery in Washington shows "Palace Ladies Playing Double-Sixes," a board game (see *Freer* 36–37).[14] One source of these courtly images was a widely disseminated text of the first century B.C.E. by Liu Xiang, *Biographies of Exemplary Women*. Such texts and the paintings they inspired presented as paragons royal women whose exemplary behavior included modesty and chastity, submission to men, encouraging the transmission of culture and avoiding distracting the emperor from his duties (Clunas, *Art* 37–38).

On that last point, the most famous "distraction" in imperial China was the imperial lady Yan Guei Fei. She was the consort of Tang Emperor Xuan Zong, whose infatuation with her was said (by notoriously misogynist Confucian courtiers) to have led him to neglect the affairs of state, which fell into the hands of unjust officials resulting ultimately in the An Lushan rebellion in 755. In the course of putting down the rebellion, the emperor was forced by his troops to have the lady put to death. Her romantic story was made famous by the poet Bai Juyi in the "Song of Lasting Regret," a poem frequently illustrated in painted handscrolls.

This is related to another common genre of history painting, which shows important incidents in court life in which officials—emperors, even—were brought face to face with the consequences of their injudicious actions. All these paintings are didactic in nature, as court painting tended to be through the long history of dynastic China, presenting Confucian paradigms of behavior (or misbehavior) and its consequences. But this is hardly the only function of art in Confucian society, as we will see below.

Art Related to The Son of Heaven

"Iconography" is the art-historical term for how the meaning of a work of art is symbolized: the content. The best-known iconographic device (i.e., symbol) of the Chinese emperor, the Son of Heaven, is the five-clawed dragon, or *long* 龍, the personification of pure *yang* 陽 that rises from the water and fills the heavens. The dragon's thundering was associated with the bringing of rain; a fine example of *yang* achieving fulfillment and tuning into *yin,* in traditional thinking.[15]

By the Ming Dynasty, the emperor's role as main harmonizer between heavenly and earthly forces in an agricultural society meant that the imperial palace was filled with ritual settings and representations concerned with the dynamic balance of *yin* and *yang* and the bringing of fertility to the Empire. In Beijing today, the Palace Museum of the former Forbidden City is filled with significant symbols: the sacrificial tripods, or *dings;* dragons and phoenixes representing *yin* and *yang,* or set up on spirit walls to ward off evil from the north. All the alignments of the palace are significant and cosmic, and all actions within the ceremonial parts of the palace were ritualized to conform to the demands of harmony and season. Different dynasties chose different emblematic colors, but in general the emperor was represented by yellow, the color of the center in the cosmology of direction. Court clothing was highly specific to rank, as shown in colors, emblems, and attachments.[16]

One major genre of imperial art surviving in great numbers, from the Song Dynasty on, is the long handscroll detailing an official occasion, such as an inspection visit to the provinces or an ancestral ceremony on an auspicious occasion. These scrolls are in-house productions of the court artists, precisely drawn and brightly colored. They may have been exhibited on official occasions to selected dignitaries, and occasionally sent as gifts, but were, for the most part, for the pleasure and use of the emperors themselves. They also served a didactic function, of course, by showing the emperors as the embodiments of the state, performing the functions expected of the all-powerful but benevolent and filial Son of Heaven and reigning dynasty.

The Arts in Confucian Society

Chinese painting is the work of the writing brush. Since this is also the preeminent tool of the Confucian scholar, there has inevitably been more attention paid to this particular Chinese art than to any other. There is an evolution in painting from the Han until later dynasties, from paintings done in hard outline enlivened by bright colors to paintings done increasingly often with the simple writing brush and ink. Over the centuries, the latter gained more prestige, since it was considered to reflect scholarly refinement and to transmit elevated values. To see how this came about, we will explore painting from different angles: theory, artist, and subject matter.

Confucian Theories of Painting

Older works on Chinese art theory tend to assume that Confucians thought of art only as didactic, and we have certainly seen illustrations of that. However, there was a discernible growth in sophisticated appreciation for the arts among Confucian scholars over the course of the dynasties between the Han and the Song.[17] Little theoretical writing about painting remains from the Han and Six Dynasties period, and what does seems to assign it three functions: illustrative, magical, and moral. This last has the longest currency. As one ninth-century author explains, "For to see the good serves to warn against evil, and the sight of evil serves to make men long for wisdom. . . From this we may know that paintings are the means by which events are preserved in a state in which they serve as models [for the virtuous] and warnings [for the evil]."[18]

The best-known utterance in Chinese art theory is the rather cryptic "Six Rules of Painting" by the early figure painter Xie He, written in the late fifth century as part of his long biography of painters. The rules are as follows:

Spirit Resonance (or Vibration of Vitality) and Life Movement. The second is: Bone Manner (i.e., Structural) Use of the Brush. The third is: Conform with Objects to Give Likeness. The fourth is: Apply the Colours according to the Characteristics. The fifth is: Plan and Design, Place and Position (i.e., Composition). The sixth is: To Transmit Models by Drawing. (Siren 19)

The precise interpretation of each rule is difficult to pin down, but taken together they might be understood in this way: A painter should capture and portray the *qi* 氣 or essential energy and life force of the subject, whether it is a person or a mountain landscape. Outlines and strong brushstrokes give structure to the draftsmanship. Effective painting requires careful attention to likeness, the use of color to enrich the ink painting, and composition. Finally, and very important, a painter must study the best models of antiquity, copying them carefully to learn their styles and to transmit them for posterity. Every succeeding treatise on Chinese painting has owed some debt to this formulation, and the principles still guide traditional Chinese painters today.[19]

In the Six Dynasties period, Confucian scholars recognized that painting embodied an artist's feeling about the thing depicted. Like poetry and song, painting was understood to be the expression of what is impossible to express in direct speech and that the wise and good observer would benefit by savoring the image of things and developing a sympathetic response. Zhu Xi (1130–1200), the leading neo-Confucian theorist of the Song Dynasty, understood that the communication of elevated feeling is a desirable aim of art, by embodying the responses of a superior person to an ennobling subject (Cahill, "Confucian Elements" 120–4). Daoist sentiment may well have played a role in this idea, and it was crucial for the development of landscape painting as an independent genre. It is hardly the case, as used to be assumed, that "landscapes are Daoist or Chan" and "portraits are Confucian," since after all, vast numbers of Chinese painters were Confucian-trained scholars or professionals, as we will see below.

Artistic creation—understood as the literati arts of poetry, calligraphy, and painting—served another very important function in Confucian thinking. It fostered a community of spirit across time and place, by putting literati in touch with their own lineage and tradition, much as literature did. With the dissemination of artist's biographies from the Tang Dynasty on, artists—professional or amateur— were acutely aware of their intellectual and stylistic lineage. Models were copied assiduously as part of any artist's training in both calligraphy and representational painting. Throughout the history of Chinese art to the present day, painters tried to be fluent in the language of the brush of approved predecessors, and kept up a dialogue across centuries through their responses and innovations within recognized traditions.

To understand the role of the arts in Confucian society, we will examine several genres of painting—portraits, landscapes, and literati themes—and also consider just who these artists were.

Portraiture

The Chinese view of the individual as a link in a family lineage, or as part of a class or professional community, makes portraiture very important; but it also limits the individuality shown in any given portrait. Ancestor or predecessor portraits were often painted posthumously, to serve in rituals of ancestor veneration. Such effigies are usually formal, the seated figure displaying little emotion, in accordance with Confucian decorum. Clothing reflects the sitter's rank and office, and only the close attention to facial features may give the portrait the feeling of individuality. Inscriptions name the sitter and affirm the continuity of lineage and the filiality of the descendants. [20]

Besides family portraiture, such effigies were also important in Chan Buddhism, where abbots and monks were often represented as part of a given monastery's lineage. Such portraits depicted the individual physiognomies with vivid naturalism; inscriptions might further describe the inner state of the sitter. Some portrait statues of abbots even contained remains of the deceased to increase the identification of image and sitter. Chan portraiture reached a peak in the Song Dynasty (960–1279).

There is little theoretical writing about portraiture before about c.e. 1700, but there are many anecdotes about artists and sitters. They stress the importance of "using form to describe spirit" (attributed to the painter Gu Kaizhi, c. 345–406). Accordingly, other modes of portraiture developed which show the sitter in other social roles aside from that of paradigmatic ancestor. There is a convention of "pictures of behavior and enjoyment," showing the subject relaxing outdoors, dating back to the fifth century C.E. Elegant and cultured gatherings are another genre—seemingly informal, but with the social roles of every figure made explicit. Beginning in the Song Dynasty, the literati were depicted—or depicted themselves—in landscape settings where the rocks, pine, and bamboo echoed scholarly virtues of strength, lasting virtue, and flexibility. Cultured garden gatherings of men dominate the portrait imagery of the early Ming period (late 14th to 15th centuries), while by the Qing Dynasty (1644–1912) such portraits often were playful or self-parodying. In all ages, Chinese portraits reflected and reinforced societal roles—within the family, the social lineage, or the class. They were didactic; their value lay in the values—usually Confucian—that they presented (Farrer 107).

Chinese Landscape Painting

Landscape painting since the Song Dynasty has traditionally been regarded as the highest achievement of Chinese artists, and a vast amount has been written about it.[21] Its origins are discernible in the tomb art of the late Zhou Dynasty, where hunting scenes are found in painted lacquer ware or inlaid in figured bronze vessels. Incense burners take the form of Mount Penglai, the island home of the Immortals in the Eastern Sea. Art historians scrutinize Han Dynasty tombs and early Buddhist murals preserved at Dunhuang (dating for the most part from the fourth through the tenth centuries) for indications of early landscape painting, seen always as a setting for figures in a narrative setting. One of our few examples of actual early landscape painting exists now only in copies, in Beijing and in the Freer Gallery in Washington, DC: Gu Kaizhi's *Nymph of the Lo River*, an illustration of a story by Cao Zhi (see *Freer* 35). In it, the landscape is indicated in a sort of shorthand, as small trees and abbreviated mountainous elements surrounding the characters in the story. A painter contemporary of his, Zong Bing, wrote one of the first treatises on landscape paintings, extolling their ability to transport the soul. He associates the Confucian appreciation of music with the Daoist appreciation of nature and spirit, in a synthesis that was to have a long life in Chinese elite thought:

> Thus by living leisurely, by controlling the vital breath, by wiping the goblet, by playing the chin, by contemplating pictures in silence, by meditating on the four quarters of space, by never resisting the influence of Heaven and by responding to the call of the wilderness, where the cliffs and peaks rise to dazzling heights and the cloudy forests are dense and vast, the wise and virtuous men of ancient times found innumerable pleasures which they assimilated by their souls and minds. What more should I desire? If I too can find this happiness in my soul, is it not better than everything else? (Siren 16)

Landscape was an established, independent subject by the beginning of the Song Dynasty (960–1279), perhaps in part because so many of the intellectuals took refuge in the countryside during the troubled times after the fall of the Tang Dynasty in 906 and came to appreciate the spiritual benefits of the natural settings of isolated Buddhist monasteries. One of the earliest remaining examples is the great "Buddhist Temple in the Hills After Rain," a Northern Song hanging scroll attributed to the tenth-century painter Li Cheng, now located in the Nelson-Atkins Gallery, Kansas City. If the value of painting lay in the presentation of elevated reactions to ennobling subject, then increasingly it was understood that contemplation of the landscape was a symbolic means of contemplating the greater cosmological ideas presented by Daoism, Chan Buddhism, and by Confucian thinkers themselves. The word for landscape in Chinese is *shanshui* 山水, "mountain-water." Confucius said, "The wise find pleasure in water; the virtuous find pleasure in hills. The wise are active; the virtuous are tranquil. The wise are joyful; the virtuous are long-lived" (*Analects* VI.XXI). The Utopian notion of the "Grand Union" remained in many intellectuals' minds: that the cosmos could be orderly without the necessity of kings and rulers and that the deep wilderness or mountain peak could recapture this perfectly ordered harmony. The legend of "Peach Blossom Spring," a favorite topic in Chinese poetry and landscape painting, captures this idea. Tao Qian (365-427), in a preface to his poem, tells the story: a fisherman follows a stream lined with blossoming peach trees, and discovers a hidden valley with a prosperous village of happy people (see *Freer* 56). They tell him that they have been hiding there since their ancestors fled the Qin Dynasty tyranny, and they ask that he please not reveal their existence to the outside world.[22] Landscape art, then, often meant more to the family or court than an exact rendering of a lovely location.

The artist-intellectual as a hermit in the mountains was an idea pioneered by Six Dynasty poets such as Tao Qian and his contemporary Xie Linyun, who praised seclusion and Daoistic notions of harmony with Nature. The sentiment was echoed by the most famous Tang Dynasty poets such as Li Bai. The famous landscape painters of the Northern Song Dynasty (960-1127) were well aware of the Six Dynasties hermits and Tang Dynasty poets. Fan Kuan, the artist of "Travellers amidst Mountains and Streams," was said to have settled in the mountains to study nature firsthand; whether this is literally true or merely a rhetorical tradition, his monumental paintings of vast looming mountains innovatively capture the insignificance of the humans who inhabit them. Many Northern Song artists (such as the great Daoist Guo Xi whose "Early Spring" in the National Palace Museum, Taipei, is one of the most famous of all Chinese paintings) wrote treatises as well. He praises landscape painting in Confucian terms:

> [I]n a time of peace and plenty, when the intentions of ruler and parents are high-minded, purifying oneself is of little significance and office-holding is allied to honor. Can anyone of humanitarian instinct then tread aloof or retire afar in order to practice a retreat from worldly affairs?[23]

The long, horizontal handscrolls invite the viewer to wander through dream landscapes, from right to left as the scroll unrolls, following the path of some just-discernable Confucian scholar walking to meet his peers in their rustic studies. Landscape art, thus, offers retreat, allowing one to satisfy the heart's longing without retiring from duties.

The spirit of the Tang poets was perhaps even more closely followed by the painters of the Southern Song court (1127–1279) such as Ma Yuan (active ca. 1190–1225) and Xia Gui (1195–1230). Ma Yuan often painted scholars standing on crags or by waterfalls appreciating the seasonal landscapes. In the Yuan Dynasty, however, as intellectuals boycotted the foreign court of the Mongol emperors, the image of the scholar as principled recluse from Confucian society was given a twist. Reclusion—retirement from an evil court—was once again seen as a preeminently Confucian act of principle. Tao Qian, the "Peach Blossom Spring" poet, served as a role model. He had retired from a corrupt court to return to his estates and cultivate his garden, a subject later painters depicted.[24] Literati artists such as Ni Zan (1301–1374) produced spare landscapes devoid of figures, as metaphors for the absence of principle in the empire. His severe style served as a model for Confucian decorum in art for many generations of intellectual painters. Other painters developed the subject of the fisherman on the river—often still dressed in his now-superfluous court dress—as a subtle criticism of court life. Later gentleman painters in the Ming Dynasty cultivated landscape styles as "bland" and, therefore, detached from worldly considerations as their brushes could produce. These attitudes served to set them firmly apart from the professional and court artists, whose styles tended to be brighter, more colorful, narrative, and emotionally engaged. This division between high-minded amateur and vulgar professional artist, seemingly so clearly drawn from the Song Dynasty onward, needs to be examined more carefully.

Artist and Artisan

Traditional Chinese theory drew a rigid distinction between artist and artisan. All manual crafts not done with the writing brush were considered to be the work of anonymous artisans. Media such as sculpture and architecture, highly regarded in Western tradition, get no recognition in the traditional historiography of Chinese art theorists.[25]

The artist, properly speaking, was an educated amateur, a *literatus* of the gentry class or above who painted and wrote poetry for his friends in his leisure time. Literacy taught him to handle the writing brush, which was also the painting brush; his fluency with the brush reflected not only his good upbringing and aesthetic sensibility, but also his moral character. His necessary equipment, beyond literacy and its tools, was cultivated good taste, a deep knowledge of ancient painting styles, and a circle of like-minded friends to appreciate and guide him. The literati must be familiar with archaic styles of painting, since imitation of approved masters was far more widely applauded than originality, at least in the Ming and Qing periods. And finally, bamboo was a favorite subject of the literati painters, since, though spare, it required virtuosity in brush handling, and was a subject loaded with the symbolism of the stoic flexibility required of a Confucian scholar-official.

Chinese art theory tends to overstate the romantic detachment of the literati painters from public life. They were, of course, nearly all members of the Confucian bureaucracy who painted as a cultured leisure activity. Theory and history tend to overstate the "amateur" qualifications of many of the most famous practitioners because of the stigma attached to professional labor: stories of literati artists scorning payment for their work abound. Such paintings were never for sale; rather, they were exchanged among friends or given in return for favors. Recent documentary evidence suggests this to be a deliberate and inaccurate stereotype; diary entries show "amateur" artists famous for rejecting unwanted attention worked in return for pay. Housing famous artists in rich households or exchanging "gifts" were not actually monetary; thus, professional activity could often be disguised.

Further, the "spontaneity" of literati artistic production has been traditionally overstated; the image of the poet tossing off a few lines on the spur of a moment's inspiration is deeply embedded. Imagine a literati producing a brilliant painting and inspiring another to append a poetic colophon on the spot. The handscrolls, often with more space occupied by poetic tributes than to the original image, lend themselves to such imagining. Spontaneous or instantaneous production occurred—it was a staple of Chan, or Zen, painting. But, recent art history scholarship suggests that sketchiness is no guarantee of spontaneity; many paintings were commissioned in anticipation of an event such as a leave-taking or a birthday and then presented to the recipient, already inscribed with poetry, as a memento. Other commissioned works included portraits, normally done by specialists, and not considered part of one's "fine art" collection.

Whether produced by artist or artisan, Chinese paintings often had an active afterlife. Appreciative collectors and circles of amateur acquaintances used treasured works of art as the centerpieces of gatherings frequently adding their own seals or inscriptions to the paintings as a tribute—a practice that fairly horrifies the modern museum professional. Many famous colophons come from such gatherings or private viewings. Not a few paintings are today treasured as much for the fine calligraphy of their colophons, or the prestigious owners of the appended seals, as they are for the original image.

Women Artists

The Chinese attitude toward art as the proper realm of the educated amateur has worked in favor of Chinese women artists, despite the legal and physical restrictions on their public activities. Quite a number of Chinese women painters are known by name today from as far back as the Han Dynasty, thanks to biographical encyclopedias compiled in the eighteenth and nineteenth centuries: Li E's *Jade Terrace History of Calligraphers* and Tang Souyu's *Jade Terrace History of Painting*, which it inspired. Tang Souyu was the wife of a distinguished scholar, also in Hang-zhou, which seems to have been a congenial city for women authors, poets, scholars, and artists. Not surprisingly, the artists are ranked hierarchically: palace ladies, wives and daughters, and concubines, with courtesans last. The biographies tend to be stereotypical in the extreme—many are praised as good wives and mothers above all, who did some painting on the side, and these are listed before—and quite separate from—painters who were concubines or courtesans. But we are able to judge their work for ourselves. A number of their works from the Yuan Dynasty on have survived in collections worldwide, including the imperial collections. The most well known is Guan Daoshen (Yuan Dynasty, 1262–1368), wife of Zhao Mengfu, noted in her own right as a calligrapher and painter of bamboo.[26]

The most prized Chinese arts, the "three treasures" of painting, poetry, and calligraphy, required only a literary education and the company of a similarly refined circle of appreciative friends to guide and inspire one's efforts. Thus painting was open to any literate woman of the gentry class, and in that class all but the most conservative families would, in fact, have their daughters educated to some degree of literacy. Since brush painting was by and large a leisured pursuit done in the studio or garden, for men or for women, it was considered a perfectly appropriate avocation for a cultured woman in her leisure time. Nuns (and monks) were known to take up literati-style painting in their monasteries. There are even stories of gentry women artists being summoned to the palace to teach the ladies there.

There was an audience for accomplished women artists, though it was more limited than the potential audience for men. Since men's and women's spheres of activity were kept rigidly separate, her primary audience might be a "ladies' poetry club" made up of her many female relatives and their friends. Some idea of the setting for this artistic and social activity can be gleaned from the *Story of the Stone*, where the lady Tan-chun's room is clearly set up as a studio, with exquisite paintings and calligraphy on the wall. Developing an audience for one's art beyond the family circle and social networks did require the intervention of a man who might distribute pictures locally, and such circumstances are recorded.

In premodern Western art history, women artists most typically were daughters of professional painters who learned the family trade. There were significant barriers to independent European women artists receiving academic training equivalent to their professional male counterparts'. Lack of access to study the nude, a crucial subject of Western art, is a well-known case in point. In China, figure painting was never a problem, since the nude is simply not among the traditional subjects of serious painting; figures are heavily draped. The problematic subject was landscape painting, at the top of the "prestige" genres of Chinese art. Chinese women of the gentry class simply did not have either the legal sanction or the physical ability (due to disabling foot binding) to go wandering in the classic landscapes of Chinese mountains. While they might well travel, it would be in closed sedan chairs while accompanying their husbands to official postings, hardly an ideal condition for making studies of rocky terrain. Consequently, the most common genres of Chinese women's painting are subjects such as bird-and-flower paintings, bamboo, calligraphy, and figural paintings of women—both domestic scenes and religious figures like Guan Yin.

One distinguished group of Chinese women painter-calligraphers is found among the concubines, and even the professional courtesans who catered to a gentry clientele. While first wives were valued for their Confucian virtues as filial daughters and wives and as good mothers, subsequent wives and concubines were valued more for their beauty and their cultured refinement. Painting, poetry, and calligraphy were elegant accomplishments for engaging the attentions of gentlemen and could serve as important avenues of communication between women and men in a rigidly segregated society.

The premier women's art of imperial China was not painting, however, but needlework, a highly prized skill taught to all women intended for marriage. Weidner even refers to the "four perfections" of educated gentlewomen, including needlework with the traditional three (*Views* 23). Some of these embroidered products are such elaborate and intricate depictions of motifs and landscapes that they resemble color paintings when reproduced. A woman was expected to enrich the domestic environment with embroidered decoration on the whole range of textiles, from clothing to furnishings. There were, of course, women among the professional artisans who produced all the fine objects not traditionally labeled "art" in imperial China. These were apt to be members of artisan families, more closely conforming to the pattern of premodern Western women artists.

Collecting Art as a Connection to the Culture

Chinese writers on the subject of art seem unanimous that old collectable objects are in some way morally ennobling, and that possessing them is an important link between the collector-owner and the classical past.

Material Culture of the Family in Later Imperial China

A number of texts from the Ming Dynasty, and later, discuss the growing market for luxury objects and household improvements.[27] These point to several things: the wealth of the new commercial elite in the Ming Dynasty, their interest in collecting both antique and modern luxuries, and the growing concern among this class for prestige and status as reflected through their collections. Many of these treatises, then, are guides for getting it right—collecting only the best things with the best pedigrees and displaying them in the most approved manner. For the person of good taste, one Ming Dynasty guide offers the following chapters: studios and retreats, flowers and trees, water and rocks, birds and fish, calligraphy and painting, tables and couches, vessels and utensils, clothing and adornment, boats and carriages, placing and arranging (flowers), incense and teas. This list should warn us against limiting our notion of "art" either to the traditional Chinese "three treasures" of calligraphy, poetry, and painting, or even to the broader Western canon of museum-quality objects.

Interestingly, "studios and retreats" are listed first. Accounts from later imperial China indicate that even lower-class families with ambitions set up some corner of the house as a "study" if only for display, so powerful was the prestige of the scholar and his highly ritualized physical surroundings. Men's spaces were furnished with the implements of writing, and the decoration reflected their presumed literary abilities and role in public life. Women's quarters had different objects and decor than did men's, reflecting the physical division of an aristocratic household by gender. Emblematic allusions to male children often filled women's spaces, reflecting their most important function within a family; a bed served as her greatest piece of prestige furniture, rather than a desk.

The importance of the garden to the material culture of the aristocratic class is underscored by chapters on flowers and trees, water and rocks, and birds and fish. We have seen that garden portraiture is an important genre, reflecting the Confucian at cultured leisure. The revival of garden culture around Suzhou in the later fifteenth century was based in large part on the study of the imperial gardens then being revived in Beijing.[28] Gardens were immensely expensive investments, especially with the rise of land prices and growth of suburban villas in the sixteenth century. Gardens were laid out with minute attention to *fengshui* 風水 ("wind-water"), the proper geomantic placement of all elements of structure and water. Placement of rocks and bamboo were often a matter of life imitating art: bamboo paintings would be studied as a guide to good taste.[29] Likewise, Ming and Qing paintings of gardens often expanded upon the mundane reality of a suburban garden, however luxurious, by setting the owner's studio and prized gnarled rocks amid an imagined mountainous landscape.

Treatises on home furnishings notwithstanding, the language of Ming Dynasty art connoisseurship reveals some discomfort over conspicuous consumption. Things, *wu* 物, are the Confucian complement to *li* 理 principle and *li* 禮 ritual, and hence by definition rather superfluous. Frugality is a Confucian virtue long praised and was enforced through sumptuary laws and periodic confiscations that held conspicuous display by lower aristocrats in check. There was also a longstanding distrust of both craftsmen and merchants, both traditionally relegated to the lowest ranks of society as earning their living not from the soil but from parasitical practices. Despite this, in the Ming and Qing Dynasties one finds lists of the best brands and the best geographic origins of objects to buy. Even "amateur" paintings, as we have seen, were actively traded commodities, particularly important for establishing *guanxi* 關係 relationships, with elaborate covers devised to cloak any hint of monetary transaction (Clunas, *Superfluous Things* 142–47).

One subject not mentioned in the treatises on art, but of potentially great interest to scholars of Confucian culture, is the home altar in later Dynastic China.[30]

Little has been written about popular religion within the family, as opposed to the public religion of the great Buddhist (and to a lesser degree, Daoist) establishments. Jesuit missionaries, with their keen professional interest in religious observance, give a number of reports concerning practices in the Ming and Qing Dynasties. Virtually every household had an ancestral altar of some sort, if only a shelf or a wooden table along a wall, containing ancestral tablets of wood, or sometimes paper tablets and portraits. Even those who did not believe in a literal way in the intervention of ancestors would occasionally leave food and drink. Ancestor portraits were a common visual element. Since the many practices that go under the name of "Chinese religion" derive variously from Buddhism, Daoism, and Confucian rites, family shrines also frequently held sculpted or paper images of members of the various pantheons. The main ritual guide of the period was the Neo-Confucian text *Family Rituals,* written by Ju Xi (1130–1200), which was considered orthodox by the state, Confucian community, and educated elite in the Ming Dynasty. In the Qing, however, the obvious impossibility of reconciling the elaborate ritual demands of the Confucian classics and Ju Xi with everyday family life caused a crisis of scholarly discussion about the uniform performance of ritual. In reality, the ritual arts and practices within the Chinese family were far less regulated, less elaborate, and less orthodox Confucian than those of the Imperial court (Buckley 209–18).

Imperial Collecting and the Chinese Cultural Heritage

If Chinese antiquities were (and are) held to be morally ennobling, it is not surprising that the emperors, as the center of the Chinese cosmos, have collected them for at least two millennia. Emperor Wudi (Western Han, ruled 140–87 B.C.E.) collected the finest calligraphy, paintings, and ancient bronzes, housing them in a specially built tower. Unfortunately, great imperial collections have been periodically destroyed in times of dynastic turmoil. Song emperor Taizong (reigned 976–997) himself a talented artist, not only collected the best contemporary work and patronized artists, but systematically searched the empire for the best available examples of calligraphy and painting for the imperial collections. Succeeding Song emperors expanded and catalogued the collection, forming the nucleus of the great imperial collections that have come down to us today. Emperor Huizong's catalogue of paintings and calligraphy lists some seven thousand items, many of them still surviving.[31] The catalogues included precise illustrations and reflected sophisticated scholarship. Emperor Huizong displayed his collection, making his paintings available to the members of his academy, and exhibiting the antiquities in a special hall. Old vessels and bells became models for casting new bronzes used in the Ancestral Temple rituals or distributed to other temples.

Foreign-born dynasties, notably the Yuan and the Qing, used their possession of China's antiquities and sponsorship of its arts as important means of cultural legitimation. Emperors learned the proper display and connoisseurship of their precious objects, recording their appreciation visibly by affixing their seals and writing appreciations in the margins of their paintings. The Qing Dynasty Qianlong Emperor (reigned 1736–1795) is especially noteworthy in this regard. He studied painting and calligraphy, patronized scholarship on the arts, and vastly expanded the imperial collection. He is notorious for his enthusiasm with the red seal and brush, often swamping precious ancient relics with the marks of his appreciation. The Qing court was also active in commissioning antiquarian art from the palace workshops.

In the nineteenth and twentieth centuries, the upheavals of Chinese history have had the effect of scattering the imperial collection around the world. During the sack of the old Summer Palace by British and French armies, virtually all the artwork on hand was looted, much of it now in foreign museums. Fires consumed more, in 1869, 1900, and 1923. The last emperor, Pu Yi, sold off more. The establishment of the Forbidden City as the "National Palace Museum" under the republic should have been the end of this story, but the most dramatic dispersal came about in the 1930s to 1949. During the Japanese invasion of China, the remaining National Palace Museum collections were boxed in thousands of crates and shipped to southern China for safekeeping, often just ahead of attack and in very dangerous conditions. After years of moving ahead of armies, the four thousand or so "best" crates were taken by Chiang Kai-shek's Guomindang forces to Taiwan and stored for safekeeping in shafts under a mountain in the suburbs of Taipei. A military triumph by the Guomindang forces would return the treasures to the mainland, but, in the absence of this event, clearly, a new National Palace Museum was needed. Opening in 1965, it housed more than 600,000 works, largely from the personal collection of the Qianlong emperor. Meanwhile, the Palace Museum collections remaining on the mainland were returned to Beijing and housed in the Palace Museum of the old Forbidden City.

We started this chapter with a consideration of "what is art?" The contents of the dispersed imperial collections give a traditional Chinese answer to that question: Neolithic jades, ritual bronzes, ceramics, and luxury objects; calligraphy and painting by the painters renowned for their moral qualities seemingly reflected in their skills with the brush. Possession of China's artistic heritage is still controversial, and still plays a role in legitimizing rule. The past and present are still tangibly linked through the medium of Chinese art, communication with the past still controlled by the central rulers, and legitimacy still conferred in part by the possession of the figurative Nine Tripods.

Glossary

Bi and **Cong** The *bi* is a flat jade disk with a hole in the center; the *cong* (pronounced *"tsung"*) is a square jade tube. They are often found together in neolithic burials and presumed to be cosmological, but their original significance is not known. In the

Lawrence E. Butler

later Bronze Age and Han China, the *bi* was understood to represent the circular heavens, and the *cong* the square of the earth.

Book of Songs One of the Confucian Classics, sometimes translated as *The Book of Poetry,* or *The Book of Odes;* transliterated as *Shijing, Shi Jing,* or *She King.*

Colophon An inscription placed in a painting or at the end of a text, usually giving facts about the place, date or circumstances of its making.

Concubine A secondary wife

Cong See *Bi* **and** *Cong.*

Ding A three- or four-legged cauldron for cooking food. From its use in ritual sacrifice offerings to the ancestors, the *ding* took on symbolic importance as part of the paraphernalia of a ruler.

Fengshui Literally "wind-water." The Chinese art of building in accordance with propitious natural forces, determined through geomancy, which aligns the inhabitant with the spirit and geography of place and dwelling.

Feudal In modern China, this is a pejorative term that is used to describe an old-fashioned person or idea.

Genre In art, a particular category or stock theme in one medium. Popular genres in Chinese painting, for instance, would include bamboo, bird-and-flower, and court portraits.

Guanxi Informal system of personal ties and network of connections.

Handscroll One of the major formats of Chinese painting. A handscroll is a horizontal length of paper or silk, painted in ink and colors with a brush, and mounted between two wooden sticks used as handles. The handscroll is unrolled section by section by the viewer, starting from the right end. **Hanging scrolls**, by contrast, are meant to hang vertically on a wall.

Hun and **Po** Two different aspects of the soul after death, important for understanding Han Dynasty tomb art. The *hun* joins the spiritual realm, while the *po* remains earthbound or tomb-bound.

Iconography In art, iconography is the study of the visual portrayal of content or meaning, or the symbols associated with a concept. Thus "imperial iconography" is the study of symbols associated with the emperor and his activities.

Li ji (Li Chi) *The Book of Ritual.*

Literati The class of educated amateurs and intellectuals of the gentry class and above, primarily but not exclusively men. A *literatus* would be familiar with the Confucian classics and, ideally, would be accomplished in all the noble arts and humanities, particularly writing, poetry, painting and music.

Orthodox Conforming to the official doctrine or opinion.

Po See *Hun* **and** *Po.*

Qin Shi Huangdi The first emperor; conquered various warring states in 221 B.C.E. to form a united China.

Sage kings The earliest rulers of China, who were also legendary originators of Chinese culture.

Shanshui A term for landscape which means roughly "mountain-water."

Taotie "Glutton." The later name given to the fantastic animal mask motif, prominent in the decoration of ritual bronzes. Its precise origin and significance are unknown;

modern researchers have proposed meanings ranging from totemistic to purely decorative.

Tso Chuen A commentary on the *Ch'un Ts'ëw,* or *Spring and Autumn Annals,* by Tso K'ëwming. *Tso Chuen* is sometimes written as *Zuo Zhuan.*

Yijing *The Book of Changes,* sometimes written as *I Ching.*

Notes

1. See especially Allen; and on the dragon as cultural symbol, Hay.

2. For a brief introduction to the bronzes, see Rawson, "Ritual Bronze Vessels of the Shang and Zhou," in *Mysteries of Ancient China.* Also see her excellent discussions of bronzes throughout her *British Museum Book of Chinese Art* or her exhibition catalogue, *Chinese Bronzes.*

3. Adapted from James Legge's translation of the *Tso Chuen,* 483. See Legge's commentary on section 19, paragraph 7.

4. See discussion of "nine bronze tripods" in Chang, 95–100, including quotes from ancient texts. For the archeology of the *ding,* see Kao, "The Evolving Shape of the Ting."

5. Based on Legge's translation, *The Ch'un Tsew with the Tso Chuen,* 293. See Legge's commentary on section 3, paragraph 4. Also quoted in Chang (95–100) along with the Nine *Ding* story from *Mo Zi,* Bk. IX.

6. For good summary discussions and illustrations, see Allen, 128–57; Bagley, *Shang Ritual Bronzes,*19–20, on the technology of casting the *taotie;* Whitfield, *The Problem of Meaning in Early Chinese Ritual Bronze;* and, most recently, Paper, 63–83.

7. I follow here the argument of Buckley, *Confucianism and Family Rituals in Imperial China,* especially ch. 1: "Introduction" (3–13) and ch. 2: "The Early Confucian Discourse on Family Rites" (14–44). Also see the numerous passages in the Confucian *Analects* concerning filial obligations surrounding mourning and its rites.

8. For Confucius's views on correct ritual practice, see the *Analects,* Book 3; and on the benefits of performing these duties in the proper filial spirit, the *Doctrine of the Mean,* chapters 16–19. For discussion of the Confucian books of ritual and their use, the *Yi Li*, *Zhou Li,* and *Li Ji,* see Buckley, ch..2.

9. Li, *The Path of Beauty,* 69–71. He quotes poetry describing these dangers in all quadrants, above and below Earth, and ascribes the aesthetic moment to "Chu-Han romanticism."

10. Quoted with adaptations from *Li Chi: Book of Rites,* trans. Legge, 364–67. Compare with the *Dao De Jing,* 18 and 19.

11. *Shi Jing,* part 5: The Books of Zhou, iv: "The Great Plan." For a discussion of how this was understood visually, see Major, "The Five Phases, Magic Squares, and Schematic Cosmography."

12. The standard work on the Wu family shrines is Wu, *Wu Liang Shrine,* from which I summarize the following discussion of iconography. Also see the important ideas by Powers,

cited above, ch. 6–9, which discuss the Wu family shrine carvings as veiled criticism of a corrupt court. His ch. 10, "Tombs of the Descriptive Tradition and Their Market" explores the patronage and construction of these tombs (279–333).

13. On the social use of Chinese portraits, see the cited works by Spiro, Farrer, and Vinograd. Vinograd provides "An Outline of Early Chinese Portraiture" on pp. 18–27, and I follow his argument here.

14. A Northern Song copy after the Tang dynasty painter Zhou Fang, acc. no. 39.37 and 60.4. Also attributed to him is a scroll of "Ladies with Flowers in Their Hair," in the Liaoning Provincial Museum, Shenyang.

15. There is an immense and growing literature on symbols in Chinese art, of uneven value. One must keep in mind that symbols often mean different things in different contexts and it is easy to overread them. With that caveat, the reader might seek guidance first from Williams, *Outline of Chinese Symbolism and Art Motives,* and relevant articles in the *Dictionary of Art* section on China. On the dragon as symbol and metaphor in Chinese culture, see Hay, "The Persistent Dragon (*Lung.*)."

16. For court costume and symbolism, see two recent exhibition catalogues: Thorp, *Son of Heaven* and *De Verboden Stad (The Forbidden City),* by the Museum Boymans-van Beuningen. The latter has a useful summary of symbolic motifs used in the art and architecture of the Beijing palace (103–17).

17. The long-time standard work on Chinese art theory is Osvald Siren, *The Chinese on the Art of Painting* (New York, 1963), originally published in 1936. Now see the works of Susan Bush, especially Bush and Shih, *Early Chinese Texts on Painting.* For a critique of the traditional wisdom about Confucian art theory, see James Cahill, "Confucian Elements." I follow his arguments here.

18. Chang Yen-yuan, author of *Record of Famous Painters of Successive Dynasties,* quoted in Cahill, "Confucian Elements" 117–18.

19. A good way into the discussion of the Six Rules is Cahill, "The Six Laws and How to Read Them."

20. The following ideas are from Vinograd's introduction (2–27), an excellent place to start reading about portraiture in China.

21. One may start with the writings of James Cahill. For the moral content of landscape, see *Hills Beyond a River;* on connections between poetry and landscape painting, see *The Lyric Journey.* For a recent and accessible introduction to Northern Song landscapes that places them within the context of "A Vision of Cosmic Order," see Fong, "Monumental Landscape Painting."

22. One easily available translation of the whole preface and poem is in *The Columbia Anthology of Traditional Chinese Literature.* The Freer Gallery of Art has a famous depiction of this story in a handscroll by the Qing Dynasty painter Dao Ji (acc. no.57.4).

23. For his treatise, see Bush and Shih, *Early Chinese Texts on Painting* 150–54. For a comparison between painting and poetry in the Northern Song, see Bush, *Chinese Literati* 22–28.

24. For example, the Freer Gallery's two narrative handscrolls of "Tao Qian Returning to Seclusion," based on a Northern Song model.

25. On the literati artists and the paintings they favored, see Sullivan, *The Three Perfections*; Cahill, *Painter's Practice;* Cahill, "Artist-Patron Transactions," and the Asia Society, *The Chinese Scholar's Studio.*

26. There has been a good deal of recent scholarship on this topic. See essays in the exhibition catalogue *Views from the Jade Terrace: Chinese Women Artists 1300–1912,* ed. Weidner; and articles in *Flowering in the Shadows,* ed. Weidner.

27. This discussion describing and analyzing the Ming treatise summarizes ideas from Clunas, *Superfluous Thing,* especially chapter 2: "Ideas about Things: Themes in Ming Connoisseurship Literature," pp. 40–81. Also see Kerr, *Chinese Art and Design: Art Objects in Ritual and Daily Life.*

28. See Clunas, *Fruitful Sites* 60–103, "The Aesthetic Garden."

29. There is a huge, growing, and somewhat suspect literature on *fengshui.* For a sober discussion of its impact on gardening see Clunas (1996), pp. 177–89, "Geomancy and the Land," from which these ideas come.

30. This discussion is based on Buckley, *Confucian and Family Rituals,* chapter 9: "Confucian Texts and the Performance of Rituals."

31. On this topic see Chiang, "The National Palace Museum: A History of the Collection." This article is an excellent introduction to the topic of imperial collecting in China, especially in the reign of the Qianlong emperor, and my ideas are largely based on it. He avoids, however, explaining the origin of the National Palace Museum in Taipei.

Works Cited

Allan, Sarah. *The Shape of the Turtle: Myth, Art and Cosmos in Early China.* Albany: State University of New York Press, 1991.

Bagley, Robert W. *Shang Ritual Bronzes in the Arthur M. Sackler Collections, I:* Washington DC. Cambridge: Arthur M. Sackler Museum/Harvard University Press, 1987.

Birch, Cyril. *Anthology of Chinese Literature, I: From Early Times to the Fourteenth Century.* New York: Grove, 1965.

Book of Songs: The Ancient Chinese Classic of Poetry. Trans. Arthur Waley. New York: Grove Weidenfeld, 1987.

Buckley, Patricia Ebrey. *Confucianism and Family Rituals in Imperial China: A Social History of Writing about Rites.* Princeton: Princeton University Press, 1991.

Bush, Susan. *The Chinese Literati on Painting: Su Shih to Tung Ch'i-Ch'ang.* Cambridge: Harvard University Press, 1971.

———. and Hsio-yen Shih. *Early Chinese Texts on Painting.* Cambridge: Harvard University Press, 1985.

Cahill, James. "Confucian Elements in the Theory of Painting." *The Confucian Persuasion.* Ed. Arthur F. Wright. Stanford: Stanford University Press, 1960. 115–140.

———. *Hills beyond a River: Chinese Painting of the Yuan Dynasty, 1279–1368.* New York: Weatherhill, 1976.

————. *The Lyric Journey: Poetic Painting in China and Japan.* Cambridge: Harvard University Press, 1996.

————. *The Painter's Practice: How Artists Lived and Worked in Traditional China.* New York: Columbia University Press, 1994.

————. "The Six Laws and How to Read Them." *Ars Orientalis* 4 (1961). 372–81.

————. "Types of Artist-Patron Transactions in Traditional Chinese Painting." *Artists and Patrons: Some Social and Economic Aspects of Chinese Painting.* Ed. Chu-tsing Li et al. Lawrence Kan./ Bloomington: Indiana University Press, 1989.

Chang, K.C. *Art, Myth, and Ritual: The Path to Political Authority in Ancient China.* Cambridge: Harvard University Press, 1983.

Chen Lie. "The Ancestor Cult in Ancient China." *Mysteries of Ancient China: New Discoveries from the Ancient Dynasties.* Ed. Jessica Rawson. New York: Braziller, 1996. 269–272.

Chiang Lin-Sheng. "The National Palace Museum: A History of the Collection." *Possessing the Past, Treasures from the National Palace Museum, Taipei.* Ed. Wen C. Fong and James C. Y. Watt. New York: Metropolitan Museum of Art/Abrams, 1996. 3–25.

Clunas, Craig. *Art in China.* Oxford History of Art. New York: Oxford University Press, 1997.

————. *Fruitful Sites: Garden Culture in Ming Dynasty China.* Durham: Duke University Press, 1996.

————. *Superfluous Things: Material Culture and Social Status in Early Modern China.* Urbana-Champaign: University of Illinois Press, 1991.

Farrer, Anne. "Calligraphy and Painting for Official Life." *British Museum Book of Chinese Art.* Ed. Jessica Rawson. New York: Thames and Hudson, 1993.

Fong, Wen C. "The Imperial Cult." *Possessing the Past: Treasures from the National Palace Museum, Taipei.* Ed. Wen C. Fong and James C. Y. Watt. New York: Metropolitan Museum of Art/Abrams, 1996. 99–105.

————. "Monumental Landscape Painting." *Possessing the Past: Treasures from the National Palace Museum, Taipei.* Ed. Wen C. Fong and James C. Y. Watt. New York: Metropolitan Museum of Art/Abrams, 1996. 121–137.

The Freer Gallery of Art: China. Freer Gallery of Art: Washington, D.C., 1981.

Hay, John. "The Persistent Dragon *(Long)*." *The Power of Culture: Studies in Chinese Cultural History.* Ed. W. Peterson et al. Hong Kong: Chinese University Press, 1994. 119–149.

Kao Jen-chun. "The Evolving Shape of the Ting." *Pearls of the Middle Kingdom.* Taipei: National Palace Museum, 1984. 20–29.

Kerr, Rose, ed. *Chinese Art and Design: Art Objects in Ritual and Daily Life.* Catalogue, T.T. Tsui Gallery of Chinese Art, Victoria and Albert Museum. Woodstock, N.Y.: Overlook Press, 1991.

Legge, James, trans. and ed. *The Chineses Classics: The Ch'un Ts'ëw with the Tso Chuen.* Vol. 5. Hong Kong: Hong Kong University Press, 1960.

————. trans. and ed. *Li Chi: Book of Rites.* Ed. Ch'u Chai and Winberg Chai. New Hyde Park: University Books, 1967.

————. trans. and ed. *The Chinese Classics: Confucian Analects, The Great Learning, and the Doctrine of the Mean.* Vol. 1. Hong Kong University Press, 1960.

————. trans. and ed. *The Chinese Classics: The Shoo King, or The Book of Historical Documents.* Vol. 3. Hong Kong: Hong Kong University Press, 1960.

Lei Congyun. "Neolithic Sites of Religious Significance." *Mysteries of Ancient China: New Discoveries from the Ancient Dynasties.* Ed. Jessica Rawson. New York: Braziller, 1996. 219–224.

Li, Chu-tsung, and James C. Y. Watt, eds. *The Chinese Scholar's Studio: Artistic Life in the Late Ming Period.* New York: Asia Society/Thames and Hudson, 1987.

Li Zehou. *The Path of Beauty: A Study of Chinese Aesthetics.* Trans. Song Lizeng. New York: Oxford University Press, 1994.

Mair, Victor. *Columbia Anthology of Traditional Chinese Literature.* New York: Columbia University Press, 1994.

Major, John. "The Five Phases, Magic Squares, and Schematic Cosmography." *Explorations in Early Chinese Cosmology.* Ed. Henry Rosemont, Jr. JAAR Thematic Studies 50/2. Chico: Scholars Press, 1984. 133–66.

Murray, Julia K. "Didactic Art for Women: The Ladies' Classic of Filial Piety." *Flowering in the Shadows: Women in the History of Chinese and Japanese Painting.* Ed. Marsha Weidner. Honolulu: University of Hawaii Press, 1990. 27–53.

Museum Boymans-van Beuningen, *De Verboden Stad/(The Forbidden City.)* Rotterdam: Museum Boymans-van Beuningen, 1990.

Paper, Jordan. *The Spirits are Drunk: Comparative Approaches to Chinese Religion.* Albany: State University of New York Press, 1995.

Powers, Martin J. *Art and Political Expression in Early China.* New Haven: Yale University Press, 1991.

Rawson, Jessica, ed. *British Museum Book of Chinese Art.* New York: Thames and Hudson, 1993.

————. *Chinese Bronzes: Art and Ritual.* London: British Museum, 1987.

————. ed. *Mysteries of Ancient China: New Discoveries from the Ancient Dynasties.* New York: Braziller, 1996.

————. "Ritual Bronze Vessels of the Shang and Zhou." *Mysteries of Ancient China: New Discoveries from the Ancient Dynasties.* Ed. Jessica Rawson. New York: Braziller, 1996. 248–65.

Sima Qian. *Historical Records.* Trans. Raymond Dawson. New York: Oxford University Press, 1994.

Siren, Osvald. *The Chinese on the Art of Painting.* New York: Schocken, 1963.

Spiro, Audrey. *Contemplating the Ancients: Aesthetic and Social Issues in Early Chinese Portraits.* Los Angeles: UCLA Press, 1990.

Sullivan, Michael. *The Three Perfections: Chinese Painting, Poetry and Calligraphy.* New York: Braziller, 1980.

Thorp, Robert L., ed. *Son of Heaven: Imperial Arts of China.* Seattle: University of Washington Press, 1988.

Vinograd, Richard. *Boundaries of the Self: Chinese Portraits, 1600–1900.* New York: Cambridge University Press, 1992.

Weidner, Marsha, ed. *Flowering in the Shadows: Women in the History of Chinese and Japanese Painting.* Honolulu: University of Hawaii Press, 1990.

88   Lawrence E. Butler

———. *Views from the Jade Terrace: Chinese Women Artists 1300–1912.* Indianapolis/New York: Indianapolis Museum of Art/Rizzoli, 1988.

Whitfield, Roderick, ed. *The Problem of Meaning in Early Chinese Ritual Bronzes.* Colloquies on Art and Archaeology in Asia, 15. London: Percival David Foundation/University of London, 1992.

Wilhelm, Richard. *The I Ching or Book of Changes.* Trans. C. F. Baynes. Bollingen Series 19. Princeton: Princeton University Press, 1967.

Williams, C. A. S., *Outlines of Chinese Symbolism and Art Motives.* New York: Dover, 1976.

Wu, Hung. *The Wu Liang Shrine: The Ideology of Chinese Pictorial Art.* Stanford: Stanford University Press, 1989.

Yang Xiaoneng. "Exploring the Imperial Arts of China." *Son of Heaven: Imperial Arts of China.* Ed. Robert L. Thorp. Seattle: Son of Heaven Press, 1988. Introduction.

Yang Yang. "The Chinese Jade Culture." *Mysteries of Ancient China: New Discoveries from the Ancient Dynasties.* Ed. Jessica Rawson. New York: Braziller, 1996. 225–31.

Zheng Zhenxiang. "The Royal Consort Fu Hao and Her Tomb." *Mysteries of Ancient China: New Discoveries from the Ancient Dynasties.* Ed. Jessica Rawson. New York: Braziller, 1996. 240–47.

4
Women and Gender

Mary Gallagher

In the opening of *The Woman Warrior,* Maxine Hong Kingston narrates the shocking story, told by her mother, of an aunt she has never met who falls victim to seemingly archaic and cruel village customs. The narrator's young married aunt, whose husband has left for America, becomes pregnant in the absence of her husband and gives birth to a child. As the day of birth nears, apparently in an effort to "cleanse" the village of the pollution brought upon it by the arrival of an illegitimate child, the villagers at first

threw mud and rocks at the house. Then they threw eggs and began slaughtering our stock. We could hear the animals scream their deaths—the roosters, the pigs, a last great roar from the ox. . . . The villagers broke in the front and the back doors at the same time, even though we had not locked the doors against them. Their knives dripped with the blood of our animals. They smeared blood on the doors and walls. One woman swung a chicken, whose throat she had slit, splattering blood in red arcs about her. . . . The villagers pushed through both wings, even your grandparents' rooms, to find your aunt's, which was also mine until the men returned. . . . They ripped up her clothes and shoes and broke her combs, grinding them underfoot. They tore her work from the loom. They scattered the cooking fire and rolled the new weaving in it. We could hear them in the kitchen breaking our bowls and banging the pots. They overturned the great waist-high earthenware jugs; duck eggs, pickled fruit, vegetables burst out and mixed in acrid torrents. The old woman from the next field swept a broom through the air and loosed the spirits-of-the-broom over our heads. "Pig." "Ghost." "Pig," they sobbed and scolded while they ruined our house.

When they left, they took sugar and oranges to bless themselves. They cut pieces from the dead animals. Some of them took bowls that were not broken and clothes that were not torn. Afterward we swept up the rice and sewed it back up into sacks. But the smells from the spilled preserves lasted. Your aunt gave birth in the pigsty that night. The next morning when I went for the water, I found her and the baby plugging up the family well. (3–5)

Could this story be true? Is this what it was like to be a woman in traditional China? How does one empathize with these people and their behavior? Trying to understand and describe accurately the essence of women's lives in any country is complex. So many things affect one's life experiences: big factors such as wealth and social class, region of the country, historical period, or smaller individual factors like one's age, physical appearance, personal talents, or even birth order. Generalizing too much (e.g., "women in China") obliterates the rich multiplicity of actual experiences. Moreover, describing life in China is particularly problematic because of its very long—over 3000—years of civilization. Anyone in America today, knowing how different U.S. society was in the 1950s, 1970s, or even 1990s, can appreciate the difficulties of such a task.

How then does one begin to learn about the lives of others? One method is to start by describing and analyzing the main social and ideological factors of a society at a particular time. Because these provide the framework and the perspective within which people act and interact, it is then possible to look at actual behavior and begin to understand it. For heuristic reasons, this chapter will describe the sociocultural bases of women's lives at two periods: one in "traditional" Chinese society, which is actually a composite from the late imperial period (Ming Dynasty, 1368–1644, and Qing Dynasty, 1644–1911), and one in modern times (late 20th century).

Traditional China

Economic, Social, and Political Factors

Traditional China was patriarchal, patrilineal, and patrilocal. This meant that men had the formal power in the society, that inheritance and descent were through the male line, and that the newly married couple resided with the husband's family. Women were subject to the authority of men throughout their lives. According to the Three Obediences, a woman was to obey her father when she was young, her husband after she was married, and her son in her old age. Female infanticide, the selling of girls, and concubinage, while not generally regarded as desirable behaviors, were nonetheless common and accepted practices.

Unlike men, women did not have a permanent place, assigned at birth, in any group. Though born into her father's family, a girl was not considered a member of this family. If a woman died before she was married, she did not get a tablet on her father's family altar and the death rituals were not performed for her. If she got married and had children, then she earned a place on her husband's family altar. Marriages were arranged by the parents, and typically the girl's opinion was not sought. It was simply assumed that she would obey her parents' wishes.

When a young woman married, the doors of her childhood home were both literally and figuratively slammed shut behind her, as her formal ties with her father's household were severed. Visits home were strictly regulated by law and custom. While theoretically welcomed into her new home as a potential producer of male descendants, in practice she was often resented for the money it had cost for her betrothal and wedding. Though her husband probably enjoyed her as a sexual partner, they seldom saw each other during the day and a warm and emotionally supportive relationship, if it developed at all, took years to form. Until she actually produced children, she became the de facto servant of her mother-in-law, who was happy to have someone to take over the heavy household chores. Indeed, a common term for marriage in Chinese is "taking a daughter-in-law." Because the mother-in-law feared that the new bride would steal away the affections and loyalty of her son, she despised her and tried to make her life miserable. But even if the bride was desperately unhappy, even if her husband beat her, divorced her, or died, she was still not welcome back in her natal home. "If you marry a chicken, stay with the chicken; if you marry a dog, obey the dog" was the common folk saying.

A clear indication of the lower power and prestige of women was the custom of foot binding. From the time of the Song Dynasty (960–1279), foot binding, supposedly started by a concubine of the emperor, became widespread. Many young girls had their feet bound, a painful process that began around age five or six, though sometimes as early as two. A long cloth was wrapped around the foot several times, bending all the toes except the big toe under the sole. For years young girls lived with the constant excruciating pain this caused. Typically mothers bound the feet of their own daughters, and though they empathized with their anguish, knew that they had to keep the bindings tight or their daughters could not make a good marriage. Over time the bones were broken, resulting in feet only three or four inches long. The sight of women teetering on bound feet was considered particularly erotic by men, whose sexual fantasies often involved touching and unwrapping the bindings of a woman's tiny "golden lilies." Foot binding produced women who were functionally crippled, so that farm labor, carrying bundles, or even walking for more than short distances caused them great pain.

Though brothers inherited equally, women did not inherit land, the major source of both income and prestige. In some parts of China and at some historical periods, women were able to retain control of their dowry, but this seems to have decreased in the later imperial period. In general there was a sharp division of labor by gender, with men doing agricultural work in the fields and dominating the outer realm of social relationships, and women occupying the domestic inner realm and responsible for child care, food processing, and cloth processing. There were of course differences among women depending in part on family wealth and on the region of China in which they lived. Women in poorer families usually faced a lifetime of onerous and unremitting hard work, and might even be sold as prostitutes, concubines, or slaves if family fortunes took a downturn. Women in rich families were not likely to be sold nor forced to perform hard physical labor, and sometimes were even taught to read and write. On the other hand their isolation in their own households was more complete than that of poorer women because they were never allowed out of the family compound nor could they be seen by or talk to any visiting males. Region of the country also affected women's lives. One survey for example found that in certain southern areas of double rice cropping, 29 percent of the farm labor was performed by women, whereas in the winter wheat millet areas of northern China women performed only 5 percent of the agricultural labor (Buck 293). There is a rough correlation between the amount of work women did in the fields and foot binding, with women in the south somewhat less likely to have their feet bound.

Besides marriage, there were a few other occupations open to women. These included becoming a slave, servant, prostitute, medium, Buddhist nun, or courtesan. As bad as marriage could be, these alternative occupations were generally worse in terms of income, prestige, safety, and security. Women who entered such occupations put themselves outside the pale of normal life and generally did so only when they were forced into it by family circumstances or sheer desperation.

Women's Behavioral Response to Their Position in Society

Women's general response to their formal position of powerlessness was to strenuously apply their energies and efforts to the one arena in which they could exert some control: the family, and particularly to that subsegment of the family that Margery Wolf (1972) labels the "uterine family," consisting of a mother and her children. The only way for a young bride to escape the isolation and resentment she found in her new husband's house, and to recreate the warmth and sense of belonging she had experienced with her mother, was to create her own uterine family. By bearing children, completely devoting herself to them, and thus psychologically binding them to her forever, a woman was able to provide the close emotional ties otherwise lacking in her life.

But the uterine family was more than just a strategy to achieve emotional security. Because women were not usually allowed their own property, investment in sons (who did not move away when they got married) was the only feasible economic security for a woman's old age. So adaptive was this strategy that even prostitutes tended to form uterine families by either adoption or bearing illegitimate children (Margery Wolf, *Women* 207). Even though they might be contributing money to their natal families, they also felt the need to build their own uterine circle of financial and emotional security.

That this strategy was successful for many women can be inferred in a number of ways. For example, most biographies of famous Chinese, including Mao Zedong, credit their successes in life to the indomitable strength, will, and steadfastness of their mothers. Looking at the subject of humor, the many jokes about hen-pecked husbands and women who run their families with an iron hand are another testimony to how women attempt to exert their influence in the family whenever circumstances permit. From a different perspective, Guan Yin, the goddess of mercy who always responds kindly to human requests, is most likely a religious parallel of the warm emotional relationship between mother and child in the uterine family.

Functionally the effect of patrilineal succession and women's coping strategy of investment in the uterine family was to force women into a competitive relationship with one another. The mother-in-law viewed any attempt by the daughter-in-law to establish a positive relationship with her new husband as an all-out attack on the security she had worked so hard to build. Sisters-in-law competed for the scarce resources available in the extended family, for if a woman was not vigilant, the members of her own uterine family might end up with less than others. The only female-female relationship of positive affect was the mother-daughter one, and this was successfully severed by patrilocal residence.

Ideology

Folk Beliefs. Another way to understand the position of women in Chinese society is to look at the beliefs and values associated with women. In general, the beliefs and values of a society explain and support the behavior that the social structure deems necessary. Common folk wisdom about girls is revealed in sayings such as: "Girls are goods on whom one loses money." "Feeding girls is like feeding cowbirds." "Girls are like maggots in the rice." "It is more profitable to raise geese than daughters." When a girl is born it is a "small happiness;" when a boy is born it is a "big happiness." These sayings emphasize the negative because they are focused on economics, and in economic terms girls were a bad investment. Because girls moved out when they got married, the family that reared a girl lost her labor and the costs of their investment in her. While children in general were highly valued, sons who stayed at home, worked the family land, and became lineal descendants performing the ancestral rituals, were of inestimably greater value.

It was also believed that women were ritually polluting (Ahern 193–214). Menstrual blood and postpartum discharge were seen as both unclean and dangerously powerful. Anyone who came into contact with these substances was barred from worshiping the gods. Several negative beliefs were associated with women's reproductive powers. Pregnant women, for example, were considered particularly dangerous and harmful to others. There was also a belief that women who had borne children or died in childbirth were punished in a special place in the underworld. Thus women were punished in the supernatural realm for doing what was the most adaptive thing they could do in the natural realm.

Orthodox Beliefs. Many people believe that the "traditional Chinese" devaluation of women began with Confucius in the classical period. However, the general purpose of the Confucian *Analects* is to talk about what is necessary for good government, and Confucius simply did not address the inner world of women and the family. Of the few references that do exist, most extol the importance of children being filial—responsible, caring, and fulfilling the rituals—to their parents (Waley 2:7, 8). A few urge men to use caution and restraint in responding to female beauty (16:17, 15:13), and one is rather patronizing in its view of women: " The Master said, Women and people of low birth are very difficult to deal with. If you are friendly with them they get out of hand, and if you keep your distance they resent it" (17:25). Overall, however, it seems that in a Confucian world the family is taken for granted as an important structure lying at the base of the society. Family relationships (husband-wife, parent-child, sibling-sibling) imitate in form the relationship between the emperor and his subjects, and individuals use the same moral traits and ritual behaviors in both.

In another classic text, the *Liji* or *Book of Rites*, the chapter on marriage stresses wifely deference and submission, but at the same time affection, partnership, and shared responsibility are seen as part of the marital relationship. Susan Mann hypothesizes that the *Liji* emphasizes natural distinctions and difference rather that hierarchy, dominance, or submission:

> A proper marriage was arranged and celebrated to underscore gender differences and to emphasize the complementary and separate responsibilities of man and woman in the conjugal relationship. Marriage was the primary human social bond demonstrating the "righteousness," or "propriety" (*i* [*yi*]), of each distinctive human role. Like all primary relationships, marriage required deference and submission (wives are to husbands as sons are to fathers and subjects to rulers). But the *Li Chi* [*Liji*] stressed that husband and wife interact to demonstrate harmony.(209)

Husbands and wives also had complementary responsibilities: women's was the regulation and harmony of families, and men's was the regulation and harmony of government.

Thus the extreme patriarchy found in Chinese culture in late imperial times does not seem to be a part of the early Chinese classics. Rather, these more excessive attitudes emerge later on in Chinese history. The cult of widow chastity is an excellent example of how beliefs and values related to women changed significantly over China's long history. As part of the Neo-Confucianist revival beginning in the Song Dynasty, the chastity, or the nonremarriage of widows, became a significant mark of a woman's virtue. Tens of thousands of "Biographies of Virtuous Women" became part of the official records during the Ming and Qing Dynasties. The lives of these "virtuous and honorable women" were generally tragic, as they were either killed or committed suicide to keep their chastity or honor intact. The state, however, had a system of rewards for widow chastity (Waltner 422). Though the specifics varied, a woman who was widowed before she was thirty and remained chaste until she was fifty could be granted a memorial arch and her family was exempt from certain kinds of taxes. Certainly, a major function of the "valorization of virtue" represented by these stories was to keep women under the control of their families and in a subservient social position (Carlitz 124).

Heterodox Beliefs. Opposed to this orthodox or official state ideology, there was in China a consistent heterodox tradition that served to negate the view that women are inferior, and to provide an alternative perspective. There is, for example, the story of Fa Mu Lan, the legendary woman warrior who took her father's place in battle and fought gloriously and victoriously. (The Chinese American author Maxine Hong Kingston created her novel *The Woman Warrior* around this legendary figure.) In many secret societies, most notably those in the thousand-year-long White Lotus tradition, women could hold office, and leadership was often passed down through a matrilineal line (Naquin 22). In the Tang Dynasty (618–907) there were many female adherents of the cult of the Queen Mother of the West, the most important goddess of Taoism, and the special patron of women, such as prostitutes, who were outside the realm of the family. As the creator of the world and one who held the secret of immortality, the Queen Mother of the West held great power (Cahill 34). The official ideology of the large-scale Taiping Revolution, 1850–1864, held that men and women were equal, that women could go to school, own land, and join in battle. Though easy to ignore because it was outside the mainstream of conventional thought, nonetheless the many strands of this heterodox tradition functioned to provide challenges and alternatives to orthodox beliefs, and thus in difficult times could absorb the worst of the contradictions concerning women.

Behavioral Studies

The ideologies just described have to do with Chinese beliefs and values about women, but without observations or behavioral descriptions, it is difficult to know the extent to which people's actual *behavior* conformed to the ideal. Because it was not within the orthodox Confucian paradigm, officials certainly would not include biographies of famous courtesans, literati women, or sexually unconventional women in their official list of "Virtuous Women." Arthur Wolf, in his study of Hai-Shan on Taiwan, presents some intriguing evidence that hints at the extent to which women did in fact control their fertility and maintain their independence. Using the Japanese-maintained household registers from the early twentieth century, he showed that most widows, including those under twenty-five, did not remarry, a fact that seems consistent with the Neo-Confucian cult of widow chastity. However, he goes on to point out that women who did not remarry bore nearly as many children as those who did—an astounding statistic, given this cult of chastity. A possible explanation for this is

> that women who had borne children and established what Margery Wolf calls a "uterine family" were reluctant to remarry. Their children gave them the right to a share of their husband's father's estate, and this in turn allowed

them an independence normally denied to women. Had they married out of
their husband's family, they would have lost both their children and their
claim to family property. They therefore preferred informal to formal
arrangements and resisted marrying a second time. (108)

A related finding is that, regardless of age, women in second marriages bore
fewer children than women in their first marriage. This can be explained by the
fact that while a woman in her first marriage was dependent on her husband's
property, in a second marriage a woman often controlled property through her
sons and could make her husband dependent on her (Wolf 108). She was thus in a
much better position than a woman in her first marriage to decide on whether or
not to have more children. Based on these and other statistics, Wolf argues that
substantial deviations from the orthodox ideal did in fact occur, and these were
due to women actually having some power, derived from their uterine family, to
make decisions about marriage and offspring.

More evidence of actual behavior that does not conform to the orthodox ideal
comes from Shunde County in Guangdong Province in southern China where the
marriage resistance movement flourished for at least one hundred years, from the
early nineteenth century to the early twentieth century (Topley 67–88). Marriage
resistance typically took the form of women forming sisterhoods. In one type, *zishunu*
自梳女 (women who dress their own hair) went through a hairdressing ritual to signify their adult status and then, before a deity, took vows to remain celibate. Another
type, *bulojia* 不落家 (women who do not go down to the family), were married
women who lived apart from their husbands without consummating their marriages.

To understand such extreme heterodoxy one needs to look at a number of local
factors. The economy was based on sericulture: fish breeding, mulberry trees, silkworms, silk spinning, and weaving. Women's feet were not bound in this area and
they performed an essential and large part of the labor. Because of ideas about pollution, unmarried rather than married women were involved in most aspects of sericulture. In the mid to late nineteenth century, domestic production of silk decreased
as industrialization began. Huge filatures were set up, again largely hiring unmarried
women. As the domestic economy declined, men began to emigrate in large numbers
and women's income became even more important for families. The local economy
was thus clearly a factor in the resistance: unmarried women could support themselves in a socially accepted manner—a very rare thing in traditional China.

Far from being opposed, many parents in Shunde County were of a practical
mind and encouraged at least one daughter to become a *zishunu*. They gained economic support and, after the daughter took her vows, did not have to worry about
her marrying and interrupting their steady income. In-laws as well did not mind
having a daughter-in-law become a *bulojia* because she was then obliged to send
money back to her husband and his family. If she decided never to return and bear
him children, she not only had to provide a concubine for him, but also had to support any children they had.

Women in Shunde got ideological support for nonmarriage from a local White Lotus sect. It spread "precious volumes" containing biographies of model women who showed that refusing to marry is not morally wrong, that childbirth is polluting and dangerous, and that chastity is desirable. In contrast to the picture of women as isolated competitors within the family, the women in Shunde formed sisterhoods and supported one another. They visited temples and attended theatrical performances together, and formed money saving associations that sponsored death benefit, festival, retirement, and mutual aid funds. Shunde demonstrates the extraordinary extent to which women rejected the traditional system of inferiority when the economic system allowed them to support themselves in a socially respectable manner.

Modern China

The twentieth century saw major changes in the structure of Chinese society: 1911 was the end of the emperors and the more than two thousand years of the imperial system; Western influence, from the mid nineteenth century on, as well as two world wars, affected people's lives drastically; and the 1949 founding of the People's Republic of China was the institutional culmination of the development of Chinese communism. For women also this was a century of great change. Footbinding largely was stopped by the 1920s, due to Western influence and the action of anti-footbinding societies. Education of girls, selection of one's own marriage partner, and women working outside the home were all part of the early-twentieth-century urban scene. In rural areas, change was slower, but the advent of Maoism brought new ideas and new structures. Mao's strategy for winning over peasants to communism involved setting up village associations to discuss the causes of poverty, and then implementing land reform. One of the successful tactics used to involve women in this process was the "Speak Bitterness" sessions in which village women gathered and publicly recounted their humiliations under the old system. This public testimony often transformed their personal anger into a collective hatred of both landlords and patriarchs, and women learned how to stick together and support one another. Nearly every ethnographer of this time describes such scenes, but perhaps the most famous is Gold Flower's story. When Gold Flower was fifteen, her parents arranged a marriage for her to a man fifteen years older in a distant village. He was a vicious man who beat her violently whenever she did not jump to serve him or his father quickly or demurely enough. In 1947 when Gold Flower was twenty-one, she hesitantly told her story to the newly formed women's association in her village. The women ran to get her husband, tied him up, and asked him if he would reform. When he answered disdainfully,

> as if by a signal, all the women pushed forward at once. Gold Flower quickly went in back of her husband. The crowd fell on him, howling, knocked him to the ground, then jumped on him with their feet. Several women fell with

him, their hands thrashing wildly. Those in the rear leaped in, tore at his clothing, then seized his bare flesh in their hands and began twisting and squeezing till his blood flowed from many scratches. Those who could not get close, dove under the rest and seized Chang's legs, sinking their teeth in his flesh.

Chang let out an anguished howl. "Don't beat me! Don't beat me," he bleated in terror. "I'll reform. Don't hurt me any more."

Under the blows of the women, his cries were soon stilled. The women backed off. Gold Flower peered down at her husband. He lay there motionless on the ground, like a dead dog, his mouth full of mud, his clothes in tatters and blood coming in a slow trickle from his nose. "That's how it was with me in the past," Gold Flower thought. Unable to restrain a feeling of happiness, she turned to the other women. "Many thanks, comrade sisters, for your kindness. If it had not been for you, I would not have been able to get my revenge."

"Don't be polite," said a girl. "This is only justice." (Belden 302)

Groups started by the Communist government, like the peasant Women's Association described above or the agricultural collective work teams, did much to end the isolation of peasant women within their family compounds, and also provided structures that placed women in cooperative rather than competitive relationships with each other.

Ideological Changes of the Mao Period: 1949–1976

The driving force of change during this period was the radical leadership group's adherence to Marxist ideology, which states that women and men are equal, and that women were oppressed in the past because they were confined to the family and had no access to socially productive labor.

One of the first major pieces of legislation passed by the Communist government was the 1950 Marriage Law. This law incorporated principles of freedom of choice and gender equality, and outlawed early marriage and concubinage. According to this law women had equal rights to choose their own spouse, to divorce, and equal ownership and management rights in community property. This law was popularly referred to as the "divorce law" because of the large number of women who attempted to take advantage of it! However, the empowerment of women contained in this law conflicted with the entitlement of poor farmers and landless peasants, who had been persuaded to support the Communists because of their program of land reform, which the peasants saw as a means of acquiring not only farms but also wives. At the same time as they were trying to push reluctant peasants from private ownership of land to collective ownership, the Communist leaders were faced with a sharp increase in the number of women petitioning for divorce, as well as resistance from "feudal" cadres (i.e., those who were patriarchal or traditional) who were reluctant to enforce the new law against their male relatives and friends. Rather than risk alienating male peasants, the Communist leadership chose to dampen enforcement of the Marriage Law and instead emphasized family and village solidarity, thereby promoting cooperative production (Ocko 320).

Full employment for women was a major agenda item for the Communists when they took over in 1949. In the cities they organized a variety of women's groups in order to promote and deal with special problems of women in employment. Far from having to encourage women to work outside the home, there were not nearly enough factory jobs for all the women that wanted them (Davin 177). The slow pace of industrial growth at the time meant that there were not enough jobs for everyone, and even men were often out of work. Government attempts to organize women for handicraft production in their own homes floundered for lack of capital, materials, and the narrow range of products and skills emphasized. The government's response to these problems was to create and promulgate the *wuhao* 五好 (five good) movement, which glorified the role of the housewife and attempted to politicize housework by giving it a recognized revolutionary value. Women were encouraged to work at home to maintain a harmonious household, to rear responsible socialist children, and to keep up family morale so that men could produce more at their jobs (Davin 163–190).

In both these instances, the same mechanism was at work. An ideologically driven Communist leadership group pressed for equality for women. But when issues of production, government policy, or family concerns conflicted with women's rights, it was always women who lost out. Equality for women became a goal that could be put off until it was more convenient. Judith Stacey interprets this as the substitution of one form of patriarchy for another in the Maoist period, while Margery Wolf (1985) sees it more simply as a "revolution postponed."

Communist policies in the Maoist period had contradictory effects on the traditional family (Davis and Harrell 1–7). Collectivization of land and labor and the elimination of most private property got rid of family farms and businesses, the economic basis of the traditional extended family. The denunciation of ancestor worship as superstition and of lineage activities as wasteful and nonproductive hit at the ideological and religious core of the family. On the other hand, more equitable distribution of food and better health care meant that infant mortality decreased, people lived longer, and population increased. Restrictions on internal migration, enacted to insure an orderly economic development, meant that males stayed put in their home village and that women still moved into the villages of their husbands. Development of a very large formal bureaucratic system to manage the whole state apparatus, also resulted in individuals developing their own informal system of personal ties and networks of connections (*guanxi* 關係) to navigate the bureaucracy. Overall these factors combined to produce the conditions conducive to the development of large, multigenerational households with extensive social and economic ties to both nearby and farflung kin. Thus while undermining some economic and ideological aspects of the traditional family, particularly patrilineality, overall the Communist policies did not seriously challenge patriarchy and patrilocality.

Post-Mao Period: 1976—Present

Ideology. The official ideology of modern China is codified in a constitution and set of laws. Those most pertinent to women are as follow:

1. Article 48 of the *1982 Chinese Constitution,* which guarantees sexual equality.
2. The *Marriage Law of 1980* changed the criteria needed for divorce. The 1950 law had stipulated that a divorce *might* be granted when mediation failed, but the 1980 law said that a divorce *should* be granted if connubial love and affection had truly been destroyed and mediation had no effect. Two things are noteworthy: one is that love and affection are acknowledged as being a major part of marriage, and when they are no longer there and mediation fails, a divorce *should* be granted. Another part of the law added that women were entitled to their own lives outside the marriage, that is they could have social or educational relationships outside the family.
3. The *Inheritance Law of 1985* guaranteed the inheritance right of daughters and widows, and confirmed the right of a widow to take property away with her into a new marriage. (Ocko 314–327)

Of course, just because new laws are enacted does not mean that actual behavior changes. Most observers conclude that China has a long way to go before equality in property rights and in spousal relations are the norm (Ocko 338; Honig and Hershatter 227; 263; 273; 340). As Margery Wolf pointed out, "patriarchy is not just a domestic ideology but a social ideology as well" (*Revolution* 163), and feudal remnants persist in the thinking of ordinary citizens as well those cadres responsible for enforcing the laws. As forms and amount of property continue to grow and as property relationships become more complicated, the courts are increasingly used for contract resolution, thus giving more opportunities to bring practice into line with the law.

Economic, Social, and Political Structures. The two major post-Mao government initiatives have been strict population control and liberalizing economic reforms, usually referred to as a "market economy under socialist conditions." China's one child policy has been fairly successful in the cities, with the average number of offspring close to one child per family, and in rural areas the average number of children is about two per family. Economic liberalization has produced dramatic changes in the standard of living: most families now have telephones, refrigerators, washing machines, and color televisions, as consumer goods have become available, plentiful, and affordable. Fewer people are employed in state-owned factories as more jobs become available in the private sector, and the economy is open to entrepreneurs.

How have these major structural changes affected women? Have these economic and demographic changes produced corresponding changes in patriarchy, patrilineality, and patrilocality? As one would expect, the answers to these questions are not always easy to see as effects have been mixed, depending, again, on variables such as social class, region of the country, and family situation.

Changes in the countryside have indeed been dramatic. Communes have been disbanded and the household has reemerged as the basic unit of production. Women still generally move to their husband's home village (patrilocal residence), and this has several effects. Parents are still more reluctant to invest in education for their daughters because they leave home, and parents feel that they must have a son who will stay at home and take care of them in their old age. When the government was requiring strict adherence to its one-child policy, women were often caught between the competing demands of their husbands and the local birth-control cadres. This was the origin of the pressure for abortion if the fetus was female, or for infanticide, abandonment, or adoption out if the infant was a girl. Currently the pressure on women has eased because a second child is allowed if the first one is a girl, and also because the central government is not quite as powerful and intrusive as it was.

Recent economic changes and loosening of the rules about mobility have led increasing numbers of rural people to look for jobs outside their local areas. Women are finding jobs as maids or babysitters in the cities, and many young unmarried women are finding factory jobs in the special economic zones of southern China. Men find contract work in construction, carpentry, transportation, or production, also often away from home. Increasingly women are taking over much of the actual agricultural work while men are engaging in small-scale entrepreneurial activity, both locally and away. Whether rural married couples live with the husband's parents depends mainly on the availability of different kinds of economic opportunities. Gao thinks that although the effects on women have been uneven, overall rural women's lives are better. She finds that there is less patriarchy as males "recognize women's competence and authority in the home, discuss important matters with their wives, subsidize their daughter's school attendance, and are beginning to help with household chores" (88). Likewise Judd, who did fieldwork in Shandong between 1986 and 1990, believes that power relations in the domestic realm are undergoing renegotiation. Though she sees that the "Three Obediences" are still a compelling determinant of gender behavior, she also found that the male patriarch did not have complete control over family finances. Women's earning power has given them more of a say.

In urban areas modernization has brought many changes in the traditional patterns, many of which show an erosion of patriarchal ideas. Urban women generally are employed away from the home for most of their lives, and they are often the ones who control family spending. Most urban residents have only one child, and if that child is a daughter, parents invest heavily in her upbringing, education, and success. Many retired elderly prefer to live with daughters rather than sons because they have a warmer social relationship with them. Neolocal residence (married couples live in a new place, not with the husband's or wife's family) is the preferred pattern in the cities, and is the most common form when housing is available (Unger 27–40). Working daughters-in-law are thus not at home to be controlled by mothers-in-law. Mothers-in-law of today complain that they have to wait hand and foot on their daughters-in-law if they want to be close to their son and grandchild!

Contradictorily, there is a lot of evidence that even in urban areas patriarchy and feudal ideas continue to persist. Women earn on average 71.7 percent of what men earn (Whyte and Parish 204–206). Women face open discrimination in job hunting, and must have higher test scores and more education to be hired over men. Women are perceived of as less desirable workers because of their "special conditions"—pregnancy, maternity leave, nursing, and taking time off when children are sick or for babysitting emergencies. Women are generally thought of as less intelligent and less clever than men (Gallagher; Honig and Hershatter 243–263).

In assessing the current state of affairs however, the Chinese people themselves express widespread optimism about the future. Both genders see their own lives as being better than their parents', and think that their children's lives, whether they are girls or boys, will be better than their own (Gallagher).

Summary

Trying to understand women's lives in China, one of the intriguing points is that Chinese women by and large have not internalized the ever-present social idea of women's inferiority. Whenever the economic or social system allows them some options, they take them. Women in China do not usually play the part of the downtrodden, pitiful victim. But why not? Certainly until recent times the political, economic, social, and ideological factors have all conspired against them. Perhaps, in a paradoxical way, the answer lies in the same Confucian ideology and traditional Chinese culture that is often pointed to as causing their oppression.

As Henry Rosemont has pointed out, though Confucian ideology is often antiwoman, it is not antitypical female gender traits, traits such as nurturance, yielding, intuition. The yin-yang symbolic concept, based on supposedly natural differences between male and female, also implies each gendered person incorporates, at different times and in different circumstances, the gender traits of the other sex. Being active is called for at some times, being quiescent at others; being logical in some circumstances, being intuitive in others; being nurturant to some people, being demanding of others. In a Chinese world each person does not have a core, innate identity, but rather each person is contingent, relational, and constantly being constructed from interactions with others. Each person performs themselves into being, through ritual role performances. Although gender hierarchies are everpresent, which gender's traits an individual manifests depends on the situation. As blatantly sexist as the patriarchal, patrilineal, and patrilocal traditional Chinese society was, women were able to resist internalization of personal inferiority, and instead model traits adaptive to their context. This enabled them as individuals to deal with their personal circumstances, and to change their behavior as those circumstances changed.

> When we Chinese girls listened to the adults talking-story, we learned that we failed if we grew up to be but wives or slaves. We could be heroines, swordswomen. . . .
>
> Night after night my mother would talk-story until we fell asleep. I couldn't tell where the stories left off and the dreams began, her voice the voice of the heroines in my sleep. . . .
>
> At last I saw that I too had been in the presence of great power, my mother talking-story. After I grew up, I heard the chant of Fa Mu Lan, the girl who took her father's place in battle. Instantly I remembered that as a child I had followed my mother about the house, the two of us singing about how Fa Mu Lan fought gloriously and returned alive from war to settle in the village. I had forgotten this chant that was once mine, given me by my mother, who may not have known its power to remind. She said I would grow up a wife and a slave, but she taught me the song of the warrior woman Fa Mu Lan. I would have to grow up a warrior woman. (Kingston 19–20)

Glossary

Foot binding The practice of tightly binding the feet of young girls in order to make the feet as small as possible.

Heterodox Not in accordance with established or accepted doctrines or opinions.

One child policy Official government policy in the post-Mao period to limit births to one child per family.

Patriarchal A form of social organization in which males have the supreme power, prestige and authority; a social system in which men dominate women.

Patrilineal Descent traced through the male line only.

Patrilocal Living with the husband's relatives after marriage.

Ritual pollution traditional belief that women's menstrual blood or pregnancy rendered them unclean, contaminated, or impure.

Three obediences According to this Confucian ideal, a woman was to obey her father when she was young, her husband after she was married, and her son in her old age.

Uterine family Margery Wolf's conception of that subsegment of the family composed of a woman and her children.

Works Cited

Ahern, Emily M. "The Power and Pollution of Chinese Women." *Women in Chinese Society.* Ed. Margery Wolf and Roxane Witke. Stanford: Stanford University Press, 1975. 193–214.

Belden, Jack. *China Shakes the World*. New York: Harper, 1949.

Buck, John Lossing. *Land Utilization in China*. Nanking: University of Nanking Press, 1937.

Cahill, Suzanne E. *Transcendence and Divine Passion: The Queen Mother of the West in Medieval China*. Stanford: Stanford University Press, 1993.

Carlitz, Katherine. "Desire, Danger, and the Body: Stories of Women's Virtue in Late Ming China." *Engendering China: Women, Culture, and the State*. Ed. Christina K. Gilmartin, Gail Hershatter, Lisa Rofel, and Tyrene White. Cambridge: Harvard University Press, 1994. 101–24.

Davin, Delia. *Woman-Work: Women and the Party in Revolutionary China*. Oxford: Oxford University Press, 1976.

Davis, Deborah, and Stevan Harrell, eds. *Chinese Families in the Post-Mao Era*. Berkeley and Los Angeles: University of California Press, 1993.

Gallagher, Mary F. "Effects of Modernization on Gender Equality: The Case of Chinese Professional Women." Paper read at the Annual Meeting of the Society for Applied Anthropology, Santa Fe, 1989.

Gao Xiaoxian. "China's Modernization and the Social Status of Rural Women." *Engendering China: Women, Culture, and the State*. Ed. Christina K. Gilmartin, Gail Hershatter, Lisa Rofel, and Tyrene White. Cambridge: Harvard University Press, 1994. 80–97.

Honig, Emily, and Gail Hershatter. *Personal Voices: Chinese Women in the 1980s*. Stanford: Stanford University Press, 1988.

Judd, Ellen. *Gender and Power in Rural North China*. Stanford: Stanford University Press, 1994.

Kingston, Maxine Hong. *The Woman Warrior*. New York: Knopf, 1976.

Mann, Susan. "Grooming a Daughter for Marriage: Brides and Wives in the Mid Ch'ing Period." *Marriage and Inequality in Chinese Society*. Ed. Rubie S. Watson and Patricia Buckley Ebrey. Berkeley and Los Angeles: University of California Press, 1991. 204–30.

Naquin, Susan. *Millenarian Rebellion in China: The Eight Trigrams Uprising of 1813*. Cambridge: Harvard University Press,1970.

Ocko, Jonathan K. "Women, Property, and Law in the People's Republic of China." *Marriage and Inequality in Chinese Society*. Ed. Rubie S. Watson and Patricia Buckley Ebrey. Berkeley and Los Angeles: University of California Press, 1991. 313–46.

Rosemont, Henry, Jr. "Classical Confucian and Contemporary Feminist Perspectives on the Self: Some Parallels and Their Implications." Unpublished Paper, 1995.

Stacey, Judith. *Patriarchy and Socialist Revolution in China*. Berkeley and Los Angeles: University of California Press, 1983.

Topley, Marjorie. "Marriage Resistance in Rural Kwangtung." *Women in Chinese Society*. Ed. Margery Wolf and Roxane Witke. Stanford: Stanford University Press, 1975. 67–88.

Unger, Jonathan. "Urban Families in the Eighties: An Analysis of Chinese Surveys." *Chinese Families in the Post-Mao Era*. Ed. Deborah Davis and Stevan Harrell. Berkeley and Los Angeles: University of California Press, 1993. 25–49.

Waley, Arthur. *The Analects of Confucius*. New York: Random, 1960.

Waltner, Ann. "Recent Scholarship on Chinese Women." *Signs* 21.2 (1996): 410–428.

Whyte, Martin King, and William L. Parish. *Urban Life in Contemporary China.* Chicago: University of Chicago Press, 1984.

Wolf, Arthur P. "The Women of Hai-Shan: a Demographic Portrait." *Women in Chinese Society.* Ed. Margery Wolf and Roxane Witke. Stanford: Stanford University Press, 1975. 89–110.

Wolf, Margery. *Women and the Family in Rural Taiwan.* Stanford: Stanford University Press, 1972.

———. *Revolution Postponed: Women in Contemporary China.* Stanford: Stanford University Press, 1985.

Works Consulted

Croll, Elisabeth. *Chinese Women Since Mao.* Armonk, N.Y.: Sharpe, 1983.

Ebrey, Patricia Buckley. *The Inner Quarters: Marriage and the Lives of Chinese Women in the Sung Period.* Berkeley and Los Angeles: University of California Press, 1993.

Gates, Hill. "The Commoditization of Chinese Women." *Signs* 14.4 (1989):799–832.

Johnson, Kay Ann. *Women, the Family, and Peasant Revolution in China.* Chicago: University of Chicago Press, 1983.

Parish, William L., and Martin King Whyte. *Village and Family in Contemporary China.* Chicago: University of Chicago Press, 1978.

Zito, Angela, and Tani E. Barlow, eds. *Body, Subject, and Power in China.* Chicago: University of Chicago Press, 1994.

5

Chinese Music and the Family

Kathleen M. Higgins

Emphasis on the family is a well-known feature of Chinese thought. Many Americans who know little else about Chinese culture are aware that it stresses respect for one's elders. Even so, we may still be surprised to learn that the Chinese associate musical tones with basic human relationships, especially those within the family. Yet the Chinese "Record of Music," a section of the *Book of Ritual,* made this claim as long ago as the Han Dynasty (c. 202 B.C.E.–220 C.E.):

> Therefore the ancient kings ... gave laws for the great and small notes according to their names, and harmonized the order of the beginning and the end, to represent the doing of things. Thus they made the underlying principles of the relations between the near and distant relatives, the noble and mean, the old and young, males and females, all to appear manifestly in the music. (108–109)

In the West, recently, philosophers have sometimes explained the common denominator of musical works in terms of family resemblance. Following Austrian philosopher Ludwig Wittgenstein, such thinkers have meant that works of music have a general, recognizable similarity that is not based on their having identical features.[1] A Sousa march, a particular Gregorian chant, and an opera aria have dissimilar structures, and yet we have no trouble classing all three as pieces of music, just as we can often recognize that individuals are members of the same family despite considerable differences among their features.

This reference to "family" is not the same as the Chinese association. The "family resemblance" image makes no reference to whether those exhibiting family relationships are siblings, cousins, or parent and child. "Family resemblance" presupposes relationships that account for perceived similarities, but the relationships themselves are not the focus of interest.

The Chinese association of personal relationships with music, by contrast, specifies particular kinds of relationships. From the Western point of view, the nature of this association is less than obvious. In what follows, we will explore the Chinese approach to music in a way that will help us to see why the Chinese consider human relationships comparable to musical tones.

The Five Tones

The straightforward basis for comparing tones and personal relationships is that the Chinese enumerate five of each. The oldest Chinese scale is pentatonic, or five-tone. The pentatonic scale still predominates in Chinese vocal music. One can get a sense of how the pentatonic scale sounds by playing only the black keys on the piano, or by omitting "fa" and "ti" when singing the scale.

This pentatonic scale is far from arbitrary. It is built of five tones within an octave (a musical interval of eight steps) that stand in close harmonic relationships to one another. This type of scale, which is highly consonant and based on natural acoustics, is also used by others among the world's cultures. Walter Kaufmann observes that the pentatonic scale characterizes indigenous melodies of diverse groups, including the Czechs, the Scots, the inhabitants of Madagascar, Native Americans, African Americans, South Americans, and South Sea island peoples.

The Chinese also consider the basic human relationships to be five in number: ruler-subject, parent-child, brother-brother, husband-wife, and friend-friend. The first basis for comparing the two series is their common number of elements. A second is suggested when we consider that the basic relationships are those formed with those to whom an individual is most closely connected. Each tone in the pentatonic scale is also closely related to other notes in the scale.

In both cases, too, the individual finds identity by means of these basic connections. The Chinese consider personal identity to be a matter of how one is related to others. You are who you are because you are the child of your parents, the parent of your children, the sibling of your siblings, the spouse of your spouse. One finds a similar kind of identity among the tones used in music. A tone has the place it does in a song, for instance, only in relation to other notes of the scale. It assumes its musical significance by relating to the other notes. Thus, a third basis for the comparison between musical tones and individuals is that identity in each case is forged through their relations.

If we examine other aspects of Chinese culture, however, we find the prevalence of the number five in classifications of all types. Five seems to represent the complete set of any type of thing. The "Record of Music" says of musical tones, "[The five notes, like] the five colours, form a complete and elegant whole, without any confusion ... The lengths of all the different notes have their definite measurements, without any uncertainty. The small and the great complete one another" (*Book of Ritual* 111). Similarly, we find "the five colors," "the five directions," "the five aspects," "the five stems" (used in calendar calculations), "the five tastes," "the five animals," "the five images of nature," "the five grains," "the five viscera," "the five smells," "the five numbers," "the five senses," and so on. Each of these groupings is also associated with the five tones and with the five human relations. What can we make of all these interconnections?

The correlation schemes indicate the importance and prevalence of analogical thinking for the Chinese. Western thought has tended to express ideas in terms of precise categories. Even when analogies are employed in Western thought, they usually refer to some specific point of comparison. Wittgenstein's notion of "family resemblance" is a good example.

In Chinese philosophy, by contrast, such comparisons are much more open-ended, inviting reflection on the ways in which the items in different categories are related. The correlations of the various fives do not pinpoint exact common features among the categories, but instead encourage imaginative exploration of each type of thing by considering the other, correlated categories as foils. In music, for example, the correlation with human relationships is not a translation key for interpreting the music; we do not mentally shift from parent-child to brother-brother as we move from one tone to another. Instead, the correlation invites us to consider the relations among tones as being similar to the relations among people. This is what we have done, for instance, when we considered how identity depends on relationship in both cases.

The open-endedness of these correlations helps to explain why "the five tones" conveys the idea of all the notes of a scale, even though the Chinese use seven-tone, or heptatonic scales, as well as five-tone scales. Heptatonic scales appear to have been used in China at least since the late Zhou (pronounced "Joe") dynasty, around 400 B.C.E. Two notes were added to the pentatonic scale for some instrumental music, resulting in a scale that resembles the major scale in the Western system. The scale possibilities are quite numerous in Chinese music. Each tone within the seven-tone scale can be used as a "final," the note of primary emphasis in a piece, and the note on which the piece concludes.

In principle, scales can also be constructed on any of the twelve notes of what in the West is called the Pythagorean scale (although in practice the Chinese do not use all of these possibilities). The Pythagorean scale corresponds roughly to the twelve tones within an octave on the piano. The scale is named, in the West, for Pythagoras (c. 581–507 B.C.E.), the ancient Greek philosopher and mathematician who discovered that strings whose lengths are in simple ratios to one another produce consonant harmonies. This discovery enabled him to generate a series of tones of decreasing harmonic proximity to a starting tone, by means of what is called "the cycle of fifths."

One starts by vibrating a string of a specific length. Then one vibrates a string two-thirds the length of the first. This second string, when vibrated, will produce a tone that is a perfect fifth above that produced by the first string. In other words, the second string produces the note "sol" in relation to the "doh" produced by the first string. One continues by vibrating a string that is two-thirds the length of the second string to sound a tone that is a perfect fifth above that string's tone. (This newly generated note is "re" in relation to the "doh" of the first string.) By repeating this process until twelve tones have been generated, one arrives at the tones that constitute the Pythagorean scale.

The Chinese, similarly, developed this twelve-tone series by around 400 B.C.E. According to legend, the twelve tones were generated by means of pitch pipes, not strings, although this is disputed. The Chinese assign analogical correlations to the twelve tones on the basis of *yin* and *yang*.

The duality of *yin* and *yang* is used by Chinese thinkers to express the nature of all interdependent oppositions. "*Yang*" originally meant "the sunny side," while "*yin*" refers to "the shaded side" of a mountain. The gradual changes of sun and shadow are reflected in *yin* and *yang,* for change alters the balance in every opposition. *Yin* gives way to *yang,* and vice versa. The primacy of the twin images of *yin* and *yang* in Chinese thought indicates the interest the Chinese have always had in change and transformation on all levels of experience. Each of the twelve tones within the octave is calculated, in the Chinese method, either by addition or subtraction. Those calculated by means of addition are associated with *yang,* while those calculated by means of subtraction are associated with *yin.*

Although *yin* and *yang* do not refer specifically to human relationships, this correlation of *yin* and *yang* with musical tones resonates with the correlation considered above. All interpersonal relationships, the Chinese assume, presuppose disparities of strength and weakness. For example, parents are initially stronger than their offspring; during that period the parents are benefactors to their child, protecting and providing for it. Later on, however, the child's physical strength surpasses that of its parents; at this stage the parents become beneficiaries to their children, who care for them in their old age. In their later years, however, parents may have more wisdom than their children, even though they are physically more vulnerable. Thus, a person can be *yin* in one respect but *yang* in another within the same relationship.

The dynamic nature of personal relationships stems from the interplay of the parties' relative strengths and weaknesses. One might argue that something similar occurs in music. The tones are mutually related through the dynamic of one tone's prominence giving way to another's. The "Record of Music" states this idea directly: "The blending together without any mutual injuriousness (of the sentiments and the airs on different instruments) forms the essence of music" (*Book of Ritual* 101).

The twelve tones represent the gamut, or full range, of pitches. They are the means by which movement within music is possible, enabling music to manifest the principles of change within nature. The Chinese considered these twelve tones to be absolute, fixed by nature. The five tones of the pentatonic scale, by contrast, are defined only relationally. In other words, the five tones stand in definite intervals to each other, so once a tone is selected as the basis for a scale, the other four are determined; but any tone might be used as the starting point. The twelve tones, however, are considered to be precise pitches, generated from a fundamental pitch, called the "yellow bell" (*huangzhong* 黃鐘). The ancients were supposed to have found an absolute fundamental tone in nature; but theorists debated about how this absolute pitch could be securely determined. During the Han Dynasty, the authenticity of the yellow bell was debated in imperial court. In this case, again, music was considered relevant to human relationships. Because they were fixed by nature, the twelve tones were seen as authoritative, and DeWoskin observes that "control of the twelve pitches . . . was an important sign of the authority to govern" (46).

Harmony in Chinese Music

Yet another basis for comparing the interplay of musical tones and the relationships of people is our desire for harmony in both. "Harmony (*he* 和)" is one of the most frequently discussed aspects of Chinese music. Westerners, however, should bear in mind that harmony in traditional Chinese music is not a matter of "harmonizing," in the fashion of barbershop quartets or early rock groups. What, then, do traditional Chinese thinkers have in mind when they refer to harmony? They mean a number of things, all of which lend a sense of unity and balance to a piece of music.

Harmony includes a sense of balance among the instruments. In this respect, the harmonious ensemble resembles the harmonious family or a balanced dish. The parts mutually respond to each other; no single element overpowers any other. Ideally, the individuality of each is preserved by its setting in the context of the whole. In this respect, musical harmony reflects the Chinese ideal of all human communities, in which the individual character of each member enhances the group as a whole.

Harmony also involves the music's ability to convey a sense of relatedness. To gain a sense of what such a relationship is, recall the case of mechanically produced jingles that accompany many computer games and some greeting cards. The tones of a song or melodic phrase are presented correctly, with regular rhythm; yet one senses that there is no musical intelligence or feeling at work within the music. Such "music" lacks harmony, in the Chinese sense.

A third connotation of "harmony" is an appropriate match between the tones and the mood of the piece. As in virtually all cultures, much Chinese music incorporates sung poetry. In the case of most successful songs in our own culture, the musical arrangement strikes us as well suited to the lyrics. We can certainly imagine incongruity between the two — a languid song in a minor key at a pep rally, for example. Sometimes musical humor or irony is achieved by deliberate incongruities. The rock band The Smiths, for example, often sets vicious lyrics to sweet melodies. Frank Zappa's music similarly juxtaposes startling lyrics with melodies derived from the cheery, predictable styles of earlier decades.

The traditional Chinese aspiration toward harmony involved the avoidance of such jarring juxtapositions. More positively, harmony is achieved in traditional Chinese vocal music when the music reinforces the message of the words. In instrumental music, harmony is achieved when the music establishes an atmosphere that suits the situation in which it is performed.

Traditional Confucian ceremonial music, accordingly, was considered harmonious when it was suitably dignified and resonant with the tradition. Such music, called *yayue* 雅樂, or "elegant music," was used in court from the Qin Dynasty (221–207 B.C.E.) until 1911. The system for this music, as it has been handed down, dates from the Han reconstruction of earlier ritual. The emphasis of the Confucian tradition has consistently been to preserve ancient practices and melodies in music, for these are designed to be appropriate for the rituals they accompanied.

Already in Confucius's time, during the Zhou Dynasty, fashionable music from outside the tradition (sometimes music brought from the West via the Silk Route) was sometimes inserted into court performances. Confucius opposed these developments. While it is not entirely clear which particular features of the imported music met with his objection, Walter Kaufmann speculates,

> In addition to melodic distortions there probably were also rhythmic changes. The imported Central Asian music, melodically simple, but rhythmically exciting and entirely different from the slow and dignified pace of indigenous ceremonial pieces, must have aroused the ire of Confucius. (100–101)

Confucius seems to have had musical grounds for considering such musical fads inappropriate for the imperial court. He also believed that music would serve its proper function only if it maintained its close connection with tradition. On both points, as we shall see, Confucius had good relationships between human beings foremost in mind.

Music's Expressive Role in Human Relationships

Confucius and other ancient Chinese thinkers associated music with human relationships on several grounds, some of which we have not yet considered. A central idea was that music expresses people's emotions and concerns. Legend held that music was invented by the Sage Kings, the earliest rulers of China, explicitly as a means of expressing the people's sentiments.

The expressive function of music is described in "The Great Preface" of the *Book of Poetry* (*The Shijing*[2]), one of the Five Classics of Confucianism. Music is an enhanced mode of expression, which "The Great Preface" describes as follows:

> The feelings move inwardly, and are embodied in words. When words are insufficient for them, recourse is had to sighs and exclamations. When sighs and exclamations are insufficient for them, recourse is had to the prolonged

utterances of song. When those prolonged utterances of song are insufficient for them, unconsciously the hands begin to move and the feet to dance. (34)

Music, in other words, is a natural outgrowth of our innate need to express ourselves emotionally. The view that music communicates more fully than words alone is common to many cultures. The structure of the Chinese language, however, offers a particular reason for thinking this. Unlike English, Chinese is a tonal language, in which inflection used is an important aspect of the word. The same consonant-vowel conjunction can be a variety of different words, depending on the tone used in the pronunciation of a syllable. Accordingly, melodic contour can be used to reinforce the tonal inflection of a word, and the contours of the music can reflect the contours of the spoken language. (In practice, the type of music determines whether or not melodic contour adheres strictly to linguistic tones. In Peking opera, for example, the reinforcement of linguistic tones by means of melodic contour is the exception, not the rule; when it does occur, however, it provides dramatic emphasis to what is being said, thus illustrating musical enhancement of the words' expressive power.)

"The Great Preface" suggests that our most powerful emotions are not adequately articulated through words alone. They need the more complete symbolism of our various expressive powers, including our musical voices and the movement of our entire bodies. This analysis reflects an *understanding* of the human being that differs from that typical in Western philosophy. Western thought has often stressed the differences between language and physical action, treating the mental and the bodily as radically different.

Chinese philosophy does not make this stark distinction. Mind and body are both manifestations of *qi* 氣 (pronounced "chee"), the vital energy that is the basic stuff of everything in the natural world. Poetry is a consciously mediated expression of *qi*; but a healthy body also expresses *qi* (if not so consciously), and Chinese medicine seeks to ensure the proper flow of *qi* in the body. The Chinese also do not distinguish thought and emotion in the manner of Western thought. The human being's expressions arise from heart-and-mind, understood as operating together.

The expression of thoughts and feelings through music is one of the most complete ways for a person to manifest him or herself as embodied *qi*. The "Record of Music" is explicit in its association of music with the manifestation of energy and also with the development of skill in managing one's energy:

The ancient kings [in framing their music], laid its foundations in the feelings and nature of men; they examined [the notes] by the measures [for the length and quality of each]; and adapted [their music] to express the meaning of the ceremonies [in which it was to be used]. They [thus] brought it into harmony with the energy that produces life, and to give expression to the performance of the five regular constituents of moral worth. They made it indicate that energy in its Yang or phase of vigour, without any dissipation of its power, and also in its Yin or phase of remission, without the vanishing of its power. (*Book of Ritual* 108)

Music's ability to give expression to human sentiments has several repercussions for human relationships. In the first place, it reveals the conditions of personal relationships. Songs indicate the way people feel about their situation, most often their situation vis-a-vis other people. We can see this by considering the number of songs we have heard that express love, discouragement, or anger within a relationship—themes also prevalent in the Chinese *Book of Songs*. We might also consider the modern siren, used to communicate urgency and emergency. Certain musical sounds were used in a similar way in ancient China. The *Analects* draw attention to such communication in the report that a guard who had conferred with Confucius told the latter's disciples, "I feel sure that Heaven intends to use your Master as a wooden bell" (III.24). Arthur Waley explains this as a reference to "a rattle, used to arouse the populace in times of night-danger, and in general by heralds and town-criers" (*Analects* 100n).

Secondly, the expressive character of music enabled rulers to determine the condition of their relationships with their people. Several ancient texts, including the "Record of Music" and the *Book of Historical Documents* (the *Shujing*), report that the rulers used music as a means of determining the moral and emotional climate in their society. Kenneth DeWoskin notes that this rationale resulted in the establishment of "official bureaus commissioned to collect songs outside of court and introduce them into courtly entertainments" (29). Although the Communist government of the People's Republic of China has discouraged adherence to Confucianism, it concurs with the traditional belief that those governing society should attend to the music produced. The government of the People's Republic has promoted large-scale efforts to collect and evaluate folk songs and music dramas.

Third, music's capacity to express emotion facilitated a sense of emotional connection between various members of society. Like the health of the body, the health of a society depends on flow, according to Chinese theory, in this case the flow of communication between the people and rulers, and between the living and the dead. Music, then, is not only a vent for expressing ourselves; it is also a powerful means of renewing all types of human relationships: those between human beings and the spirit world, those between human beings and nature, those between members of families, and those throughout society.

Xunzi (Hsun Tzu) describes the bonding power of music:

When music is performed in the ancestral temple of the ruler, and the ruler and his ministers, superiors and inferiors, listen to it together, there are none who are not filled with a spirit of harmonious reverence. When it is performed within the household, and father and sons, elder and younger brothers listen to it together, there are none who are not filled with a spirit of harmonious kinship. And when it is performed in the community, and old people and young together listen to it, there are none who are not filled with a spirit of harmonious obedience. (*Hsun Tzu* 113)

Confucius's insistence on music that maintained continuity with tradition can be partially understood in this light. The music of antiquity, understood as the invention of the Sage Kings, was a means of retaining contact with the thinking and practices of an earlier, wiser age. In effect, music renewed the connections that the living had with the founders of their culture and all intervening ancestors, as well as their bonds with each other.

Music as Educator

Confucius also had another rationale, however. He believed that besides renewing each individual's sense of connection with others, music could promote harmony within specific relationships. This idea draws inspiration from the observation that the rhythm of music coordinates various individuals in dance. Music, in effect, can produce an image of noncoerced complementary action, the ideal for harmonious interaction.

The actual state within society, however, may fall short of the ideal. Like many contemporary ethnomusicologists, the Chinese tradition has typically contended that music can provide a mirror for seeing how relationships actually stood. Confucius acknowledges that music can be a symptom that a society's relationships are unhealthy. Thus he criticizes the music of the Zheng people, for example, on the grounds that it is licentious (*Analects* XV.10).

How, if music mirrors actuality, can music display relationships in their ideal condition? The seeming contrariness of these goals dissolves when we observe the importance of the notion of the Way (*dao* 道) in Chinese thought. The Way, the ultimate pattern of all things, is the central concern of the Daoist tradition in Chinese thought, which emphasizes attending to the patterns of nature and deemphasizes human society as such. Confucian thought, which is often contrasted with Daoism, is also concerned with the Way; the main difference is that Confucians place emphasis on manifestations of the Way in human relationships instead of in nature.

When Confucius looks to music as an image of the ideal, he is seeing it as a reflection of the Way, the fundamental pattern of reality. As the "Record of Music" says in the passage cited above, "the underlying principles of the relations . . . all . . . appear manifestly in the music." The correlations of virtually every aspect of human experience with the five tones of music are premised on this notion that music displays reality's basic structure.

According to Confucius, learning to attend to these principles is crucial to helping one to develop the sensitivity essential to conducting one's relationships harmoniously. He describes his ethical ideal in terms of being focused on the Way, and he considers music an indispensable means for achieving this condition. "The

Master said, 'Let a man be first incited by the Songs, then given a firm footing by the study of ritual, and finally perfected by music'" (*Analects* VIII.8). A person who is guided by the Way will behave appropriately in all respects, being cognizant of principles underlying the flow of the universe. Confucius takes moral goodness to be the evidence that a person has been receptive to what the music reveals: "The Master said, 'A man who is not Good, what can he have to do with ritual? A man who is not Good, what can he have to do with music?'" (III.3).

Listening is a prominent image for insight and ethical maturity throughout the ancient Chinese classics. DeWoskin observes that the Chinese attached "special importance ... to hearing as the central link between the mind and the outside world and exploitation of hearing and aural sensitivity as a metaphor for perspicacity in general" (7). Confucius's description of his own development suggests that the refinement of one's sense of hearing is one of the ultimate stages of spiritual maturity:

> The Master said, At fifteen I set my heart upon learning. At thirty, I had planted my feet firm upon the ground. At forty, I no longer suffered from perplexities. At fifty, I knew what were the biddings of Heaven. At sixty, I heard them with docile ear. At seventy, I could follow the dictates of my own heart; for what I desired no longer overstepped the boundaries of right. (*Analects* II.4)

Music promotes interpersonal harmony, not only by displaying the ideal and revealing the patterns underlying the flow of reality, but by developing the right habits. Music develops the individual's self-control and sensitivity, both of which are important in interpersonal behavior. Music also regulates particular relationships. "The Great Preface" describes this role of sung poetry:

> Therefore, correctly to set forth the successes and failures [of government], to move Heaven and Earth, and to excite spiritual Beings to action, there is no readier instrument than poetry.
>
> The former kings by this regulated the duties of husband and wife, effectively inculcated filial obedience and reverence, secured attention to all the relations of society, adorned the transforming influence of instruction, and transformed manners and customs. (*Book of Poetry* 34)

Like the *Analects*, the *Book of Poetry* attributes educational powers to music. Music is described as a means of inculcating respect for elders, teaching the young, and educating society as a whole in new customs and habits.

Music plays a role in maintaining customs within a society. Many ethnomusicologists have noted the "conservative" character of music, in the sense that repetition of the same tune and melodies is a staple of music in virtually every culture. The repetition of the same music from one generation to another functions in many societies, including China, to link the generations and to give its members a sense of embodying a living tradition by repeating enduring musical formulas on important occasions throughout one's life. Music is also a mnemonic device. It facilitates memorization, as any English-speaker who has mentally returned to the "ABC" song to recall the order of the letters is aware.

A repertoire of important songs, besides functioning to strengthen societal bonds, ensures the memorization of lyrics that assert ideas that are especially significant in most societies. The *Book of Poetry's* suggestion that music can mold new habits in the members of a society, I suspect, is premised on the observation that music enhances the listener's learning of messages conveyed by lyrics. In the twentieth century, the government of the People's Republic of China has explicitly sought to change the thinking of people across the nation by supporting the composition and proliferation of songs that praised work and revolutionary ideals. While the particular ideas being promoted are new, using music for this purpose has ancient roots in China.

Assuming One's Place in the World

So far I have emphasized the Confucian tradition, with its stress on the importance of music for promoting good societal relationships. I will conclude by noting two other Chinese traditions, each of which corroborate the Confucian view that music is important to a person's achieving proper relationships with the larger world, though disagreeing with Confucius about what those relationships should look like.

I have already made mention of the Daoist tradition and its concern with recognition of the Way. Daoist thinkers often understood this aspiration as being incompatible with attachment to society's values. As a consequence, much Daoist thought encourages a retreat from political life and social artifice. In this respect, the Daoist view resembles the "return to nature" philosophy that Jean-Jacques Rousseau popularized in the West in the later eighteenth century.

Two important Daoist concepts are particularly useful in helping us to understand how this philosophy would establish a prominent role for music. One of these is the notion of nonaction (*wuwei* 無爲). Nonaction is not inactivity. Instead, it is moving with the flow of nature. Human aspirations that attempt to "master" or "dominate" nature are misguided, the Daoists contend. The ideal condition is to offer no resistance but to allow the currents of the Dao to work through one.

The second important concept is that of being natural, of expressing one's nature as it is, without camouflage. This concept is termed *ziran* 自然 , and is often translated as "self-so-ness" or "self-so-ing." To be *ziran* is to be spontaneous and unaffected in one's behavior. One acts without attending to the principles and habits that one has learned through social conditioning. Social conventions are more often an impediment than an aid to interpersonal harmony. Harmony in one's relationships is, of course, ideal; but this is achieved only when one allows one's nature to express itself directly. The mediation of ritual practices is unnecessary.

For the Daoists the correlation schemes came to be seen as a means of communing with nature. Daoist thought often focuses on the mysterious, ineffable nature of the Way. Music's ability to express more than words can convey is seen by the Daoists as a reflection on the limitations of language and analytic categories for reflecting the true Way. Daoist thought about music also emphasized music's manifestation of the interconnectedness of all things by means of sympathetic resonance between separated objects, and by its power to move listeners, even at a distance.

Daoist thought was conducive to a particularly interesting musical subculture of China, the cult of the *qin* 琴 (pronounced "chin"). The *qin* is standardly a seven-string, unfretted zither, with intervals indicated by decorative marks on its top surface. It is one of the earliest types of indigenous zithers, and it has the prestige of being allegedly used by the Sage Kings. In a number of stories, nature virtually offers the materials used in making the *qin* to its inventor. Because it derives so directly from nature, the *qin* is thought to have tremendous powers to influence human beings, even natural forces.

During the Han Dynasty, the *qin* was considered the symbol of correct music, and it was taken to be essential for ceremonies. Confucius was a *qin* player, and is even said to be the composer of some traditional pieces of *qin* music. The Confucian tradition placed high value on the *qin*, seeing the restraint and control involved in playing it as resembling the ideal of ethical behavior.

A cult of the *qin* developed, however, that drew more inspiration from Daoist thought than from Confucianism. This development was related to the *qin*'s association with the literati. The literati were cultivated scholars, particularly those outside the established power structure, a position idealized in Daoist expressions of skepticism about political structures. Daoism encouraged aloofness from the ways of the social world, and the ideology that developed around the *qin* romanticized a reclusive way of life.

The *qin* lends itself to such romanticism because it is a very intimate instrument, whose tones are often softer than ambient sounds around it. Playing the *qin* is a quintessentially solitary pursuit, occasionally shared with another kindred person. The romantic image of the isolated scholar, practicing the traditional six arts of the gentleman, is a frequent theme in Chinese art and the *qin* is a frequently depicted accouterment.

Playing the *qin* is also a practice of nonassertiveness. Mastery of the touches for the *qin* is supposed to stem from the performer's attunement with the Dao. The Dao, in effect, directs the playing. The *qin* is also particularly well suited to association with the Daoist ideas of nonaction and self-so-ness. The *qin* is a highly sensitive instrument, which sometimes sounds when the wind passes through its strings or when it sympathetically resonates with environmental sounds. Played by nature in this way, the *qin* manifested the idea of allowing the Way to course through oneself. DeWoskin observes that a whole mythology has developed around the image of a *qin* that is "nonsounding" (138–144). Sound is taken to be only the coarse external manifestation of something that is much more subtle, which the true sage can recognize even in the *qin* that does not sound.

The Daoist notion of self-so-ness is also evident in the lore of the *qin*. The nuances of individual touches are the focus of *qin* connoisseurship. The *qin* is a highly expressive and personal medium, and it is accordingly seen as a means of giving spontaneous voice to one's nature. The very lines of one's fingerprint shape the nuance of given touches, suggesting a very direct expression of the particular person performing.

The individualism of the *qin* cult was denounced in this century by another school of thought that has reflected upon music, contemporary communism. Communism has had direct practical effects on recent musical practice in China. It has eliminated the class structure that supported musical patronage, supported musicological fieldwork, promoted music that expresses revolutionary political ideals, and repressed forms deemed reactionary.

Of interest to our discussion is the Communist leadership's adherence to traditional notions of music's impact on societal relations. Its treatment of Peking Opera illustrates the government's conviction of music's power to influence and the steps it has taken to control it. Peking Opera is a regional form that developed in the Beijing area, although it developed a following in other parts of China as well. A spectacular form that emerged from lowbrow popular entertainments, Peking Opera gained credibility with the social elite when the imperial court began incorporating it into official entertainments. It became a guaranteed crowd pleaser, in part because it usually includes acrobatic acts, especially in connection with battle scenes. Traditional Peking Opera makes use of stock characters who are identifiable by the way their faces are painted, their elaborate symbolic gestures, and their basic styles of movement. The Communist regime made various attempts to reform Peking Opera. At first these efforts were limited. "Reactionary" pieces were eliminated from the repertoire, and unsocialist gestures such as kowtows were abolished; the basic productions, however, remained traditional. In 1956 there was even a brief period of liberalized policy toward opera, during which there was a flurry of performances of traditional operas to enthusiastic audiences.

The subsequent crackdown movement was directed by Mao Zedong's wife, Jiang Qing. She considered traditional plots objectionable because they reflected the outmoded class structure, fostered Confucianism, and sometimes encouraged superstitions, like belief in ghosts. Under Jiang Qing, these traditional operas were replaced by new, "model" Peking Operas.

These "model" operas were committed to the aesthetic ideal of socialist realism, the theory that art should portray revolutionary developments and thereby contribute to the ideological education of those who watched it. The plots focused on communal life, class struggle, and the Chinese revolution. Socialist realism promotes art that is easily understandable by the masses; accordingly, the traditional vocabulary of symbolic gestures was eliminated in the new opera. The model operas were never very popular. Besides resisting popular desire for the traditional plays, they were often much longer than opera had traditionally been, often two hours long or longer. Mao's death and Jiang Qing's removal from power in 1976 ended the repression of Peking Opera; but the form has not recovered its vitality.

The government's conviction that traditional Peking Opera was a threat to socialism and that it should be subject to government policy are telling. These beliefs reveal that however revolutionary the society the Communist leadership envisions, it has no doubt as to music's central importance for their efforts. Music's role as the regulator of human relationships and the educator of societal habits remains unchallenged. Like the legendary rulers of antiquity, the Communist leadership sees music as the touchstone for determining their society's real condition and their own position within it.

The Chinese character for "music (*yue* 樂)" is also the character for "joy (*le* 樂)." The dual nature of this character is apt for the Chinese view of music. Music is the natural means for expressing such emotions as joy. Music also regulates the human world in a way that renders it joyous. We have observed the many dimensions of the Chinese reflection that musical tones resemble human relationships. Chinese philosophical speculation about music reminds us of the joy of harmonizing with others, in both musical and other contexts.

Confucius rhetorically asks in the *Analects*, "Music, music! Does it mean no more than bells and drums?" (XVII.11). He implies that music is vastly more than ordered noise. Music represents the ways human beings are related, reflecting society's conditions and its aspirations. It provides occasions for personal expression and for coming together as families and communities. Its organizing principles also reflect the order of the world of nature, the largest community in which we are members. Music moves like ripples in a pond, resonating through the larger world, relating human beings to each other, and ultimately to everything.

Glossary

Book of Poetry One of the Confucian classics, sometimes translated as *The Book of Songs,* or *The Book of Odes*; written as *Shijing, Shi Jing,* or *She King.*

Cycle of fifths The cycle of tones generated sequentially by leaps of a perfect fifth (which are dropped, if necessary, to keep the tones all within the same octave). Eventually, this method returns to a tone that is close to the tone with which the process begins. The fact that it does not return to exactly the same tone has struck philosophically minded musicologists, both in China and the West, as disturbing, and perhaps as an indication that the universe is not fundamentally orderly. Consequently, many efforts were made to rectify this situation mathematically, some of which involved subdividing the octave into as many tones as 60 (in one case, even 360).

Final The note of primary emphasis in a musical composition, which is also the note on which the piece ends.

Huangzhong Literally, the yellow bell. The yellow bell is the fundamental pitch, which can
 be used to generate the twelve tones of the chromatic scale. The *huangzhong* is absolute, rooted in nature, but there has been much historical debate about how the precise pitch of the *huangzhong* can be determined.

Pentatonic scale A five-tone scale constructed of tones that stand in close harmonic relationships with each other and, accordingly, form consonant intervals with each other.

Pythagorean scale Roughly, the twelve tones of the chromatic scale. Chromatic scales can be
 formed by playing all twelve keys within an octave on the piano. The name refers to the
 Greek philosopher and mathematician Pythagoras, who discovered that strings of
 lengths that are in simple ratios to one another produce consonant intervals. This discovery enabled him to generate a sequence of tones in order of decreasing consonance
 with the original tone, a sequence known as the cycle of fifths. [See "cycle of fifths."]

Qin A zither, usually with seven strings. For the Confucians, the *qin* came to be a symbol for
 correct music. For the Daoists, playing the *qin* became a central practice in a cult of
 personal cultivation.

Shujing (*Shu Ching*) *The Book of History*

Socialist realism The doctrine that art should serve to promote the achievement of an ideal
 socialist order. At certain times during the Communist regime in the People's Republic
 of China, the composition of music has been regulated by this ideal. The composition
 of music by committee and the production of operas and songs that promote socialism
 have been some of the results.

Wuwei The Daoist virtue of nonaction. The idea is that one ought not to exert one's will to
 force conditions to come about. Instead, one should move along with the flow of nature, allowing the Dao to operate through one.

Yue Music (performed); enjoyment. (The same character is used to express both ideas.)

Ziran Spontaneity; unaffected naturalness; "self-so-ing." *Ziran* is the ethical ideal, according to the Daoists.

Notes

1. See Vance Cope-Kasten's discussion of Wittgenstein in his chapter "Meeting
Chinese Philosophy."

2. Alternatively *Shi Jing*, or *She King*. See entry on *Book of Poetry* in glossary.

Works Cited

Analects of Confucius. Trans. Arthur Waley. New York: Random, 1989.

Blacking, John. *How Musical Is Man?* Seattle: University of Washington Press, 1973.

Book of Poetry. See Legge, *She King.*

Brace, Timothy Lane. *Modernization and Music in Contemporary China: Crisis, Identity, and the Politics of Style*. Ph.D. dissertation. University of Texas at Austin, 1992.

DeWoskin, Kenneth. *A Song for One or Two: Music and the Concept of Art in Early China*. Ann Arbor: Center for Chinese Studies, the University of Michigan, 1982.

Ellis, Catherine. *Aboriginal Music: Education for Living*. St. Lucia: University of Queensland Press, 1985.

Han, Kuo-huang, and Lindy Li Mark. "Evolution and Revolution in Chinese Music." *Musics of Many Cultures: An Introduction*. Ed. Elizabeth May. Berkeley: University of California Press, 1980.

Herndon, Marcia, and Norma McLeod. *Music as Culture*. Darby, Penn.: Norwood, 1980.

Hsun Tzu. Basic Writings. Trans. Burton Watson. New York: Columbia University Press, 1963.

Kaufmann, Walter. *Musical References in the Chinese Classics*. Detroit Monographs in Musicology 5. Detroit: Information Coordinators, 1976.

Legge, James, trans and ed. *The Chinese Classics: The She King or Book of Poetry*. Vol. 4 Hong Kong: Hong Kong University Press, 1960.

Rowell, Lewis. *Thinking about Music: An Introduction to the Philosophy of Music*. Amherst: University of Massachusetts Press, 1983.

Yo Ki, or "Record of Music." *The Sacred Books of China* in 6 vols. *The Sacred Books of the East* in 50 vols. Ed. F. Max Muller. 28. *The Texts of Confucianism*, Part IV: *The Li Ki*. Trans. James Legge. Delhi: Motilal Banarsidass, 1885; reprinted by Clarendon, 1966.

6

Chinese Folktales and the Family

Howard Giskin

What is folk literature? This question seems a good place to start in a consideration of literature in the folk tradition. Chinese folk literature is a part of a body of world literature in the great folk traditions that have existed for many thousands of years, in a diverse range of cultures. It is likely, in fact, that folk literature is the oldest form of literature, far predating written forms of literature, and written language itself. Chinese folk literature can be traced back to the very origins of the Chinese culture, and can be plausibly argued to give us a number of clues about what it means to be Chinese. One persistent Chinese concern has been the family, and Chinese folktales show a continual interest in the integrity of this basic societal unit. In beginning to understand the role of folktales in Chinese culture, and just how concerns about the family run through China's folk literature, it is important that we start by taking a more general look at the genre of storytelling.

Folktales have been around for a very long time. In fact, we can imagine our primitive ancestors, long before Chinese or Americans existed, sitting around campfires telling stories to ward off the dark of night. Language, by some estimates, has existed in its modern form for at least one hundred thousand years, and where there is language there are stories. It is not hard to imagine what our primitive ancestors told stories about, though the exact details cannot of course be known. They must have told stories about what mattered to them, about the things they wondered about, why the sun and moon rose, about the stars and the natural world, about hunts long past and great ancestors, and possibly about hunts yet to come.

As time went by, these stories began to get collected into the body of material we know as the folk tradition. An important thing to remember about these early stories is that they were passed down orally from one person to the next for hundreds of generations, and that the people telling and hearing the stories saw them as important, worth preserving, and as Charles Hammond argues, "alleged to be true as part of an unself-conscious tradition" (26). It is not hard to imagine why ancient people wanted to remember these stories and enjoyed telling and listening to them. Most important, perhaps, is the simple fact that the stories people told were fun to listen to. Who hasn't enjoyed listening to a bedtime story as a child, or listened to a scary or funny story by a campfire at night. Stories transport us to another world, allowing us to envision realities that can only be dimly felt in everyday life; stories also help us to explain things about life that we have a hard time understanding. After all, there have always been many things that we don't understand. In addition, before the written word was invented, and even in orally based cultures today, folktales preserve and pass on much important information about a culture, such as how the people in that culture deal with issues of right and wrong, marriage, family life, good and evil, and many other day-to-day aspects of life.

Folktales differ from other forms of literature in several ways. Folk literature is seldom the work of any one person in particular, but rather is the accumulated work of many persons over many generations. For this reason, oral tales tend to vary from place to place and time to time. It is not unusual, in fact, to find dozens of variations on one root story in the same culture, and some folktales occur in literally hundreds of forms throughout the world. The Cinderella tale is a good example of a story whose analogues are found in many cultures around the world. If we think about how folk literature is transmitted from one generation to the next, we realize that devising ways to remember stories is a key part of folktale telling. Folktales tend to be simple in structure, and frequently use techniques of repetition and stock phrasing in order to help people easily remember the tales (Ong 34). Characteristic of folk literature also is the tendency to include a moral component. Folktales aim to teach us something about the complexities of life, and in this sense can be considered as portraying lessons gleaned from many generations' reflection on life's difficulties. Folktales are the accumulated wisdom of a culture, and present a society's way of dealing with day-to-day life over a period of decades or even centuries.

Folktales are also similar to written literature in several important ways. Folktales are literature because they do what we expect literature to do, to entertain us while teaching us something valuable about the world we live in. In addition, while they are simple in structure compared to other forms of literature such as novels or short stories, they nevertheless frequently contain considerable subtlety in the form of moral teachings, psychological insight, use of myth, symbolism, metaphor, and other literary strategies seen in traditional written forms of literature. Folktales also act as a form of coded communication in which important cultural values and lessons are guarded and kept in the possession of the society which may not be able to write down this material. Most importantly, perhaps, folk literature acts as a cultural glue by allowing the different members of a society to share stories, ideas, values, and emotions in an intimate or communal setting. Folktales, in short, having existed long before books were invented, and even before written language, are one of society's original teachers; they are still told today in villages and homes around the world, and most certainly in China.

One aspect of folk literature that makes it particularly suitable for transmitting lessons from one generation to the next is the universal quality of much of what one finds in this genre. While the range of human emotions varies somewhat from culture to culture, it is generally agreed that there are certain basic emotions that all humans possess. Since folktales deal with everyday life it is natural that they should deal with feelings of happiness and sadness, grief and fear, pity and anger, hope and resignation, and all the other emotions that people feel. Chinese folktales show us the particular mix of emotions and sentiments that are characteristic of traditional Chinese life. We might even say that the collective folk literature of a society is akin to its cultural blueprint, which no other culture possesses in exactly the same interwoven pattern of complex form.

Certain recurring themes mark folk literature. Carl Jung and later Joseph Campbell noticed that while folktales differed in many of their details, they contained a surprising number of similarities across cultures. Jung believed that these similarities were due to archetypes, or shared inherited experiences of humanity that are in some way present in humans at birth. Campbell drew upon Jung's idea of archetypes in his extensive research in myth and folklore of cultures around the world in order to show that human experience has a common basis. Not only do all cultures have myths that explain the origins of geographic features, animals, weather, good and evil, and other aspects common to human experience, but gods and goddesses, heroes and villains, virtuous orphans, prodigal sons, evil step-mothers, monsters, demons, mischievous spirits, and cruel landlords, are all found in abundance. Whether similarities in folk literature and myth are due to the presence of archetypes in the human psyche, or some other method of transmission of common themes, both men demonstrated the universal nature of many of the themes found in folk literature.

As we would expect, Chinese folktales show many of the common concerns of folk literature from other parts of the world; but they also bear the stamp of uniqueness that comes from China's ancient continuous tradition. Chinese governments over the centuries have made efforts to collect folktales from the countryside in the belief that in some way the folk literature could be used to gauge the concerns and interests of the people, and in this belief they were probably correct. Chinese folktales, in fact, while dealing with what may be considered general concerns of the Chinese people as a whole, also reflect regional or even local preoccupations, and thus could be used by emperors and government officials to keep in touch with those they governed. Emperors and officials who ignored the teachings of folk literature did so at their own peril, since historically in China, ignoring the needs of the people typically led to the downfall of an individual or an emperor, and a series of bad emperors could bring a dynasty to an end. So folk literature is a good gauge of the feelings and needs of the people. Yet folk literature helps us to understand China not only because it teaches us about its people, but also because we learn about Chinese history and a way of life that remained relatively constant for thousands of years (at least from the standpoint of the peasants). Folktales are part of the cultural web that keeps the society unified and helps Chinese people know what it means to be Chinese, and folktales evolve with the changing nature of society, helping present generations of Chinese retain a connection to their ancient, and more traditional, past (Wang 839; 845). Learning about Chinese folktales is especially important now both for Chinese and non-Chinese alike because of the many changes economic reform and the introduction of Western ideas are bringing to China today.

While Chinese folktales can be classified a number of ways, a useful method of grouping the stories is by theme and subject. While this manner of categorization allows some crossover in content, it also permits the broadest treatment of the folktales in their cultural and human context. Chinese folktales can be conveniently grouped into tales about dragons, love, magic, the supernatural, history and legend, as well as in categories for fairytales and fables. In this chapter our examination of dragon and love tales will allow us to see clearly the importance of family relations in Chinese folktales, and help us to understand how the metaphor of family plays such a central role in Chinese culture on the whole.

Communal Resolution of Difficulties: Dragon Tales

Stories about dragons are a good place to begin in our discussion of Chinese folktales because dragons have been part of Chinese culture for just about as long as Chinese culture has existed. The dragon is one of the most complex symbols in Chinese cosmology, but since the Han Dynasty (206 B.C.E.–220 C.E.) the dragon has symbolized most prominently the power of the emperor (Hay 133–37; Eberhard 83). Nevertheless, the dragon also retains its connections to forces of nature, and is seen in folktales both as a helper of humans as well as a cause of destruction (Lai, "Symbolism" 333; 340–41).

The presence of the dragon in Chinese culture can be traced back at least six thousand years with the discovery near Zhengzhou, Henan, in 1987 of a 1.78 meter dragon statue dating from the fifth millennium B.C.E. Yangshao Culture. A 1971 archeological discovery of a jade dragon in Sanxingtala, Inner Mongolia has been dated to about 3,500 B.C.E., suggesting that if the concept of the dragon did not originate in China, it migrated there at a very early date, or perhaps originated independently in several parts of the world (Zhao, *Study* 17). Qiguang Zhao argues for the striking longevity of the dragon in Chinese culture by pointing out that the appearances of Chinese dragons through time are nearly identical, and only differ in relatively insignificant details such as the fins and claws. Though separated by three thousand years, a Shang dragon looks quite similar to a Qing dragon, except that the latter is somewhat more elaborately fashioned and well proportioned (*Study* 22–23).

Zhao further argues that originally the dragon may have been a totemic emblem comprised of parts of the various animal totems of the newly united Sinitic tribes of the Yellow River Valley, created by the legendary first ruler of China, the

Yellow Emperor.[1] However the dragon originated, the Chinese dragon was gradually standardized. Wang Fu's (ca. C.E. 85–162) classic description of a dragon includes the "nine resemblances," which stipulate the dragon as having "the horns of a deer, the head of a camel, the eyes of a devil, the neck of a snake, the abdomen of a clam, the scales of a carp, the claws of an eagle, the paws of a tiger, and the ears of a cow" (cited. in Zhao, *Study* 18).

Interestingly, according to Zhao, we must distinguish between the mythological dragon and the folktale dragon, the former which, for two thousand years, has been a symbol of imperial authority, and which is seldom killed. In *The Book of Changes* the mythological dragon is seen as a "symbol of the spiritual, dynamic, arousing force that manifests itself in the sublimity of the Creative," a source of productive, but at times fearful power, which represents not only good fortune but also truth (*Study* 72; 79; 83–84). In contrast, the folktale dragon can be either good or evil, can be killed, and is often associated with elemental and chaotic power (*Study* 128; 129; 134–135). Though folktale dragons appear physically similar to mythological dragons, they often represent very different ideas (*Study* 133).

Let us begin our study of folktale dragons with a story called "Dragon Pond," which is said to have taken place in a town called Dashiqiao in northeastern China.

> It was summer and the peasants were working in the fields. Furious dark clouds suddenly covered the sky, like wild horses running on the plain. The wind blew very hard, and branches swung from side to side. The peasants hurried home to shut their doors tightly.
>
> It was so inky black that nothing could be seen. People looked out their windows in surprise. It rained heavily. Thunder sounded as if it would deafen their ears; lightning flashed as though it would blind them. To the peasants' surprise, they saw something enormous fall down to the ground from the heavens as the lightning flashed, then they heard a loud thud as it landed. It rained hard for another hour, then gradually the sky began to clear. Eventually the rain stopped. A beautiful rainbow appeared, and the sun came out from behind the clouds. Everything looked fresh, and men, women, and children went outdoors again.
>
> The peasants were very surprised to find a big new pond near the road with a very large animal lying in it. It had long, thick hair on either side of its mouth and a head like a horse's, but much bigger. It also had a pair of huge antlers. Its body was more than one hundred meters long, covered with thousands of fishlike scales, each more than one meter in diameter. The creature had four large talons shaped like a rooster's, as well as a long tail.
>
> An old man recognized the creature as a dragon who was in charge of rain. There are many kinds of dragons, and they all have different jobs. Some are in charge of fire, some of rain, some of sand, and so on. They are all ruled by the Emperor of Heaven and live in the seas, rivers, lakes, and even wells. At times they fly above the clouds, or even change form into people or other

animals. Of course, dragons have magnificent palaces in the water. In ancient times, emperors of China regarded themselves as descendants of dragons. This was a sign of absolute power. Many temples were built to honor the dragon, and when it was dry people would pray to dragons for rain.

This dragon was dying. The people realized that he must have committed a serious crime against the Emperor of Heaven and had been punished by being hurled down to earth by the emperor's troops. That is to say, the emperor had taken back the dragon's supernatural powers. The people pitied the dragon from the bottom of their hearts. They felt that they must help him get back to heaven. Wasting no time, they knit a big mat of dried reeds and covered the dragon with it to prevent the sun from burning him. Then they went back to the village. Two men were left to take care of the dragon. One of the old men told the villagers to make preparations to send the dragon off, so they beat drums, blew horns, burned spices, and prayed to the Emperor of Heaven to allow the dragon to go back.

The villagers did this for nearly three days. On the third day a thick fog filled the village. As the day passed, the fog became thicker and thicker, so thick people could not see each other. When the fog finally disappeared, several villagers ran to see the dragon but found it had vanished. All of the townspeople gathered around the pond in astonishment. The new pond remained but the dragon was gone. It was a real miracle, and the people cheered.

As the years went by, the villagers found that the pond was never dry, even when the rains did not come. Moreover, the pond was rich in fish, shrimp, and crab. To memorialize this strange event, the villagers of Dashiqiao call this place Dragon Pond. (6–7)[2]

This charming story of a dragon who falls to earth and is helped by kind peasants highlights the central role of community (family in its more inclusive sense) in Chinese culture, and functions as a parable of the interdependence of heaven and earth in the Chinese cosmos. Dragons in Chinese culture are often associated with the titanic forces of nature, especially hydrological: rain, the seas, and rivers (Hay 123; Zhao, "Hydraulic" 234–35). Indeed the coming of the dragon in the above tale is introduced by the advent of a violent storm that sends the villagers scurrying into their houses to avoid getting soaked, or worse. The suddenness and intensity of the storm suggests that we are dealing with unpredictable and powerful forces of nature. The imagery in the first two paragraphs of this story is striking in its evocation of nature's awesome power, and reinforces the sense that the peasants are dealing with something they can neither control nor fully understand.

The first two paragraphs of this story also function on another level, however, in which the violent storm with its images evocative of anger and struggle ("furious dark clouds suddenly covered the sky like wild horses running on the plain"; "branches swung from side to side"; inky blackness; deafening thunder; blinding lightning) foreshadows the ejection of the dragon by the Emperor of Heaven. The final sound of a (sickening) thud, followed by the gradual letting up of the rain and clearing of the skies, as well as the appearance of a beautiful rainbow, signals that the struggle that has taken place is over. The villagers have witnessed one of nature's awesome spectacles, while the reader (or listener) of the story is taught something about the smallness of human beings before the forces of nature.

Yet this story also teaches that, while human beings have little direct control of certain forces in their environment, their behavior, moral behavior in particular, has a direct effect on reality. The image of the massive dragon lying helpless while the peasants examine it elicits sympathy for this great creature; the villagers are shown to be compassionate and kind-hearted, and though they realize that the dragon has been punished by the Emperor of Heaven, they do not hesitate to help in any way they can. More importantly, however, in helping the dragon they show that in some inexplicable way heaven itself (and here we may think in terms of nature, or the cosmos if we prefer), depends on how the peasants act. The villagers' cooperative effort to save the dragon and send it back to heaven further underscores the deeply communal nature of their task, one they would have no chance of accomplishing were they not able to work harmoniously. From a Confucian standpoint, the peasants' behavior is appropriate and exemplary.

Most interestingly, perhaps, the Confucian principle of family or clan unity and cooperation (mutual codependency) is implicitly elevated to the level of a cosmological principle; the great and powerful things in the universe (heaven; the dragons) are dependent upon the weak and small (human beings), and vice versa (a *yin/yang* opposition). This is important because the humble peasants can justifiably feel that they have done something special, actions that they are uniquely suited to perform. Implied also is the *yin/yang* idea that all things contain their opposite, shown through the weakness of the dragon (normally seen as strong), and the strength of the peasants (normally weak in the face of natural calamities). Curiously also, it is the peasants, not the Emperor of Heaven, who show compassion through their actions, again implying that the human perspective is indispensable for the harmonious functioning of the universe. The peasants ask the Emperor of Heaven to take the dragon back, and in so doing work for the restoration of balance (the violent storm at the start of the story signals a disruption of the harmony in heaven, and consequently on earth); "they beat drums, blew horns, burned spices, and prayed," and all this "for nearly three days."

Finally, when the dragon is allowed to go back to heaven, the peasants are left with the pond that appeared when it fell to earth in town. The pond, "rich in fish, shrimp, and crab," and never dry, is the dragon's gift to the kind villagers, but also emblematic of the codependency of heaven and earth. In a cosmic act of reciprocity, the peasants' active compassion in restoring the dragon to its rightful domain brings them good fortune in the form of the pond. Thus the lesson at the end of this tale is a profoundly moral one, teaching that compassionate action, performed selflessly, and in cooperation with others, brings positive results. This lesson is important in China, where the preservation of social order (what the Chinese would call "acting in the spirit of cooperativeness") has traditionally been seen as crucial because of the dire consequences of the disruption of the food supply (the villagers' reward in this story is food, a fact not irrelevant considering China's perennial concern with feeding its population).

Communal responsibility for the well-being of family, clan, and society as a whole, is frequently seen as a central concern in Chinese folktales, and other dragon tales draw upon the Confucian ideas of mutual codependency and personal self-sacrifice (cardinal family and clan virtues) in an effort to show the benefits of working selflessly to accomplish a difficult task. When communal effort, however, fails to bring about the solution of a problem, it often falls upon one or several individuals to resolve the difficulty facing a family or village. In a sense, selfless action in the service of the family, clan, village, or society is the natural counterpoint to coordinated group action in the face of a threat to the integrity of the family or village. In "Land and Sea," the idyllic life of a village ("people made their living by fishing and growing crops . . . villagers were very kind to one another . . . people had a happy and quiet life") (9), is interrupted by a dragon who asks for food, then destroys houses and eats farm animals or even children. A girl in the village named Jiuhua (whose name means "chrysanthemum"), and her boyfriend Shoushan, both of whose fathers had been killed the day before their wedding by the dragon, set out to kill the dragon, despite the pleas of the villagers to leave it alone. They manage to stab the dragon while it is asleep in a cave, which causes the wounded creature to

> [shoot] out of the cave, running as fast as he could. He flew into the sky to try to get rid of the couple, who were now hanging onto his back. They held the dragon's body tightly as he racked his brains to figure out how to get free of the couple. Finally, the dragon dove deep into the ocean hoping to drown them. They knew they could not survive long underwater, but still they hung on. On the seventh day the dragon died, but the couple had already been dead for days. Even after they died, they still clung tightly to the dragon. Eventually the dragon turned into a freshwater spring, the girl into an island, and the young man into a hill watching the island from across the land. (9)

In this story, Jiuhua and Shoushan make the ultimate sacrifice in giving their lives to save their village. The teller of this story concludes "Land and Sea" by adding that a "statue of Jiuhua now stands on the beach . . . smiling and holding a chrysanthemum in her hand, still defending the peace" (10), proof that the villagers remember and appreciate her gift (and Shoushan's) of their lives. This pattern of self-sacrifice for something larger than oneself appears often in Chinese folktales.

Romance in a Confucian Society: Tales of Love

Love in traditional Chinese society, as it is portrayed in folktales, is often bounded by rigid Confucian stricture. The rules and regulations relating to marriage in China before 1949 were rather complex and governed in great detail how and under what circumstances people could marry (Wolf 215). Wolfram Eberhard writes that "marriage was not something that young people entered upon of their own free will. Rather it was a 'political' act of union between two families, and therfore hardly something that could be left up to the whims of the inexperienced" (179). The preparations for marriage frequently resembled those of a business agreement, and included a marriage broker who facilitated negotiations between the families, an astrological consultation, exchange of gifts, and a dowry. Finally, even after the marriage, if the bride turned out not to be a virgin, she would be promptly sent back home (Eberhard 179–81; Hershatter 238).

Yet love seems to be one area where storytellers have felt free to show aspects of behavior that go against the rules of traditional society. The reason is simple: despite vigorous attempts on the part of parents to discourage "improper" matches, nature apparently all too frequently took its course, often with dire consequences. While the results of romance are often tragic in Chinese folk literature, lovers are sometimes allowed the happiness they desire. Let us examine one such tale called "River Snail Girl."

Once upon a time, when Shanghai was only a small fishing village, there lived a poor man named Aming whose parents had died when he was a child. Aming lived alone in the village facing the sea. Every day he went to the sea to fish to make his living. Although he was very poor, he tried his best to help whenever people asked something of him.

One day after fishing, Aming was on his way home when he caught sight of a black thing lying on the side of the road. As he approached he saw that it was a big river snail that had somehow gotten away from the water. "This snail will surely die for lack of water if I don't take it home with me," he thought to himself.

He picked up the snail and continued on his way. As soon as he reached home, he wiped the mud off the snail's shell, then carefully placed it in a jar with water. From then on, he often changed the water so that the snail would have a clean place to live.

Several months later, one night after Aming had worked hard at the sea near his house, he suddenly saw a column of smoke rising from his chimney. He was so surprised that he ran home. As he entered the house and searched, he found no one there at all. On the table, however, there were several bowls of delicious-smelling food.

"Maybe a kind soul has come to prepare food for me. I must find and thank them," thought Aming.

Strangely, the same thing happened on the second day, then on the third, fourth, and fifth days. By this time Aming was incredulous about what was happening, so he decided to ask the villagers who had done his cooking for the past five days. To his surprise, no one admitted to making his meals. Aming decided to find out for himself.

One sunny day, Aming brought out his net and went fishing as usual. After a while he returned home and hid outside his house. Crouching down, he peered into the window so that he could see clearly what was happening inside the house. To his great astonishment, he saw a very pretty girl cooking at the stove. The girl looked like a fairy. At the sight of her Aming rushed in and seized her by the arm. The girl was surprised and wanted to flee, but she could not because Aming held he so tightly.

"Who are you, pretty girl?" Aming asked excitedly. "Why are you helping me?"

Looking at the ground, the girl said shyly, "I'm just the river snail you saved. I found you to be a warm-hearted man and wanted to do you a favor to thank you. Would you permit me to stay here with you?" The girl's cheeks turned bright red, but this only made her more beautiful.

"Truthfully," Aming replied, "I have begun to fall in love with you. But I am very poor. I am an orphan and my parents died when I was still a little boy. I am afraid I am too poor to provide well for a wife."

"Honest man," the girl answered, "perhaps you have mistaken me for someone else. I want to spend my life with you, living through all of the suffering and joy that life has to offer. Do you believe me?"

"Yes," replied Aming with great joy, "you are a wonderful girl and today is the happiest day in my life."

Soon Aming and the young girl got married. After the wedding, Aming went to the sea to fish as before, and the girl stayed home. They both loved each other deeply. Aming and his lovely wife lived a happy life in their seaside village. (63–64)

This story is atypical of love tales in Chinese folk literature in that it has a happy ending. This is worth examining, as the happy outcome of the story can shed light on some other aspects of folk treatment of love in China. First, however, let us look at "River Snail Girl" in detail. The first important aspect of the story we notice is the fact that Aming is an orphan. This is a crucial piece of information, because it allows us to begin to situate the story in the traditional backdrop of Confucian society. The fact that Aming has no parents, and apparently no relatives, releases him from any obligations a son has to his family, especially his parents. This, essentially, leaves him free to marry as he wishes. Also key to our understanding of his situation is the fact that we are told he is poor, which means that it will be difficult for him to marry. So we see that, as of the first paragraph of the tale, Aming is outside the reach of many of society's rules governing proper marriage. Not that he would intentionally go against such rules, for Aming is not shown as rebellious in any way, but rather that no one would really care about how he marries (only family or clan would have an interest in trying to regulate such matters). So in some ironic way, Aming is made freer by the misfortune of losing has parents, and his poverty. Curiously, then, the story becomes a kind of Confucian fantasy in which the strict laws that govern even intimate affairs (in Confucian society marriage is primarily a social event, a joining of families) are suspended, and a couple are allowed to fall in love and marry. Also important is that Aming is a kind and simple man, for he is shown at the start of the story to be worthy of good fortune. As Whalen Lai suggests, however, in his discussion of the popular Madame White Snake story, the results of such a fantasy were often far less happy ("Unpacking" 59). Fatima Wu, in an interesting discussion of fox tales by Pu Songling (1640–1715) argues for a didactic purpose that approximates that of "River Snail Girl," the creation of an ideal world in which the weak and oppressed receive "emotional and poetic justice," and are "protected by a certain magical power. Not only are they able to escape oppression, but they are given a chance to redress the injustice done to them" (144). "River Snail Girl" portrays just such an idealized vision of reality.

Ironically, the *absence* of family in "River Snail Girl," coupled with our realization that the situation portrayed in the story is atypical, serves to remind us of the central role of family in governing marriage (and thus love) in traditional Chinese society. Importantly, however, despite Aming's lack of family, he still displays exemplary behavior toward others in a manner consistent with what, in Confucian society, would be called "a good upbringing." In short, Aming, while formally unsuitable for marriage into a good family for lack of parents, nevertheless clearly is shown to be an ideal mate; for he is kind, earnest, compassionate, hardworking, and simple in his tastes. And here the folktale seems to acknowledge a failing in the traditional Confucian system governing marriage: there are good, decent people who, because of misfortunes not of their own making (like losing one's parents), may be denied the fulfillment of a married life. So Aming, in all ways except the physical requirements of having parents, lives up to Confucian family values. Why, then, shouldn't he get married like everyone else? The story, I believe, performs the dual function of answering this question and responding to the awareness that, even in the traditionally rigid Confucian marriage structure, young people still occasionally fell in love.

The story suggests that society (with the help of a little magic, perhaps) holds a place for good people who might not otherwise fit in, and more philosophically, that there is a moral justice in the world that insures that worthy people get taken care of. Stories of this type present a vision of the triumph of the human spirit over the rules of society, though it is worth noting that love stories that end happily all seem to involve some sort of magic. If there is a sad aspect to "River Snail Girl" it is that Aming can only marry a fairy, someone who is equally removed from the strict rules governing marriage in Chinese society. The story ends happily for Aming to be sure, but its implications for others in similar situations are rather bleak. Few orphans could expect to achieve the marital bliss of Aming, and in folktales from the Han Dynasty on, women were virtually excluded from forming liaisons with "immmortals." As Whalen Lai notes, female immortals could still grace young men with their favors, while by Confucian times male immortals had lost this freedom. "Men could have affairs with heavenly maidens," Lai argues, "but to have women sleeping with gods and producing offspring would create havoc with the standard patrilineal genealogies!" ("Unpacking" 58). Typically, in fact, Chinese folktales

about love tend to play out the tragic consequences of the inevitable conflict between romance and Confucian values. In traditional Chinese life, love was considered neither an appropriate nor sufficient reason for marriage, and typically families
took strenuous precautions to prevent illicit romantic liaisons from developing, and
harsh, even cruel, measures to dissolve them should they occur.[3] Chinese love tales
with happy endings are rare, and clearly the primary focus is on the many impediments to romantic love in Chinese society. Ironically, however, even tales that end
tragically stress the power and enduring qualities of love, again suggesting that the
human spirit is capable of overcoming the harshest constraints. Unsympathetic parents, the cruel mother-in-law, poverty, lack of status, and death through misfortune,
are some of the factors that keep lovers from being together.

A brief but poignant tale, "Shennu Peak," typifies the sadness that pervades
Chinese folktales about love. Deeply in love, a young couple Anhu and Ahua (even
their names suggest their closeness) are separated when Anhu goes out fishing as
usual on the Yangtze, only to drown when his small boat overturns in a storm.
"Ahua," we read, "climbed a rock to look down on the Yangtze, but she saw nothing.
. . . She waited and waited, and still Anhu did not return" (49). The story tells us that,
after waiting many days for her husband to return, she turns into a rock, which
people called Beauty Peak, then later Shennu Peak as a reminder of Ahua's sorrowful
wait for Ahua.

More characteristic, however, of sad love stories in the Chinese folk tradition are stories in which lovers are thwarted by parents who reject a son or daughter's beloved. The tragic results of such a situation are schematically played out in
the short tale, "A Story from My City," where many years ago, we are told, there
lived a beautiful young lady who had long, dark hair and big, beautiful eyes. She
was kind and warm-hearted, and her father was a general who commanded many
soldiers.

> One fine day the lady went out on her horse. Suddenly a carriage passed
> and startled her horse, who bolted wildly away from the castle. A young man
> appeared and restrained the horse, but not before being slightly hurt by the
> animal. The woman invited the man to the castle to rest. They got to know
> one another and soon fell in love. They were both kind, the lady was beauti-
> ful, and the man was brave.
>
> About a year passed and the young man went to see the young lady's father
> to ask for his daughter's hand in marriage. The general was very surprised,
> then he laughed. He told the man, "How do you think you can marry my
> daughter? You are dreaming! You have nothing. You are poor."
>
> The young man was not discouraged and went to the father again and
> again. The father became angry, telling his soldiers to take the young man to
> prison. The young lady heard what had happened to the young man and was
> saddened. Finally she killed herself. When the young man discovered what
> she had done, he too ended his life, unable to live without her. (32)

The tragic details of the father's rejection of the young man are arrived at in short order in this tale, but still there is enough detail to infer several important aspects about the situation of the young lovers; the young man is unsuitable for marriage to the general's daughter because he has no status in the society. As one would expect, the two lovers are not concerned with such matters and insist on pursuing the relationship. As the results seem to suggest, the tale may be meant to discourage young people from blindly following their desires while also acknowledging the powerful and unpredictable nature of romantic passion. Given the context (the young man is poor and the girl's father is an important general), it is clear that the general will not, and possibly cannot, allow his daughter to marry the young man. Both lovers should know this, of course, yet they persist. Perhaps the story is meant as a cautionary tale.

The story of Zhu Yingtai and Liang Shanbo (38–39) (which narrates in painful detail the rejection of a clever but poor scholar by the parents of an unusual young girl) presents a curious picture of the best and worst of Confucian society. Again, this tale can be seen as both a warning about the dangers of defying the norm and a confirmation of, even reveling in, the indomitable nature of the human spirit. It is amazing that a single story could contain such apparently diverse points of view, but perhaps because folktales evolve organically out of complex real-life situations this is possible. Implicit in this story is the realization that going with one's deepest heartfelt desires can be costly in terms of happiness or even life itself, but that by not following one's desires one risks living a lie. The story suggests that for a certain segment of the population, a very small segment, perhaps, the Confucian social arrangement is clearly not the best. Yet the presentation of Zhu and Liang's misfortune is not an explicit condemnation of the Confucian order, only an admission that it does not fit everyone; there is a tinge of sadness, verging on resignation in the tone as the story ends, suggesting that no matter the tragedy, or personal suffering of the two lovers, fate too plays a role. In this sense the events of the story (Liang dies while studying in a far-off city and Zhu commits suicide), however tragic, are inevitable. The result is a bittersweet sadness, lightened perhaps by the image of two butterflies rising from the couple's fresh graves, but still painful to the heart.

And yet there is much positive about this story in its unconventional portrayal of the two lovers. Zhu Yingtai, especially, is shown as outstanding in her intelligence and surprisingly persistent and steady in her pursuit of what she wants in life. While it is clear that her parents disapprove of her actions, it is not nearly as clear that she is not in many other ways a good daughter; the one small but significant hint that Zhu Yingtai does not neglect learning household duties and skills expected of woman at the time, is the mention that she is "good at sewing"; in fact, both Zhu and Liang are in many ways exemplary in Confucian terms, but the story lets us know early on that certain conditions make life as it exists in that time and place, unsuitable for them. Zhu's failing (ironically) is to possess a fine, inquiring mind and strong will, while Liang's peasant parentage destines him as unsuitable for a young lady of even modest background.

Other tales stress the overpowering effect of traditional Confucian family-re-
lated expectations on newly married couples, but especially the wife, who was forced
to move in with her husband's extended family, where the mother-in-law often
lorded it over the new wife, at times making life nearly intolerable for her. In "Mo
Chou Woman" (47–48) ("Mo Chou" means "without worry"), a simple, kind orphan girl becomes the wife of a wealthy, handsome young man named Jiao Ping. Because Jiao Ping works in a distant town and has to leave Mo Chou alone with his
mother, who hates Mo Chou for her poverty, the mother is able to brutally mistreat
Mo Chou. The story ends tragically, when the mother-in-law attacks Mo Chou with
several large needles and blinds her, after Jiao Ping has returned home unexpectedly,
finding Mo Chou black and blue all over from the beatings she has received. Mo
Chou bolts out of the house and jumps into the lake, and though Jiao Ping races after
her, it is too late. He cannot save her and drowns along with Mo Chou.

As we have seen, not all Chinese folktales about love end tragically, though
many do. Yet, even the saddest Chinese love stories seem to leave us with the sense
that some indefinable, perhaps even indomitable aspect of the human spirit remains when all else is lost. This is curious in a culture that preferences the communal. It points to the primal irreducibility of the experience of love. In some oddly
ironic yet genuinely Chinese way, the private tragedy of the lovers is turned, ultimately, into a sacrament, a kind of shared act of sympathetic repentance (through
storytelling) for the suffering inflicted by society on the couple. And in this way
(through the creative act of acknowledging this suffering), some collective forgiveness is achieved.

Through folktales we are able to glimpse the hopes and aspirations, as well as
the fears and concerns of a people. Chinese folktales help us to understand the Chinese people and their history by providing a unique window into the collective experience of an ancient yet vibrant culture that is still relevant today. Perhaps in
learning how the Chinese have dealt with issues of family, community, and culture
over the centuries we can learn something about ourselves as well. For it is a truism
worth restating, that only when we see ourselves reflected in the mirror of others
do we know our own true face.

Glossary

Archetype In Jungian psychology, a collectively inherited symbolic image or pattern of
    thought that appears across diverse cultures and times.

Book of Changes An ancient classic text, the *Yijing* is one of the Five Classics of Confucian-
    ism; believed to have originated in the twelfth century B.C.E., the *Yijing* contains a dis-
    cussion of Zhou dynasty divination, and sets out a cosmology that involves humans
    and nature in a unified system.

Confucian society A society based on the teachings of Confucius (Kongfuzi), a teacher, philosopher, and political theorist (551– 479 B.C.E.) from the state of Lu. Confucius's teachings formed the basis of Chinese education for 2,000 years, and have influenced all civilizations of East Asia.

Dragon (*Lung*) In Chinese folklore, a supernatural snakelike creature capable of both good and bad deeds; the dragon is associated with rain and floods, and was traditionally associated with the emperor.

Emperor of Heaven The heavenly analog to the earthly emperor. The Emperor of Heaven rules his "subjects" just as the earthly emperor does.

Folk literature Traditional knowledge and beliefs of cultures that are transmitted by mouth; includes prose, verse narrative, poems, songs, myths, fables, and proverbs, as well as drama, and ritual.

Folktale A story transmitted orally that is typically anonymous, and whose time and place are often but not always vague. The existence of folktales is nearly universal among preliterate cultures and in many places has survived in literate societies.

Folk tradition The inherited oral history of a culture.

Yangshao culture A neolithic culture of North China characterized by dwellings with sunken floors, domestication of the pig, and carefully worked pottery.

Yin/yang In Chinese philosophy, male and female principles associated with nature, that influence persons and things.

Notes

1. Zhao writes, "Here I use the name of the Yellow Emperor as a representative of any prehistorical tribal chief. The creator of the dragon as a combination of tribal totems may be anybody or any group of ancient people" (18).

2. All folktales are drawn from my *Chinese Folktales*. (Reprinted from *Chinese Folktales* by Howard Giskin, 1997. Used with permission of NTC/ Contemporary Publishing Group, Inc.) References will be given by page numbers only.

3. Recent stories by Chinese authors suggest that traditional morality still exerts significant pressure on young couples. Writing in 1985 concerning the generation of writers who flourished from 1978 to 1981, Kam Louie suggests that after thirty years of Communist rule "marriages are still often arranged by 'introduction' on the basis of economic and social status." Many stories, he adds, "also show the tragedies that can occur for those who try to resist the system" (85–86).

Works Cited

Eberhard, Wolfram. *A Dictionary of Chinese Symbols*. Trans. G. L. Campbell. New York: Routledge, 1986.

Giskin, Howard. *Chinese Folktales*. Lincolnwood: NTC/Contemporary Publishing Company, 1997.

Hammond, Charles E. "Waiting for a Thunderbolt." *Asian Folklore Studies* 51.1 (1992): 26–49.

Hay, John. "The Persistent Dragon (*Lung*)." *The Power of Culture: Studies in Chinese Cultural istory*. Ed. Williard J. Peterson, Andrew H. Plaks, and Ying-shih Yü. Hong Kong: Chinese University Press, 1994.

Hershatter, Gail. "Making a Friend: Changing Patterns of Courtship in Urban China." *Pacific Affairs* 57 (Summer 1984): 237–251.

Lai, Whalen. "From Folklore to Literate Theater: Unpacking Madame White Snake." *Asian Folklore Studies* 51.1 (1992): 51–66.

———. "Symbolism of Evil in China: The K'ung-Chia Myth Analyzed." *History of Religions* 23 (May 1984): 316–43.

Louie, Kam. "Love Stories: The Meaning of Love and Marriage in China." *After Mao: Chinese Literature and Society, 1978–1981*. Ed. Jeffrey C. Kinkley. Harvard Contemporary China Series. 1. Cambridge: Council of East Asian Studies, Harvard University, 1985: 63–87.

Ong, Walter J. *Orality and Literacy*. New York: Methuen, 1982.

Wang, C. K. "The Transmission and Transformation of Chinese Popular Traditions." *Tamkang Review* 19.1–4 (Autumn 1988–Summer 1989): 835–51.

Wolf, Margery. "Marriage, Family, and the State in Contemporary China." *Pacific Affairs* 57 (Summer 1984): 213–236.

Wu, Fatima. "Foxes in Chinese Supernatural Tales: Part I." *Tamkang Review* 17.2 (Winter 1986–Spring 1987): 121–54.

Zhao, Qiguang. "Chinese Mythology in the Context of Hydraulic Society." *Asian Folklore Studies* 48.2 (1989): 231–46.

———. *A Study of Dragons: East and West*. New York: Peter Lang, 1992.

7

Chinese Literature in the Confucian and Modern Traditions

Fay Beauchamp

"Metaphor, the revealer of nature, is the very substance of poetry. The known interprets the obscure, the universe is alive with myth" (Fenollosa 23). These sentences on Chinese poetry helped lead an American poet, Ezra Pound, to revolutionize modern poetry. Using the notes the scholar Ernest Fenollosa bequeathed to him in 1908, Pound translated Chinese poetry into English; in the decades that followed, poetry in English became more vivid, precise, enigmatic, and unruly. Pound saw in Chinese poetry concrete images that evoked ideas and feelings without directly expressing abstractions. Pound scolded two other great modern poets, W. B. Yeats and T. S. Eliot, for being wordy, and through them influenced how poetry was perceived worldwide. Modernization is often thought of as a process of westernization, but modern poetry has been profoundly influenced by the Far East.

This chapter explores how speakers of English have interpreted and translated Chinese literature, how American students might approach Chinese poetry and fiction so they can engage in interpretations themselves even though they do not know Chinese. It looks at images from the *Yijing, The Book of Changes,* then poetry anthologized as *Odes* or *Songs,* references to poetry by Confucius, poems from the great age of poetry, the Tang Dynasty, and finally, two writers from the modern period, Lu Xun and Ding Ling. Because Chinese tradition involved extensive memorization of works such as the *Yijing,* the *Odes* and the *Analects,* it can be said that all Chinese poetry is, in a sense, related. It is therefore appropriate to think of Chinese poetry as an organic whole, which rather than evolving in a strictly linear fashion, has grown and been nourished in familylike fashion. Similarly, Chinese poetry was thought to enhance family relationships between men and women, children and parents; and poetry used metaphor as its "chief device" to make life "pregnant with art" (Fenollosa 23).

Metaphor and the Written Character

Fenollosa thought that each Chinese ideogram acted as a metaphor.[1] If a square with a line in it represents the sun 日, and the sun represents the more abstract word "day," and "day" can mean a certain time in the past, the concrete image of a square represents an abstract idea, just as in the West the picture of a rose or a heart can represent love. In Chinese writing, images are combined, so that the square for sun behind the drawing for tree means "east" 東 (when the sun rises in the east, you can see it on the horizon behind a tree). Fenollosa thought that every Chinese ideogram radiated meaning and that Chinese readers always understood abstractions through concrete representations of things. This theory has been attacked because scholars have said that relatively simply drawn words like "east" are the exception, but it is possible that classic Chinese poetry used a more limited vocabulary where these "simple cases" predominate.

What is unarguably true is that calligraphy and poetry are interrelated. In the West, readers don't care very much how words look on the printed page. In China how poetry is drawn matters considerably. Written for centuries with brush and ink, the handwriting—calligraphy—has been valued for its beauty, for its ability to convey emotion. Westerners see poetry written on top of Chinese paintings and consider the writing like graffiti, even if it was written by an emperor. For Chinese, the written form is part of the art of poetry. A first step for a novice to Chinese poetry, then, might be to look at some Chinese ideograms and decide whether the visual images do suggest the meanings, whether the image of the horse 馬 does convey the ideas of being alive, powerful, moving.

The Source of Writing in Divination and the *Yijing* as Poetry

In the West, some poets and artists have said that poetry or art should not always be interpreted: "Art should not mean, but be." In the 1880s the American painter James Whistler attacked works of art that were supposed to teach morals or to be didactic in any way; instead art was supposed to exist for "art's sake." Ironically, Whistler saw Asian art as "decorative" or "realistic" in ways that did not need interpretation, but there is a very old tradition in Chinese/Confucian literature, going back to the very origins of Chinese writing, that words need to be carefully interpreted, that poetry serves to guide people in everyday decisions.

Chinese writing began with the "reading" of lines in oracle bones or in tortoise shells. While lines were first found by chance in natural objects, they were soon created by people, by scratching the bones or shells. People examined these artifacts to get advice—not just to admire their beauty. In the *Yijing*, an early work of divination, each trigram signifies a natural image; each image has a symbolic meaning. For example the trigram called "*Qian* 乾, the creative," is associated with the image "sky" as well as a cluster of other symbols—strength, father, head, stallion, and red. The *Yijing* helps a person to be conscious of an "unrealized thought" or desire, according to the psychologist Carl Jung (Wilhelm xxxix). Even though each image—light, earth—has a fixed symbolic meaning, interpretation still depends on the interpreter. There is a message—the image is not just decorative or realistic; its meaning, however, is deeply ambiguous.

The *Book of Poetry*

The roots of Chinese poetry may be found in the ideograms themselves and the images of the *Yijing*, but the first flowering of literature is traditionally considered to be the collection of poems translated by James Legge as *The Book of Poetry*, by Ezra Pound as the *Confucian Odes*, and by Arthur Waley as the *Book of Songs*. Most modern Western critics consider this anthology to be "a haphazard collection" of poems created in many different areas of China over six hundred years, from the twelfth to the seventh centuries B.C.E. (Dembo 4). For hundreds of years, however, Chinese readers studied these poems in a book they believed was arranged and edited by Confucius in the fifth century B.C.E. How exactly the 305 poems were presented in four large categories was important in their interpretation. Those in the first group were considered ritual hymns, for example, through which leaders in the Zhou (Chou) Dynasty gave actions political "legitimacy and meaning" (Owen, *Anthology* 21). Western translations of these poems give a number that shows their original order, but almost all the translators into English group them differently to show different patterns and ideas.

   In the Confucian context, the poems were read not just for entertainment, but to give guidance to people's actions. *The Book of Poetry* has a "Great Preface" that was credited to Confucius, even though it was almost certainly written down hundreds of years after his time. This preface states that poetry "correctly [sets] forth the successes and failures [of government] to move Heaven and Earth, and to excite spiritual Beings to action" (Legge 34). While poetry expresses genuine feelings, it also is the means by which "former kings . . . regulated the duties of husband and wife, effectually inculcated filial obedience and reverence, secured attention to all the relations of society, adorned the transforming influence of instruction, and transformed manners and customs" (34). This quotation seems to show that not only were the poems grouped, figuratively speaking, in family relationships, they were also perceived as promoting literal families. "The Great Preface" grew out of *The Analects* itself. In XVII.9, Confucius tells his disciples to learn the *Odes* because a quotation can stir the imagination and can express complaint (Lau 145); Confucius then emphasizes how the *Odes* bring harmony both to the family and to the state; "Close to home they let you serve your father; farther away, they let you serve your lord" (Owen, *Anthology* 58). This Chinese tradition, therefore, turns to the *Odes* as a guide to morality, how not to swerve "from the right path" (Lau 63). Readers of *The Book of Poetry*, however, might want to ask whether the poems should be interpreted as promoting morality or whether their amusing and imaginative qualities should be seen free of didactic content.

"Boat of Cypress"

To carefully analyze a poem from this collection, a student who cannot read Chinese needs to look at a number of translations to become aware of the different possible interpretations. Each word has different connotations or associations; a translator can choose among many English words for each Chinese word, but seeks to establish a pattern so that different words reinforce or enrich the metaphorical or symbolic meaning of the poem as a whole. An analysis of two translations of the "The Cypress Boat" helps to explain this process:

Translation 1	Translation 2
It floats about, that boat of cypress wood;	That cypress boat is drifting,
Yea, it floats about on the current.	drifting with the flow:
Disturbed am I, and sleepless,	fretful, fretful, I cannot sleep,
As if suffering from a painful wound.	as if from a painful grief,
It is not because I have no wine,	though I've no lack of wine
And that I might not wander and saunter about.	to ease and amuse me.
My mind is not a mirror;—	My heart is not a mirror,
It cannot [equally] receive [all impressions].	you can't just peer into it!
I, indeed, have brothers,	I too have brothers,
But I cannot depend on them.	though not the kind to rely on.
If I go and complain to them, I meet with their anger.	I go to them with pleas, only to meet their anger.
My mind is not a stone;—	My heart is not a stone,
It cannot be rolled about.	you can't tumble it around;
My mind is not a mat—	my heart is not a mat,
It cannot be rolled up.	you can't just roll it up!
My deportment has been dignified and good,	My conduct was pure and proper,
With nothing wrong which can be pointed out.	you cannot fault me there.
My anxious heart is full of trouble;	My grieving heart pains and sorrows,
I am hated by the herd of mean creatures;	I'm hated by those petty people.

I meet with many distresses;	Trouble—I've seen plenty;
I receive insults not a few.	suffered insults—not a few.
Silently I think of my case,	Silently I brood on it,
And, starting as from sleep, I beat my breast.	awake, beating my breast.
There are the sun and moon,—	You sun, you moon,
How is it that the former has become small, and not the latter?	why do you take turns hiding?
The sorrow cleaves to my heart,	Sorrow around my heart
Like an unwashed dress.	like an unwashed robe—
Silently I think of my case,	silently I brood on it,
But I cannot spread my wings and fly away.	helpless to rise and fly away.
(Legge 38–40)	(Watson 22–23)[2]

Students given these two versions described very different situations for the speaker of the poem. For the Legge translation, the students thought the speaker was a military man who was angry at brother officials. When pressed to explain how they arrived at this interpretation, they said that the reference to a "painful wound" made them think of war (although they saw that the words "as if" meant the person did not have a physical wound); "saunter" seemed like a masculine way of walking, sort of bold and nonchalant; the dignified "deportment" seemed to belong to a stiff officer who has a "case" built against him that has given him reason to complain.

In the second version by Burton Watson, students thought the speaker was a woman. When they compared the two versions, they noticed that wine would just "amuse" the speaker, not lead her to sauntering, that she goes to brothers with more gentle "pleas" not complaints, that "pure" seems more a defense against a charge of sexual misconduct, and that in general the speaker in the poem seems more emotional—she is fretful, grieving, and brooding, where the speaker in the first translation silently "thinks" of his case. When asked to make up a story about the Watson translation, students thought a woman was turning to her brothers— literal members of her family, when pressured to marry a respectable man when she loves someone else.

The biggest difference between the two translations might be the choice of how to translate *xin* (*hsin*) 心; in looking at the Chinese ideograms in the Legge edition even someone who doesn't know the language can see this simple character repeating in the poem. Some translators dealing with this word in prose translate it as heart/mind/soul. A poet, however, has to choose one word so it fits the pattern of a poem. In English, heart is the center of emotions, feelings, love; mind is the opposite—the center for rational thought. Westerners do think of the heart as more feminine and the mind as more masculine, although why they make this association makes for good classroom discussion. In three key places where Legge uses "mind," Watson uses "heart." In discussing this word, it can be said that the Chinese original is more ambiguous as to the situation being described—the poem evokes both a story about love and about politics. In choosing either heart or mind, the translator is beginning to interpret the poem; a student, therefore, needs to look at more than one translation to see the different possibilities for what it means.

Students often ask about poetry, "but what does it really mean?" In this case James Legge has published notes of what Chinese commentators have said about the poem. A scholar named Choo He in the year 1177 C.E. wrote at length that the speaker was a certain woman Chwang Keang who was neglected by her husband in the year 756 B.C.E. in the state of Wei. Legge lines up against the obscure Choo He the most famous philosophers in Chinese history—none other than Confucius and Mencius—to argue that Choo He was wrong; Legge says that Confucius and Mencius held the view that this poem is a "complaint of a worthy officer, neglected by his ruler" (Legge 41). This is the interpretation that Legge supports in his translation decisions. In the twentieth century, however, an American scholar interested in Chinese women, Patricia Ebrey, summarizes other commentators who consider this poem to be the oath of "Kung Chiang, a widow who resisted her parents' pressure to remarry" (195).

This survey of the commentary seems to show that, approximately two thousand and seven hundred years after this poem was composed, readers are not going to know whether the author or the topic was a man or a woman. The power of the poem may be that all of us, regardless of our circumstances, can identify with that first metaphor of the boat—even if we are made of material as beautiful and resilient as cypress, we often feel buffeted about, drifting, lost. The metaphor of the cypress boat is more powerful than the interpretations put into abstract language. But it is interesting that the Chinese were keenly interested in the act of interpretation. Many works of literature have a long record in China of being read on more than one level, one private and of the heart, and the second public and political. As we will see in Chinese literature in the twentieth century, this interpretive scrutiny often gets writers in trouble—the most expressive work of personal feeling can be interpreted as an allegory of discontent at government policy! On the other hand, for women writers and narrators, such as the modern author Ding Ling and her character Sophie that the second part of this chapter discusses, critics sometimes just see personal feelings and private lives. To see more than one level of meaning, to explore the possibilities of political and social commentary as well as personal expression, enriches the understanding of literary texts.

Du Fu and Tang Dynasty Poetry

Even a limited introduction to Chinese literature is incomplete without reference to what is considered its highest achievement, poetry written in the Tang Dynasty

(618–907 C.E.). Fifty thousand poems written in this period survive, and from them, the poetry of Du Fu (Tu Fu, 712–770 C.E.) is considered the greatest — the most creative, with a multiplicity of styles and topics (Owen, *Great* 183). Introductions to Du Fu routinely associate him with Confucian beliefs (Mack 1:1312), putting family relationships at the core of his value system; it seems especially appropriate, therefore, to question how many of Du Fu's lyric poems—with intense emotion dependent on the beauty of words—can be based on a topic so often felt to be a stable part of ordinary existence, everyday family life.

Part of the answer lies with the decades that inspired Du Fu's most powerful poems. They were years of dislocation, rebellion, civil turmoil, and violence. Before 755 the Tang Dynasty represents China at its zenith. The capital was Chang'an, now famous under the name Xi'an where fields of terracotta warriors have been found buried. Chang'an not only militarily controlled territory thousands of miles away, but was viewed as a cultural center for art, music, and poetry by millions of people, from Central Asian states eastward to Japan. The Silk Road brought Buddhist sutras, precious metals and jade, and tributary princesses to Chang'an; further to the East, Japan was enthralled by Tang Dynasty religious sects, brocades, paper and ink, stringed instruments, poetic forms, and the central figure of an emperor.

While biographies of Du Fu emphasize vicissitudes, it should be recognized that he was, with a grandfather famous as a court poet, born at the center of a vast empire. Raised to be in the scholar-official class, his education was Confucian. In order to pass the civil service exams at the highest level, he memorized and analyzed a well-established Confucian canon, including at the core *The Analects* and *The Book of Poetry*. Composing poetry was a requirement of the Tang examinations, illustrating how Western divisions between critic and author, or more significantly divisions among philosophy, government, and the arts did not pertain in East Asia. Only because Du Fu's life and times kept him from the bureaucratic posts he initially sought, did he concentrate so much of the energy of his heart and mind on poetry.

The traumatic event that changed the direction of Du Fu's life was the An Lushan rebellion of 755. The very reach and vastness of the Tang empire caused dissension, which led to the capture of the capital itself. An Lushan was a general for the Chinese emperor, but his roots were Central Asian; he was considered a barbarian, the literal translation of the Chinese word for foreigner. Another famous poet of the Tang, Bo Juyi (Po Chu-i, 772–846 C.E.) wrote a poem describing An Lushan dancing the Central Asian "whirl" (Owen, *Great* 457–58). Bo Juyi's "Song of Lasting Pain" (Owen 442–47) describes how Emperor Xuanzong allowed his Prized Consort Lady Yang (Yang Guifei) to be throttled because she was associated with An Lushan; this poem became the starting point of the most revered Japanese novel, Murasaki's *The Tale of Genji* written in the year 1000.

Some of Du Fu's most poignant poetry takes as its subject matter the disruption of family life caused by the An Lushan rebellion. Wife and children became the focus of lyric poetry, perhaps because they were so imperiled. One of China's most noted poems, available in many different translations, is called by Stephen Owen "Moonlit Night" (Mack 1:1314). The center of Du Fu's personal life, his family, is conflated with the center of the country, the capital, Chang'an. Du Fu mourns, "While far away I think lovingly of daughters and sons, / Who do not yet know how to remember Chang'an." The An Lushan rebellion kept Du Fu away from both his family and from the occupied capital.

The primary image of "Moonlit Night," however, concerns Du Fu's wife, who, separated from Du Fu, watches the moon that Du Fu also views. She is sensually described as "scented fog" with moist "cloudlike" hair and translucent "jadelike arms"—that is, she is described through metaphors comparing her to cloud and jade. Through the image of the woman gazing at the moon, Du Fu conveys his feeling without the abstractions "I love you," "I miss you," "I long for you." Longing is a key component of Chinese and Japanese love poetry (Norma Field's study of *The Tale of Genji* is called *The Splendor of Longing*); when the wife is absent, she becomes the poet's special object of desire. A similar poem written by Li Bo (Li Po 701–762 C.E.) is well known in America through a 1915 translation by Ezra Pound, "The River Merchant's Wife: A Letter" (Rouzer 2–3), where the wife longs for the absent husband. As has been said here earlier, the "Cypress Boat" is sometimes interpreted as a neglected wife's lament to her absent husband. In the Chinese tradition such reverberations are an important component to the appreciation of a particular poem. Ironically Pound's poem has been taken as the epitome of modern poetry, and in the 1950s and 1960s classes routinely analyzed and evaluated it independent of any cultural context because of an American critical tradition, called New Criticism.

Even more than "Moonlit Night," however, a poem Stephen Owen entitles "Song of Peng-ya [Bengya]" illustrates well the specifically Confucian values which Du Fu holds. A saying very commonly used in China even today is from the beginning of *The Analects*: "Is it not a joy to have friends come from afar" (Lau 59); this phrase extoling hospitality is only one theme of "Song of Peng-ya," which shows how Du Fu's political, social, and personal concerns unite in a way which is an essential attribute of Confucian morality. Havoc in the state causes havoc in a family; hospitality and friendship create a haven where the order that is restored becomes a metaphor that conveys the abstract goals of good government.

"Song of Peng-ya" narrates the flight of Du Fu's family through the chaos of civil war. The terror of the situation becomes vivid in the relationship of father and children, conveyed through concrete details:

> My baby girl gnawed at me in her hunger,
> And I feared wild beasts would hear her cries:
> I held her to my chest, covered her mouth,
> But she twisted and turned crying louder in rage.
>   (Mack 1:1313)

One might think it would be roaming soldiers Du Fu would fear, but the wild beasts make it seem that the countryside itself is reverting to an uncivilized, savage state. Unlike poets associated with Daoism such as Li Bo whose "mists and bright wisps" lead him to "another world/ that is not of mortal men" (Owen, *Anthology* 402–403), Du Fu's time of emotional intensity occurs in raw nature—among thunder, mire, and rain. Value exists in family relationship, with the "little son [who] did his best to take care of things, / With purpose went off and got sour plums to eat" (Mack 1:1313) The fruits of the wild are sour; it is by clinging together and sharing responsibility and emotion that the family pulls through. The social aspect of the ideal state is represented by the home of Du Fu's old friend, Sun Tsai. Ritual is followed when paper flags are cut "to summon our souls"; Sun Tsai's family—his wife and children—establish emotional connections though tears of empathy, a very human bond.

Comparing this poem to one with a similar high position in the Western canon, William Wordsworth's "Tintern Abbey," reveals similarities and differences in the East Asian and Western traditions. An autobiographical immediacy exists in both, complete with layers of memory; Du Fu begins "I remember" and moves to a line, "Since we have parted, a year has run its course." Much has been said about contrasting Eastern and Western conceptions of self, but the reflective individual recollecting times of personal intense emotion, apparently without creating a fictional persona, is evoked in both poems. In Owen's translation the resemblance is highlighted by an abrupt shift of pronoun, where Du Fu addresses the absent Sun Tsai: "And I make this vow to you, / That forever I will be your brother, your kin"; Wordsworth similarly addresses his sister who is with him in memory, and calls her his dear friend. Du Fu makes a brother out of his friend, a member of his scholar-official class; Wordsworth similarly extols friendship, a European Romantic value as much as it is a Confucian one, but by making his sister his friend.

The comparison of the two poems also leads to reflecting on how Du Fu lets the reader consider the social/political turmoil in his country. Since the 1980s, now that New Criticism's rules against using cultural context have been lifted, the Wordsworth poem has been interpreted to have social, political references to the chaos of the French Revolution, the separations it caused, and the revolution's attack on tradition, exemplified by the ruined abbey itself. Similarly, Du Fu uses a personal episode to illuminate a precise moment in the history of a country. He begins "I remember when first we fled the rebellion" and toward the end reminds the reader, "And still the barbarian weaves his calamities," a reference to An Lushan. Stephen Owen writes about Du Fu:

Chinese critics from the Song Dynasty on often refered to Du Fu as the "poet historian"; and indeed, if a reader is interested in the particular details of the period of the An Lu-shan [An Lushan] Rebellion, he or she will find in Du Fu comments on current events and powerful images of the historical moment eliciting an immediacy that always eluded the historian proper. The Confucian interpretation of the Classic of Poetry as bearing witness to the history of the Zhou Dynasty lent authority to such a use of poetry; Du Fu saw himself in the role of the engaged witness of a general political and social situation that reveals itself in particulars. (*Anthology* 413)

One can relate what Owen is saying here to part of the quotation from Fenollosa that begins this chapter, "the known interprets the obscure." What happens to a country in one particular historical moment is obscure: evidence comes in fragments and generalizations are false because they are so likely to reflect the bias of the historian. The more abstract the word, the more bias exists: was An Lushan a barbarian or even a foreigner? But when Du Fu describes his baby girl gnawing at him in hunger, there is truth in that image. The reader understands the pain of political chaos and understands the need for good government that can create social stability.

Comparing poems from two independent traditions, East and West, runs the risk of blurring what is distinctive in one culture or even in one poet. Yet it should be noted that while the Chinese critical tradition, as Owen summarizes it above, consistently saw Du Fu as a social historian, Western critics have rarely valued poetry as history. Du Fu does want to escape the political calamities by having wings "to fly off," an ending which resembles the ending of the "Cypress Boat"—an allusion that ties many poems together. But Du Fu wants to "alight" before his friend's eyes, a friend in this world who lives in a real house with many gates, a house where one can enter and get his, and his children's, feet washed. His commitment to the real world also separates him from the Daoists or Buddhists in his own culture; he does not want to escape the human world for other states of consciousness or no consciousness. Like Confucius and unlike Western Romantic poets, Du Fu does not want to "associate with the birds and beasts" (*Analects* XVIII, 6). Du Fu sees social pain and struggle, yet will not leave the bonds of friends and family "while the Way is to be found in the Empire" (Lau 150).

American teachers of Asian literature have recently tried not to introduce students to Chinese literature using only Western methods of critical analysis or seeing greatness only when works reveal so-called universal truths. It is very easy to use literary criteria built from centuries of Western thought, and then to distort and demean Asian writing when it does not meet expectations that have little to do with Asian traditions. For teachers and students who do not know Asian languages, this problem is particularly severe. We need to be very careful of translations, and to compare different translations to see how they may be reducing ambiguity and interpreting the texts by the English words they choose. Comparing Chinese poetry to Romantic poetry might lead to distortions, yet not to do so eliminates the insights that can be gained by this process of critical analysis. As this chapter has shown, often the familiar can introduce the unfamiliar, fresh juxtapositions lead to new ideas, and the known can help interpret what seems at first to be obscure.

To use a Chinese framework of criticism, however, one begins by placing a poem in its cultural/historical context. Du Fu, for example, must be seen, not only at a particular moment in Tang Dynasty history, but also as the student and the master of texts in the Confucian canon—the *Yijing*, *The Book of Poetry*, and *The Analects*. In Western criticism, the technique of allusion has been denigrated since the 1798 *Lyrical Ballads*, when Wordsworth and Coleridge ridiculed Milton's peppering of his poetry with Greek and Biblical references. This attitude perhaps slowed down the realization of how much modern Western poetry is indebted to China, even to the extent that Ezra Pound's translations have been treated as his own original work. Western criticism has valued the novel and the unique. Du Fu was, indeed, original, creative, and unique, but his poetry is best appreciated when allusions to previous Chinese poetry and philosophy can be understood. The literati, scholar-official class, including Du Fu, had a very specific set of works they admired, conserved, and transformed.

A student can learn some Chinese, learn the ideogram for heart/mind/soul (*xin* 心), and know each time she reads "heart" that the word truly beats with the other meanings as well. A reader can recognize sun 日 and moon 月 and feel their brightness when the ideograms are together 明, and recognize the sun even when it is tangled in the branches of a tree on the eastern horizon, 東. Metaphors can speak to us directly even when we gaze —separated by distance, by time, by loss — at the moon from different vantage points.

Chinese Fiction: 1918–1948

In 1911 the group then ruling China, the Manchus, were forced to give up their power and declared an end to the Qing Dynasty. There would be no more emperor holding together China as one family; no more examination system establishing with certainty which family of books, what canon should be admired, analyzed, memorized, and drawn upon by a nationwide network of literati-officials who provided the daily governing of the country. Civil war broke out, and the next thirty-seven years were marked with struggle, terror, and death. It was also a time of conflicting ideas, when China was questioning many of the ideas that have been presented in the various chapters of this book. There were strong rival groups asking what was the right way to live, what should community mean, what was the value of art or music. There were arguments about the purposes of literature, of what made good literature. The fiction of the period also captured and described all the other arguments—about family, community, government, about self, selfishness, and isolation, about the need to rebel and the fear of rebellion and chaos.

There were many writers of fiction during this period, and except for one man, Lu Xun, there has been little agreement about which writers are better or more important than others. This lack of agreement is not surprising for such a time; many people have given judgments, but an American student reading different evaluations will see conflicting reports which seem to depend not just on whether the critics are Western or Chinese, but whether the critics are Nationalist

Chinese or Communist, living in Taiwan or Hong Kong or mainland China, or immigrants to United States from these areas, whether they are male or female, and in what decade they were born. All critics have their own world view, their own ideology or belief systems, but for this period the conflicts that seem to influence evaluation are extreme.

This section presents one writer, Lu Xun, who stands out among the rest, explores the influences on him, and then chooses one author, among many, that he clearly influenced. For the second author, Ding Ling, there is lack of agreement over whether her fiction is any good, which part of it is better than other parts, and even what it means. But partly because Ding Ling has been seen as a leading woman author, there is more information about her in English than about other modern Chinese writers. In the twentieth century, many political/cultural movements attempted to transform women's lives. Ding Ling's life itself, as well as how this woman portrayed her world as a woman writer, has fascinated critics, biographers, and historians.

The May Fourth Movement

Lu Xun has been associated with a group of intellectuals, many of whom took part in student demonstrations in Tiananmen Square in Beijing on May 4, 1919, to protest the Treaty of Versailles which, at the end of World War I, gave Japan rights to parts of China as colonies. The treaty revealed how weak China was politically and economically in relation to the rest of the world; reactions to the treaty accelerated the internal process of criticizing Chinese customs that seemed to have held it back from developing industrially as Europe and Japan had done. As a harsh critic of the old China, Lu Xun was admired by Chinese dissidents regardless of whether they later followed Mao Zedong's Communist Party or Chiang Kai-shek's Nationalist Party, the Guomindang.

Lu Xun specifically criticized Confucianism, which has already been portrayed in this book as the ideology, the philosophy, which gave coherence to the traditional Chinese world from government to literature, art, and music. As Confucianism had evolved over centuries, it had codified duties and expectations far beyond what Confucius had said in *The Analects*. In attacking Confucianism, Lu Xun was influenced by a journal called *New Youth*, published by the most influential students and teachers at Peking University; article after article analyzed and criticized Confucianism.

Confucian family values were held responsible for China's political and economic weaknesses. A key essay that conveys this focus is Chen Duxiu's "The Way of Confucius and Modern Life," which appeared in *New Youth* in December 1916. This essay criticized the Confucian ethical norm that holds that "sons and wives possess neither personal individuality nor personal property" (DeBary 153). Chen Duxiu asked: "When people are bound by the Confucian teachings of filial piety and obedience to the point of the son not deviating from the father's way . . . and the women obeying not only her father and husband but also her son, how can they form their own political party and make their own choice?" (154). While modern scholars such as Patricia Ebrey document the evolution of the subjugation of women after the eleventh century, Chen Duxiu attacked many practices described in the Confucian *Book of Rites*, such as those pressuring widows to remain unmarried. Chen Duxiu contrasted Chinese customs to Western mores where "daughters-in-law, particularly, have no obligation to serve parents-in-law" (155), and where "social intercourse between men and women is a common practice" (154).

Lu Xun's Writing

It was an editor of *New Youth* who persuaded Lu Xun to publish fiction. In the preface to his first collection of stories, *A Call to Arms*, Lu Xun records a conversation with an editor of *New Youth*, Jin Xinyi, who asked him to write for that journal. Lu Xun replied:

> "Imagine an iron house having not a single window and virtually indestructible, with all its inmates sound asleep and about to die of suffocation. Dying in their sleep, they won't feel the pain of death. Now if you raise a shout to wake a few of the lighter sleepers, making these unfortunate few suffer the agony of irrevocable death, do you really think you are doing them a good turn?"
>
> [The editor replied] "But if a few wake up, you can't say there is no hope of destroying the iron house."
>
> [Lu Xun continued] "True, in spite of my own conviction, I could not blot out hope, for hope belongs to the future. . . . So I finally agreed to write, and the result was my first story 'Madman's Diary.'" (*Complete Stories* ix)

This preface makes clear that for Lu Xun the purpose of fiction is to bring about social/political change. There is a key image—an iron box—and Lu Xun's decision to write can only be understood if the reader interprets that box as a metaphor for China—cut off from the rest of the world with a deadly isolation. The iron box is like a guarded "stronghold" of traditional values, an image Lu Xun elaborated on in 1930 (Denton 19). By waking up those who are sensitive, the light sleepers, literature might have a transformative role that gives strength to Chinese inhabitants sufficient to change what Lu Xun portrays as a rigid cosmos to one more open, adaptive, and free. Through changing individuals, waking their imaginations, the world would be changed. It should be noticed, however, that Lu Xun's words need to be interpreted—because he is using a metaphor, his language, like classical Chinese poetry, is ambiguous. He uses the phrase "light sleepers"; when a translator calls these sleepers "individuals," there is an emphasis Lu Xun himself

may or may not intend. The story about the iron room is a parable; critics have interpreted Lu Xun's advice for China in different ways.

"A Madman's Diary," Lu Xun's story that immediately follows his preface in
Call to Arms, is one of the first modern short stories to be written in China. The story
starts with an introduction clearly establishing that Lu Xun himself is not the journal
writer, the madman who writes confusedly with different colored inks. Since the
madman "can't sleep at night" (*Complete Stories* 3), the reader associates him with the
"light sleepers" of Lu Xun's preface—the imaginative people who are ready to change
China. While he can't sleep, the madman passes the time reading. The object of Lu
Xun's satire becomes clear: the madman reads a history book that has "no chronology
and scrawled all over each page are the words: 'Confucian Virtue and Morality'" (4).
Confucianism here is not seen as one philosophy in China over the centuries, along
with Daoism or Buddhism for example, but the philosophy that dominated all
aspects of life. Since the words are scrawled defacing every page, Lu Xun seems to be
saying that Confucianism has spoiled China. The madman continues, "Since I could
not sleep anyway, I read intently half the night until I began to see words between the
lines. The whole book is filled with the two words—'Eat people'" (4).

It seems puzzling at first why Lu Xun would blame Confucianism, a system
that exists to promote morality, for "eating people"—for consuming or devouring
individuals. The madman/narrator is most afraid of his elder brother, the relative
in Confucian terms he should respect and love; he suspects this brother of having
eaten his younger sister, and wanting to wolf him down as well. Confucian morality states that younger siblings should respect and obey the older brother as children respect and obey their parents. These relationships are supposed to bring
beneficial order to the whole society. The narrator is hallucinating when he sees the
words "Confucian Virtue and Morality" and "Eat People" on every page of the history of China: Lu Xun, however, is making a satirical point. He sees the hierarchies
supported by Confucianism crushing people's spirit only for the welfare of those in
power—the strong who devour those weaker than they.

Women's Issues

While Lu Xun was exceptionally well educated in the classic Chinese texts, literature from the West was a crucial catalyst in leading Lu Xun to challenge Chinese
traditions. As a young man Lu Xun studied in Japan from 1901 to 1905 and
immersed himself in the hundreds of European works of literature being translated there. One issue then hotly debated by intellectuals in both Japan and China
involved the role of women. Lu Xun, himself, became a harsh critic of the roles traditional Chinese women were forced to play. On his return from Japan his family
arranged a marriage to a woman with bound feet; Lu Xun supported this woman
financially but refused to live with her. His short story "The New-Year Sacrifice"
(1924) is uncompromising in showing a woman's misery in an arranged marriage;
she is physically forced to marry, forced by three men to have sexual intercourse

with her husband even after she "bashed" her head in her attempt to escape (163). The story indicts Confucian morality because the traditional rituals and the rules, such as those against widows remarrying, support the indifference of the villagers, none of whom oppose what happens to the woman. As the villagers begin to ridicule the woman's story of suffering and allow her to die from poverty, society as a whole is held responsible for her pain.

In examining how Lu Xun became an advocate of women, even using the surname of his mother "Lu" instead of his father's last name, it is worthwhile analyzing briefly one Western work of literature questioning women's relationships to family that clearly influenced Lu Xun, the participants in the May Fourth movement, and women who became writers, such as Ding Ling. This influential work is Henrik Ibsen's *A Doll's House*, first produced in Norway in 1879. In 1918 a special issue of *New Youth* was devoted to Ibsen and his advocacy of women's emancipation. The 1933 novel *Family* by Ba Jin gives a detailed account of how Chinese students in various Chinese cities shortly after 1918 discussed the play's challenge to traditional views of marriage, arranged productions of the play, and endured riots and arrest as a result. We know the play influenced Lu Xun directly because in 1923 Lu Xun gave a lecture, "What Happens after Nora Leaves Home?" where he is pessimistic about the plight of Chinese women even if they leave home as Nora did.

While virtually all accounts of modern Chinese literature refer to *A Doll's House*, few look at the play itself to see what so challenged Chinese views of family and society. Primarily, the play establishes just the sense of self that commentators on Chinese philosophy have said does not exist in China. This Chinese/Confucian way of looking at personality, that there is no independent self to be involved in relationships with others, was directly challenged by Ibsen's play.[3]

The doll's house of the title has some similarities to the iron box that is Lu Xun's primary image for China in his seminal preface. Ibsen's main character, Nora, is frequently compared to a caged squirrel or bird. This Norwegian play describes a family very similar to that of the Confucian ideal: the husband provides moral leadership and physical comforts for his wife and lets her run the household. Yet at the end of the play, she rebels against the moral duties which kept her in line.[4] Nora's final statement of duty only to herself, her own development as a human being, for Chinese of Lu Xun's generation directly challenges Confucian values, which put family in a central position. Nora establishes a core sense of self, independent of family roles, and she defends her actions ethically in the name of this autonomous self. While Ba Jin begins to have women characters who are influenced by Nora, women writers more creatively explored how a Chinese woman might also leave home and family.

Ding Ling

Every modern writer of fiction in China—between 1918 and 1948—was influenced by Lu Xun, since he introduced the modern short story form in China. Lu Xun's stories dominate anthologies published in English of modern Chinese writers—

and there were originally two collections that appeared in the United States, one edited by Edgar Snow, *Living China*, published in 1937, and a second edited by Harold Isaacs, *Straw Sandals*, put together with the help of Lu Xun in 1934 but published in 1974. In these collections there is one woman writer singled out in the introduction, Ding Ling. Already by 1934 she was emphasized not only for her fiction, but also because of events in her life.

Born Jiang Bingzhi in 1904, she became known by her pseudonym, Ding Ling, for her early 1920's short stories, which drew the attention of intellectuals in the main cities of China. Her colloquial language, frank discussions of sexual feelings, and her individualist tone caused controversy. This early fame secured for her a turbulent life in revolutionary China: her husband who shared her literary activities was arrested and after a month executed by the Nationalist Guomindang in 1931; Ding Ling was kidnapped by the Guomindang and held under house arrest starting in 1933; she was released in 1936 and through a long trek in disguise joined Mao Zedong in Yan'an where she was at first welcomed as a heroine. For twenty years she wrote fiction considered to have Communist values, yet she was denounced by the Communists relatively early in 1954 for reasons that are unclear. She lived a life of labor and frequent imprisonment for twenty years until "official rehabilitation" in 1979, and then at age seventy-five, Ding Ling emerged somewhat broken in body, but in interviews, engaging, whole, and determined to write again. She died in 1986. For such a writer, interpretation of her stories had life-and-death consequences. The introductions, commentary, and critical analysis referred to in this chapter were often framed by respect given to someone who was among the disappeared. That she survived through decades where millions died — fighting in the civil war between the Nationalists and the Communists, the "Great Leap Forward" in the 1950s, and the Cultural Revolution in the 1960s and 1970s — makes it difficult to regard her work dispassionately. Opinions about her life are often strong, and assessment of her fiction varies as widely.

Conflicting Critical Evaluations of Ding Ling

Many Americans interested in China might meet Ding Ling's name first in the writings of Jonathan Spence, a Yale historian often considered brilliantly idiosyncratic. For Spence, Ding Ling is a modern heroine. In *The Search for Modern China* (1990), Spence uses Ding Ling as a case study of those who had been "caught up in the dreams for a New China that lay at the heart of the May Fourth movement" of 1919 (410). In using Ding Ling in this way, Spence drew upon his earlier 1981 book *The Gate of Heavenly Peace*, where he chose Ding Ling as one of three "individuals whose lives were not so obviously central to the course of the revolution but who nevertheless described their hopes and their sorrows with particular sensitivity, and whose personal experiences help to define the nature of the times through which they lived" (xiii). Spence's respectful account of Ding Ling's life and work contrasts most sharply with a critic writing in 1961, C. T. Hsia, who says of her later Communist fiction, "As a story-writer, [Ding] Ling is much worse than Chiang Kuang-tz'u [Jiang Guangci] or Kuo Mo-jo [Guo Moro], who at least wrote lucidly in spite of their great shallowness; she belongs with such early women writers as Huang Lu-yin [Luyin], who could not write one decent paragraph in Chinese" (269). Other critics strongly disagree. Tani E. Barlow, who thought Ding Ling worthy to be collected, retranslated, and published in United States, calls the same later work "a stunning achievement" (40). In "Ding Ling's Fiction: Ideology and Narrative in Modern Chinese Literature," Yi-tsi Mei Feuerwerker calls Ding Ling's novel *The Sun Shines on the Sanggan River*, which won a Stalin prize for literature in 1951, "a remarkable excursion of the fictional imagination" (122). Various factors could help explain these conflicting opinions. Barlow and Feuerwerker are women explicitly interested in the connections of political and feminist issues; C. T. Hsia is a man of an earlier generation. While both Hsia and Feuerwerker are Chinese-Americans, Hsia came from Taiwan where the forces defeated by the Communists retreated; Feuerwerker's research was partly supported by the Chinese Academy of Social Sciences in Communist mainland China. Students need to look at critics' evaluations somewhat skeptically because all critics have different points of view, which are highly subjective.

While the twentieth century started with Chinese intellectuals being drawn to the idea that an individual such as Nora could value herself independently from family relationships and community opinions, Feuerwerker's 1982 study seems to show how Chinese Communism shares an outlook similar to the traditional Confucian views of self and society. Feuerwerker states, "Basic to the outlook [of the novel *The Sun Shines on the Sanggan River*] is the sense, always important in China, that each individual achieves his identity through being a member of his community." She elaborates, "Such a view . . . see[s] the self, performing in and shaped by society, as nothing more than a structure of the roles it plays." Feuerwerker apparently agrees with this view of self, since she further states, "This approach to personality contravenes the cherished 'bourgeois' notions of the autonomous and unique individual character, long the staple of the Western realistic novel" (125). Here the ideas in Ibsen's *A Doll's House* are dismissed as Western, yet in Lu Xun's generation Chinese writers were making such ideas part of revolutionary China.

Extended Analysis of "Miss Sophie's Diary"

Considering Ding Ling important in her efforts to describe the conflicts of modern China, not the certainties of later Communism, Jonathan Spence chose to highlight one of Ding Ling's early stories "The Diary of Miss Sophie," which was said to have "stunned a literary generation" (cited in Feuerwerker 43) when it was published in 1927. The story has been interpreted as the failure of a modern independent woman to sustain herself. Critics, however, frequently mistakenly assume the writer, Ding Ling, is the narrator, Miss Sophie. C. T. Hsia dismisses the story by saying, "Apparently lonely and confused, [Ding] Ling pours all her resentments and exasperations in the diary mold of her fiction" (262–63). Feuerwerker sees this story as an expression of the "ideology of modernism," a "solipsistic exercise in self-negating circularity," a "senseless" text that ends in a conclusion of "despair and self-pity" (50). Some contemporary Chinese critics thought the sexual eroticism was "unmediated confessional autobiography" (Barlow 24). Barlow states that "Ding Ling worked for the rest of her life to prove that ["Miss Sophie's Diary"] was not autobiographical" (25), and Barlow herself seems to doubt this defense. Even the sympathetic Spence seems to think the story is autobiographical in that he assumes that Ding Ling was depicting herself as a Nora-type heroine after she left home. Spence implies that Ding Ling heard Lu Xun's lecture on Nora when she was auditing some of Lu Xun's classes in Beijing (*Heavenly* 216–17). But Spence cannot understand why, if Ding Ling herself was enjoying the life of "discovery and freedom," her character, Sophie, has such a "dispiriting" experience (*Search* 411). A reinterpretation of this story explains this discrepancy, but also demonstrates how a complex set of allusions, metaphors, and images needs to be carefully analyzed to appreciate the full impact of a Chinese short story. Even while modern Chinese writers turned against Confucian family hierarchy, they maintained a Confucian tradition, seen clearly with Du Fu, where an individual account illuminates the political/social situation. The analysis of one of Ding Ling's stories that follows shows how a careful analysis in a cultural context leads to understanding China in a crucial period of transition, not just understanding one woman idly choosing among lovers.

The story "Miss Sophie's Diary" does begin claustrophobically. The diarist, the writer, Sophie, is alone, enclosed in a room, a sick woman stuck in bed. The first paragraph reads:

> It blows again today! The wind awoke me before daybreak. And now the servant comes in to make the fire. I know I'm not going to be able to sleep anymore. I also know if I don't get up I'll soon be dizzy. I'm too fond of mulling over many strange things when I lie under my quilt. The doctor told the best thing is to sleep a lot, eat a lot, and not to read or think, but this is precisely what I can't manage to do. I can't ever get to sleep before two or three in the morning, and I'm always awake before it's light. It's impossible not to think of the many irritating things that come to one's head during weather like this. (*Miss Sophie's* 12)

Some critics have quoted from this paragraph to show that Ding Ling herself was over-sensitive, but in the context of modern Chinese literature dominated by Lu Xun, this beginning can be seen as ironic, controlled, amusing. Could Miss Sophie, the diarist, be one of the light sleepers that Lu Xun describes? These are the select few, the only ones who have a chance of destroying the suffocating iron house. The kindly doctor thinks, of course, that it would be better for Sophie to get plenty of sleep, not to read and not to think, to dull her consciousness, in short. Being truly awake leads to suffering, but the opposite is a living death, unconsciousness.

The fourth paragraph can be interpreted in a way that confirms the connection of this story to Lu Xun's preface. Sophie continues, "But it's terrifyingly lonely when there are no sounds, especially inside these four whitewashed walls. Wherever you sit they blankly block your view. If you try to escape by lying on your bed you're crushed by the ceiling, which is whitewashed too" (*Miss Sophie's* 14–15). The metaphor of the iron house has been brought to imaginative life. The four blank walls are surrealistic, dreamlike; they are a literal impossibility; there is not just no window, there is no door. The doorless room is terrifying—a modern woman may need to establish her independence by walking out a door and slamming it as Nora did when she left her family, but how can she if there is no door?

If the allusion is to Lu Xun's preface, it also has other literary reverberations. Barlow refers to Flaubert's Madame Bovary (50), but understanding references to Russian authors leads to consideration of the text less as a realistic one about love, and more as a satiric text about broader issues. The image of the claustrophobic room evokes comparison to Dostoevsky's 1864 "Notes from the Underground" where the narrator begins, like Sophie, by establishing he is "sick"; he wonders if he should refuse his doctor's treatment (1105). He has settled down in "a corner," in a room which is "nasty, squalid" (1106), an image that has been interpreted as representing the human condition in modern society. When this narrator takes pride in "the overly acute consciousness of one's own humiliation"(1108), he resembles Sophie who feels "defiled" yet "in full possession of [her] faculties" at the end of her story (Isaacs 169). Dostoevsky footnoted his work to make clear that his persona/narrator was "fictitious of course . . . a representative of the current generation" (1105). In China, Ding Ling's work of surreal irony was read as a realistic account of Ding Ling's own experience, a fact which caused considerable difficulties for her.

While Dostoevsky influenced both Lu Xun and Ding Ling, references to Nikolai Gogol's 1835 "Diary of a Madman" are even more explicit. Ding Ling's title "Miss Sophie's Diary" suggests connection to both Gogol and Lu Xun; all three have a persona write in first person with an idiosyncratic, informal style, a style which was new to Chinese prose fiction. While Barlow traces the name Sophie to Rousseau's French Sophie (26), Sophia is a common Russian name, and Sophie is the name of the main female character in Gogol's "Diary of a Madman." Further, the main character in Gogol's story is in love with her, but the attractive and lively Sophie, drawn to a worldly man, ridicules the narrator, just as Ding Ling's Sophie laughs at her suitor, Wei.

From the beginning Ding Ling poses a question of where Sophie will go when winter passes, when she will finally be able to leave her room. Sophie has two suitors who keep her in a state of indecision and inaction. One of them is Wei, a sincere man, with Confucian virtues, who materializes in her room from time to time, buys her such artifacts of the scholar literati as "good paper and . . . good brushes" (*Miss Sophie's* 20) and "[sheds] his tears drop by drop on the back of my hand [making] me laugh with pleasure like a savage"(19). In fact, Wei's main activity is to weep over this woman, a trait he shares with traditional Chinese heroes of literature, from Bo Juyi's Tang Dynasty "Song of the Lute" through Baoyu who cries with the ill Daiyu for volumes in *Dream of the Red Chamber*. Sophie, however, is unsympathetic to this tradition—it only irritates her and makes her laugh.

Sophie's second choice is Ling Jishi, whose "tall body, his tender pink face, his soft lips, and his charming eyes could allure a lot of women who were vulnerable to beauty" (43). The novelty of a woman writer describing a female character bowled over by such a man's "languid manner" entranced her young Chinese readers. Described as a Westernized Chinese, Ling's passions are "debates; tennis tournaments; going to study at Harvard; becoming a diplomat, an ambassador or a minister; . . . going into the rubber business; becoming a capitalist" (44). He is also morally corrupt, wishing to spend "his money in the whorehouse to buy a moment's physical pleasure, or [sit] on a well-upholstered settee with his arms around a scented body, smoking a cigarette . . . [before going] back home to his wife" (43–44). Ding Ling's presentation of Ling is not very consistent, for all we see Ling doing is also appearing at her bedside, patting her hand, teaching her English, and finally giving her one unchaste kiss. As a psychological portrait, this is silly, yet as political allegory the story is provocative. There is liveliness to the story because Sophie cannot stand the sincere (Confucian) alternative, Wei, and is shown as attracted to Western materialistic values through the portrayal of her physical desire for Ling's "red lips" (Isaacs 160). Ding Ling's descriptions of Sophie's longing for physical gratification may have gone beyond her allegorical intent, since contemporary readers were shocked, and perhaps distracted, by their explicit personal nature.

In the final paragraph of the story Sophie seems disgusted with the life she has been leading. Some readers, like Spence, think Sophie is like Nora after Nora leaves home, because Sophie seems isolated, living by herself without family. But it is only at the end that Sophie makes a decision and walks out her door for good. The door she takes leads to the South in a clear rejection of the capitalist West and traditional East. Sophie says "I don't want to stay in Beijing and I don't want to go to the Western Hills, I'm going to take the train southward, where no one knows me." (In the terminology of the *Yijing*, North signifies death, and South is Kun, the receptive, Earth, mother, female.) Ding Ling was sending her heroine directly into revolutionary China, a revolution Ding Ling, herself, soon embraced.[5]

Even though Sophie will continue to "waste what's left of my life," like China she nevertheless rejects both Western capitalism, perceived as hollow and materialistic, and a traditional China that will nurture her only while she is sick. The reader feels Sophie is on her way to something new, neither Western nor Confucian. Sophie's laughter at Wei (traditional Confucianism) and Ling Jishi (Western capitalism) may seem spiteful and self-centered, but in rejecting both men she responded to Lu Xun's "call to arms" for the light sleepers to aspire to destroy the iron house.

Ding Ling had an extremely hard life after she published this 1927 story. Other stories show the pain she felt when her husband was executed, when she had to give up her baby to her mother's care. Sometime in the 1960s Ding Ling was kept in solitary confinement for several years. That she emerged still wanting to write, that she came to United States on a visit and talked with the playwright Arthur Miller is remarkable, and a testament to her unbending spirit.

Summary

While attitudes have changed in modern China toward Confucianism, toward religious practices such as using the *Yijing*, toward family hierarchy and women's roles, and toward an empire governed by an emperor and a scholar-official class, many literary values have remained. As we have seen, the *Book of Odes* remained, until recent times, a much quoted source of wisdom and inspiration to Chinese writers and scholars, and while its influence has waned during the postrevolutionary period, there are signs of renewed interest in this as well as other traditional works. In general, the continuity of Chinese literature through the ages cannot be denied, an impressive fact considering the long span of time between the earliest writings and the present. While writers like Lu Xun and Ding Ling are best understood when the full ambiguity of their fiction is recognized, and when symbols, metaphors, and allusions are carefully studied to derive different possibilities of interpretation, we must also see them as what in China can only be called recent manifestations of perennial concerns that have taxed the minds and spirits of Chinese throughout the ages—in short, as unique representatives of an ancient and evolving culture.

Glossary

Allusion A reference to a literary or historical person, event, or text; often the reference is not explained so that knowledge of the reader is necessary to understand its significance.

Ambiguity Language which suggests more than one meaning, leading the reader to consider alternative interpretations; even contradictory meanings might be intentional so that different layers of a story or poem will be perceived.

May Fourth Movement Refers to May 4, 1919; this term describes a radical anti-traditional movement which sought to change the foundations of Chinese culture, namely the Confucian ethical tradition. It is thought to have been started by foreign educated students and may have indirectly led to the creation of the Chinese Communist Party in 1921.

Metaphor A comparison between two basically unlike things where the second acquires the emotional or imaginative associations of the first. Often a concrete image conveys an abstract idea, and the abstract idea gains the associations of the concrete image. For example becoming a leader is an abstract process, carving jade is more concrete. By comparing the two, becoming a leader is perceived to be a process of great value requiring artistic skill, patience, judgment, experience, and so forth.

Modern Literature For both the Far East—China and Japan—and in Western Europe and the United States, the period 1918 to 1948 was characterized by a self-conscious attempt to reject past traditions and to value what was new and different. Thus a term which literally means new, up-to-date, was used during this period to characterize art, literature, and political/economic change. In the Far East modernization was influenced by Western ideas related to government, technology, and women's roles, for example. It should be recognized that Western modern poetry was as profoundly influenced by the Far East as was Frank Lloyd Wright's modern architecture or the earlier Impressionist art in establishing a radical departure from past forms and values.

Nationalist Party (the Guomindong) Formed in 1912 with leadership from Sun Yat-sen, this political group formed an army under Chiang Kai-shek and split with the Chinese Communist Party in 1928. Defeated in 1949, this anticommunist group moved to Taiwan where it is still a dominant party.

New Criticism Primarily an American movement of literary criticism, which developed in the 1930s and dominated American college teaching of literature until the 1970s. One of its founders, I. A. Richards, emphasized the value to poetry of metaphor and ambiguity rather than knowing the biography or cultural background of a poet. Richards was greatly influenced by Ezra Pound's work on Chinese poetry and went to China to study Chinese philosophy and literature in 1930.

Ode A relatively short poem marked by imagination, melody, and emotion. In discussing Ezra Pound's use of this term to translate the Chinese, Dembo emphasizes, "Poetry to the ancient Chinese seems to have been an art in which the art of words and music formed a single unit" and notes that the English word "ode" was originally a song meant to be sung (xiv). In Chinese there is a rhyme scheme which translators rarely attempt, partly because patterns of sounds of Chinese and English are quite different; rhymes occur in Chinese much more frequently so that a rhyme scheme constricts the choice of words less.

Yijing *The Book of Changes*, sometimes written as *I Ching*.

Notes

1. For more on Chinese ideograms, see Linda Pickle's chapter "Written and Spoken Chinese: Expression of Culture and Heritage."

2. From *The Columbia Book of Chinese Poetry*, translated by Burton Watson. Copyright 1984, Columbia University Press. Reprinted with permission of the publisher.

3. See Vance Cope-Kasten's chapter "Meeting Chinese Philosophy" for a more detailed discussion of the Confucian conception of self.

4. Ibsen writes,

HELMUT: Isn't it your duty to your husband and children?
NORA: I have another duty, just as sacred.
HELMUT: You can't have. What duty do you mean?
NORA: My duty to myself.
HELMUT: Before everything else, you're a wife and mother.
NORA: I don't believe that any longer. I believe that before everything else I'm a human being—just as much as you are. (227-28)

5. Like Ding Ling, Sophie is from the South; Sophie's woman friend, Yun, who has died, was there. While not entirely clear what Sophie might be running toward in political terms, in the year before the publication of "Miss Sophie's Diary" in December of 1927, both the cities and the contryside directly south of Beijing were in turmoil seeking political and social change. In 1925-26 Mao Zedong was active in organizing peasants in Hunan, Ding Ling's home province.

Works Cited

Barlow, Tani E. Introduction. *I Myself Am a Woman: Selected Writings of Ding Ling*. Ed. Tani E. Barlow and Gary J. Bjorge. Boston: Beacon, 1989

De Bary, Wm. Theodore, Wing Tsit Chan, and Chester Tan. *Sources of Chinese Tradition*. Vol. 2. New York: Columbia Univeristy Press, 1960. Chapter 24.

Dembo, L. S. *The Confucian Odes of Ezra Pound: A Critical Appraisal*. Berkeley: Univeristy of California Press, 1963.

Denton, Kirk A., ed. *Modern Chinese Literary Thought: Writings on Literature, 1893-1945*. Stanford: Stanford University Press, 1996.

Ding Ling. *Miss Sophie's Diary and Other Stories*. Trans. W. J. F. Jenner. Beijing: Panda, 1985.

Dostoevsky, Fyodor. "Notes from Underground." *Norton Anthology of World Masterpieces*, Expanded Edition. Vol. 2. New York: Norton, 1995.

Ebrey, Patricia. *The Inner Quarters: Marriage and the Lives of Chinese Women in the Sung Period*. Berkeley: University of California Press, 1993.

Fenollosa, Ernest. *The Chinese Written Character as a Medium for Poetry*. Ed. Ezra Pound. San Francisco: City Lights, 1968.

Feuerwerker, Yi-tsi Mei. *Ding Ling's Fiction: Ideology and Narrative in Modern Chinese Literature*. Cambridge, Mass.: Harvard University Press, 1982.

Hsia, C. T. *A History of Modern Chinese Fiction: 1917-1957*. New Haven: Yale University Press, 1961.

Ibsen, Henrik. *A Doll's House and Other Plays*. Trans. Peter Watts. London: Penguin, 1965.

Isaacs, Harold R. *Straw Sandals: Chinese Short Stories 1918-1933*. Foreword by Lu Hsun. Cambridge, Mass.: MIT Univeristy Press, 1971.

Lau, D. C., trans. *The Analects of Confucius*. London: Penguin, 1979.

Legge, James, trans. and ed. *The Chinese Classics: The She King or The Book of Poetry*. Vol. 4; Hong Kong: Hong Kong Univeristy Press, 1960.

Lu Xun. *The Complete Stories of Lu Xun*. Trans. Yang Xianyi and Gladys Yang. Bloomington: Indiana University Press, 1981.

Mack, Maynard, ed. *The Norton Anthology of World Masterpieces*, Expanded Edition. Vol. 1. New York: Norton, 1995.

Owen, Stephen, trans. and ed. *An Anthology of Chinese Literature: Beginnings to 1911*. New York: Norton, 1996.

———. *The Great Age of Chinese Poetry: The High T'ang*. New Haven: Yale University Press, 1981.

Rouzer, Paul. "Li Bai: Chang gan xing (Song of Long Gully)." Unpublished manuscript.

Spence, Jonathan D. *The Gate of Heavenly Peace: The Chinese and Their Revolution, 1895–1980*. New York: Viking, 1981.

———. *The Search for Modern China*. New York: W. W. Norton, 1990.

Watson, Burton. *The Columbia Book of Chinese Poetry*. New York: Columbia University Press, 1984.

Wilhelm, Hellmut. *The I Ching [Yijing] or Book of Changes*. Trans. C. F. Baynes. 1950; Princeton: Princeton University Press, 1967.

Works Consulted

Ding Ling. *I Myself Am a Woman: Selected Writings of Ding Ling*. Ed. Tani E. Barlow and Gary J. Bjorge. Boston: Beacon, 1989.

———. *The Sun Shines over the Sanggan River*. 1948; Trans. Yang Xianji and Gladys Yang. Beijing: Foreign Languages Press, 1984.

Field, Norma. *The Splendor of Longing in the Tale of Genji*. Princeton: Princeton University Press, 1987.

Kent, Leonard J., ed. *The Collected Tales and Plays of Nikolai Gogol*. New York: Modern Library, 1964.

Lau, Joseph S. M., and Howard Goldblatt, eds. *The Columbia Anthology of Modern Chinese Literature*. New York: Columbia University Press, 1995.

Kalgren, Bernhard. *The Book of Odes: Chinese Text, Transcription and Translation*. Stockholm: Museum of Far Eastern Antiquities, 1950.

Pound, Ezra. *The Confucian Odes: The Classic Anthology Defined by Confucius*. New York: New Directions, 1954.

Snow, Edgar. *Living China: Modern Chinese Short Stories*. Westport, Conn. Hyperion,1937.

Waley, Arthur. *The Book of Songs*. 1937; New York: Grove, 1960.

Wordsworth, William. *The Pedlar, Tintern Abbey, The Two-Part Prelude*. Cambridge: Cambridge University Press, 1985.

8

Jia 家, "Family," and the Chinese House

Judy Schaaf

Chinese culture is distinctly "other" to most Westerners, a recognition that can strongly persist through one's improving familiarity with Chinese history, culture, and place. The humanist tradition in the West trains in the belief that human nature transcends the local and specific, that there is fundamental human experience that people from all cultures, and with every variety of personal history, share. Although the Chinese share a cultural experience that is among the most encompassing and ancient in the world, their ways of knowing the world unmoor them from this kind of certainty. Reason, dichotomy, classification, empirical knowing, the idea of the given—features of Western thinking—do not characterize Chinese apperception. The coherence of a Chinese world is aesthetic rather than logical, and its values comparatively anarchical. The usual Western approach to understanding the unfamiliar, to compare it with what one knows and what one believes to be alike, will thus not work well to give one a sense of a Chinese world. As one scholar of Asian cultures puts it: "In a Chinese world, most acorns become squirrels, not oak trees" (Ames). And even the squirrels seem different.

The landscapes of Europe and North America are historical texts. Traveling through the urban or rural scene, one reads the human past inscribed most obviously in the architecture, but just as reliably in other evidence of the appropriation of natural space: in canals and fences, second-growth forests, parks and preserves, the sinuous tangle of highways, and the solid plats and grids of cities, homesteads, suburbs. "Unlike the cities and countryside of the West, which may be read as museums of changing architectural styles, the cultural landscapes of China" have been "remarkably ahistorical" (Knapp, *House* 1). They are now, however, landscapes under vigorous revision, into which a palpable history, connecting China with the rest of the world, is entering. Yet Chinese tradition persists through change and informs it. One European architect, perceiving that continuity, expressed it this way: "Anyone in China seeing for the first time a residential garden of one of the former prosperous scholars and artists in Soochow is overwhelmed by an impression quite alien to European experience.

What is so striking is the visual unity of the scene as a whole. Whereas we in the West are accustomed to seeing, next to Renaissance palaces (of the nineteenth century!), a Baroque facade and then modern blocks of concrete, we find in China, thanks to the continuity of their tradition, only one style of architecture. Each building merges into the rest—even empty space is drawn into the pattern" (Blaser 77).

There is, of course, not really only one style of architecture in China but there is remarkable coherence in the Chinese architectural aesthetic. The West's syncretic architectural traditions, resulting from cultures merging through conquest, influence, and cohabitation, contrast with China's continuities, its cultural cohesiveness, its persisting and gradually developing architectural aesthetic. It is useful to begin at home, literally, to understand any culture. Chinese cultural tradition is centered in, and radiates from, the family, the familial project of home. Because traditional Chinese houses express powerfully the values of Chinese familial tradition, their forms have persisted through millennia, evolving but essentially unchanged. Even as the pressure of the last century has opened China more to the world, the traditional forms of its domestic architecture endure—through profound political change, the difficult demands of increasing urbanism, and a developing world market economy. This chapter examines some traditional features of the Chinese house and explores aspects of the tradition in change. Its purpose is to offer a place to begin to learn about the Chinese family.

The Chinese home is a place of repose, a living space in both senses of the term. Chinese domestic architecture expresses a continuity and simplicity that clarify the daunting complexity and antiquity of Chinese culture. Despite significant variations in regional design, which respond to topography, climate, and cultural infusion, the traditional Chinese house has an essential pattern persistent across both place and time. Its basic aspects traceable to Neolithic times, the Chinese house draws the family together while distinguishing its elements and respecting its hierarchy. The dwelling is so closely identified with its inhabitants that the same word, *jia* 家, represents both the family and its house. To study Chinese domestic architecture is thus one way to study the Chinese family.

The first section below sketches features that belong to Chinese domestic architectural tradition generally. These features—of siting, building technique, proportion, and decoration—establish a baseline for understanding essential Chinese elements of domestic architecture. The next two sections explore very distinct traditional Chinese houses, the urban northern courtyard house (sometimes called the Beijing house) and the earth-sheltered dwelling of the loess soil area of northern China (sometimes called the cave house). These represent pervasive and ancient, though not comprehensive, patterns of Chinese housing, the elements of which are being adapted in new construction for a contemporary, more urban China. The concluding section examines some factors influencing change in China's domestic architectural tradition and looks at some modern adaptations of these traditional forms. Throughout, the chapter explores the Chinese familial ethic expressed in the domestic architectural tradition.

Traditional Elements of the Chinese House

The essential elements of Chinese architecture sketched below—elements of siting, building technique, proportion, and decoration—transcend not only regional differences but also functional differences. "Common and distinctive elements characterize Chinese building plans whether humble dwellings, palaces, or temples from earliest times to the present day. Regional and even local environmental, historical, or ethnic conditions have bequeathed patterns of striking diversity; however, these are insufficient to mask the common tradition" (Knapp, *House* 5).

Confucian Tradition

There is a common tradition of domestic architecture because there is a common Chinese familial tradition. The Chinese family has traditionally conjoined generations, although the idea of the large extended family dwelling in a commodious compound with dependents and servants, the portrait drawn in fictions like the eighteenth-century work usually called *The Dream of the Red Chamber* or the twentieth-century historical novel *Family*, by Ba Jin (Li Feigan), is now under revision. Scholars studying household registers and other historical information are learning that during "most of the two millennia of the imperial period, the average household was fluctuating between five and six, with a very large portion of nuclear families" and "an overwhelming proportion of households were centered around a married couple with possible 'extensions' such as retired parents or single persons (brothers, sisters, or a widowed mother)" (Cartier 308–309). The Chinese family, nevertheless, is traditionally inclusive, not insular, and strongly hierarchical, its behaviors guided by Confucian tradition.

That tradition is ingrained in Chinese culture in the forms of social custom, the rules of engagement for Chinese both within and without the family. But the tradition is not merely applied externally or prescriptively, as such tradition might be in the West, as a code of etiquette. Rather, the tradition actually shapes the world—deeply informs experience, as a body of expectations for the performance not only of the human contract, but also of natural, even cosmic, phenomena. Put simply, the Confucian tradition is the Chinese world.

It is not the purpose of this chapter directly to examine this tradition, which, either explicitly or implicitly, is presented from a different perspective in each of the chapters of this volume. But it is helpful to remember three key features of the Confucian tradition when trying to understand the Chinese family through exploring its home. These features are individually identified here, but they are philosophically inseparable, and discussion of one flows inescapably into consideration of the other two. The Confucian tradition is *ordering*, it is *performative*, and it is *adaptive*. Although these terms are inexact and partial, they give a fair preliminary sense of the character of Confucian tradition. They also provide a conceptual outline for a discussion of the Chinese domestic architectural tradition. Confucian order is manifest in the elements of the shared architectural tradition discussed in the first section below. The performative nature of the tradition is suggested in the next section, which presents the two vernacular styles of the courtyard house and the earth-sheltered house, discussing how Chinese live in these domestic environments. The adaptivity of Confucian tradition is evident in the last section's treatment of the contemporary use and redesign of the Chinese house.

Most fundamentally, the Confucian tradition orders the extant and active phenomena of the world. Its hierarchy of interdependent parts describes a fluent, fully functional universe where relation, and consequently value, do not have the same kinds of meanings they would in the West. It is the first, and usually most difficult, task of a Westerner trying to understand Chinese difference to let go the assumptions of relative worth that belong to Western ways of living in the world, of negotiating its values.

To Chinese, the self is not an isolated individual placed within the frame of a social scheme, although the Confucian hierarchy of relation may make that appear to be the case. The self is, instead, the center of social relationships that are continually achieving shape through the self's own creative transformation. One never masters the art of any relationship, not even briefly. Relationships are processes, continual challenges. The Confucian order, which privileges reciprocity rather than simple authority, provides the enabling context for the art and acts of becoming human. The exemplary person pursues harmony, not sameness, not the image of a role model. There are no specific, discrete models of the *junzi* 君子, or highly realized person. There is no script for the evolving self, in the sense in which European or American cultures script that evolution through personal ethics, secular law, and religious code.

Second, the Confucian tradition performs its principles which exist only through their continual enactment. In China, social experience negotiates shared values within the context of a canonical tradition in which the canon is continually reexamined, to achieve right thinking for each particular time and place. In this sense, the Confucian tradition is radically liberating. The rituals of performance are not mere prescriptions for behavior or guides for the direction of one's attention to the world, but are more like contexts for that behavior and attention. Certainly, prescriptions exist, in places like the *Liji*, or *Book of Rituals*, a compilation of the second century B.C.E., mentioned below. But one has only to sit patiently with a Confucian analect for a time, exploring its suggestions, its evocations, to realize that Confucian experience is not at all static and prescriptive, but instead flexible, exploratory, and, in the root sense of the word, educative.

Third, the Confucian tradition grows by adapting to change. It is accretive, synthetic, forgiving, absorbing. It is in this sense truly a living tradition, and it can be understood as having survived so vigorously for so long significantly because of this feature. The Confucian way of meeting difference, even conspicuous opposition, is to embrace and incorporate that difference. That character of the tradition was established in the third and fourth centuries B.C.E. by Xunzi, a conservative Confucian thinker and the first systematic Confucian philosopher, who appropriated and reshaped the elements of prior and competing philosophies. The adaptive capacity of the Confucian tradition makes and keeps it viable.

These three seminal features of Confucian tradition are expressed in the domestic architectural tradition described below, even where elements of the architectural tradition antedate Confucius, who clarified and developed the great cultural tradition already more than a thousand years old in his time. The Chinese house is a kind of Confucian text itself, expressing traditional understanding in a manner consonant at once with the spiritual and physical needs of the indweller. To enter a traditional Chinese house, even to approach one traditionally situated, is to enter the Chinese world.

Siting

Siting is the most basic shared element of domestic architecture in China, the one least subject to change across regions. The principal axis is from east to west, with the dwelling facing south. Climatic and other environmental conditions help determine this, as does the millennium-old philosophy of *fengshui* 風水, literally "wind and water," with its respect for the spirit of a place and the harmony to be achieved with the spirit of the people who dwell there. *Fengshui* manuals elaborately indicate the allowances and requirements of the complex code with respect to siting a building auspiciously. The principles are more complex and sophisticated than any summary can fairly indicate, but essentially *fengshui* posits

> a universe animated by the interaction of *yin* and *yang* in which an ethereal property known as *qi* ("life breath" or "cosmic energy") gives character and meaning to a place. . . . Accessibility to this mystical ecology is through the medium of a *fengshui shi* or *fengshui xiansheng* ("wind and water interpreter"), sometimes called a geomancer, who can perform the arcane monitoring of building sites. . . . The *fengshui* characteristics of a site are linked to those who will utilize it by relating the time and date of the principal's birth to the particulars of a site. The temporal and spatial personalization of a site isolates for an individual and his family the fund of good fortune that accrues therefrom. In a world of limited resources, *fengshui* provides a means of assuring a reasonable share of good fortune that includes wealth, progeny, good harvests, and official positions. (Knapp, *Rural* 109–10)

Put most simply, *fengshui* offers a way in which one can enter the spirit of a place, can become an indweller there.

Fengshui informs building practice at all economic levels, and of all architectural kinds:

> Observations of common houses throughout urban and rural China confirm a widespread understanding of the attributes of *fengshui*. The great

range of topographic conditions throughout the country naturally militate against a single pattern of siting because the hilly areas of the south and the open plains of central and northern China present quite different environmental circumstances in which *fengshui* can operate. Yet there is no doubt that even uninitiated farmers site dwellings in broad conformity with *fengshui* criteria, using them as rules of thumb rather than restrictive prescriptions. (Knapp, *House* 59)

The principles and practice of *fengshui* apply to Chinese gardens as well as houses, and even to the classic village landscapes of China. "Although it may appear that villages in general display a lack of orderliness, a great many rural settlements indeed have an 'order' derived from geomancy, or *fengshui*. ... Chinese practices of siting demonstrate an environmental awareness, a regard for recurring patterns of nature, and the imposition of an order ... to create village landscapes of beauty and practicality" (Knapp, *Landscapes* 5).

Fengshui, with other traditions, has been dismissively criticized in China since the Maoist era.

A common theme in discussions and in print is the need not only to acknowledge China's *rich* building and planning traditions, but also to go beyond them. For the most part, what appears in print concerning *fengshui* belittles its practice and its practitioners together with other superstitious practices that must be uprooted. Yet professional planners and villagers together generally continue to order new and old settlements in ways that reflect an understanding of traditional *fengshui* elements. (Knapp and Shen 70)

China's official disavowal of *fengshui* principles has been countered by the Western embracing of them. An article in *Fortune* magazine comments playfully on this phenomenon, as expressed in three American examples of the enterprising use of *fengshui*. A California developer, unable to sell five $650,000 homes, hired a *fengshui* consultant, followed her advice about reshaping the landscaping, and sold them all within three months. A New York investment management firm invoked on its business the blessings available through *fengshui* by creating a rock garden with a waterfall as its reception court. Solectron, a California manufacturer of computer circuit boards, inaugurated its new facilty in 1991 with a *fengshui* ceremony. The *Fortune* article, published the next year, comments: "The price of Solectron's shares has since more than tripled. Go figure" (Kirsch).

Building Standards

Traditional Chinese building techniques have evolved over several millennia, as evidenced by the archaeological and historical record. Timber-frame construction, for example, is evident in a relief on a bronze vase of the Zhou dynasty, Warring

States period (403–221 B.C.E.) (Liang 24), and is depicted on clay models of houses from tombs of the Later Han Dynasty (first and second century C.E.).

As Fu notes:

> Judging from known archaeological remains and sites, Chinese traditional architecture may be traced back at least 7,000 years. Though great difference in geographical and climatic conditions cause marked diversity in the architecture of various regions, a unique system based upon wooden framework gradually took shape over several millennia of innovation and synthesis. (10)

Our understanding of the earliest forms of domestic architecture actually depends on the uniformity of principles, techniques, and building materials in Chinese architecture generally, because the earliest physical evidence of domestic architecture dates from the Han period:

> Although the Anyang excavations of palaces and other buildings of the eleventh century b.c. show north-south orientation, axial arrangement and a columnar system of timber construction, and although there are a few indications about houses from fragments of ornamentation on bronze vessels and the like, between the eleventh century b.c. and the end of that millennium, it is really not until the Han Dynasty (206 b.c.-a.d. 220) that anything very graphic appears. From that time, however, besides an actual excavated house floor in Sian and some drawings or low reliefs of houses or parts of houses found on tiles, on stone, and on bricks, there are a fairly large number of pottery models of houses. (Boyd 87)

Early graphic evidence of domestic structures includes a tenth-century painting by Gu Hongzhong [Ku Hung-chung] (910–980) called "Evening Party at Han Xizai [Hsi-tsai]," which "portrays a number of delightful scenes in the interior of a great Tang house" (Boyd 92), and paintings from the Song and Yuan periods, mostly depicting townhouses in the courtyard style. The earliest extant examples of domestic houses belong to the Ming Dynasty (1368–1644). These two-story, shallow-courtyard dwellings near "Hui-chou [Huizhou] at the south-eastern extremity of Anhui province in central China, west of Shanghai," housed mostly merchants and some minor officials (93).

Although the building traditions were deeply embedded in building practice well before they were encoded in text, two records of building practice are known to have survived, and both were published under imperial order. The older is the *Yingzao fashi*, or Building Standards for classic Chinese architecture, which were set forth by Li Jie, a Song Dynasty superintendent of construction at the court of Emperor Huizong, in the early twelfth century. The textual editing was complete by 1100, and the work was published in 1103. The later code is the *Gongbu Gongcheng zuofa zeli*, published in 1734 by the Ministry of Construction of the

Qing Dynasty. Both of these works came into being not to teach craftsmen how to build, but to "facilitate the accounts of public buildings for which the ministries were responsible" (Glahn 48). Not one of the fine arts whose rules and development are documented in Chinese histories, architecture is a craft performed essentially by carpenters responsible for building maintenance as well as construction.

A description of the contents of these texts suggests the character of Chinese architectural tradition, as well as its antiquity. The *Yingzao fashi*

> consists of 34 chapters preceded by an introduction by the editor, Li Jie, on preliminary work and calculation. The first two chapters list 49 terms for construction members, with quotations from literary sources dated from the Zhou Dynasty. The rest of the work can be divided into four parts: rules, labor, materials, and drawings. The first part (chapters 3–16) deals with construction methods for different structural members. The second part (chapters 17–25) discusses work units, that is, the amount of work for each different category that a skilled artisan is expected to carry out in one day. The third part (chapters 26–28) lists the amount of material needed for each type of work and the ratio of ingredients for mortar, plaster, pigments, and glaze. The fourth and last part (chapters 29–34) consists of drawings illustrating details of construction as well as plans and cross-sections of buildings. Each of the four parts is subdivided into twelve sections: moats and fortifications, stone work, carpentry, joinery, wood carving, turning and drilling, sawing, bamboo work, plastering, painting and decoration, brick work, and the manufacture of tiles. (Glahn 48–49)

The Qing text has seventy-four chapters. The first twenty-seven describe construction methods for building frames of different sizes. Chapters 28 through 41 concern bracket sets. Chapters 42 through 47 treat stone and tile construction. Chapters 48 through 60 discuss material, and the last fourteen chapters concern labor.

> In comparison with the Qing manual, the Song *Yingzao fashi* is far better organized and illustrated. The editor, Li Jie, was Vice Director of the Ministry of Public Works Office of Building and well informed about Chinese building. Having received in 1097 an imperial order to edit a manual for public building, Li questioned artisans, who explained everything to him, as he states in his introduction to the *Yingzao fashi*. Because Li himself was in charge of erecting palaces and government buildings in the northern Song capital of Bianliang (modern-day Kaifeng), he was in an excellent position to inquire about building technology. (Glahn 50)

These classic texts, as well as a growing body of contemporary architectural and archaeological scholarship, detail the features, variations, and historical and cultural contexts of the ancient Chinese art of building, whose principles apply at once to public and private construction. Here, we will simplify by describing some basic elements of the construction, proportion, and decoration of the Chinese house, exploring briefly the idea of family expressed in these traditional techniques.

Timber-Frame Construction

This chapter focuses on traditional Chinese houses that employ wood-frame construction, with distinct structural and cladding elements such as load-bearing pillars and non-load-bearing walls. These pervade throughout China and exemplify the oldest identified Chinese housebuilding tradition. The details of these timber-frame houses distinguish Chinese from other Asian domestic housebuilding traditions. In China, structures with load-bearing walls, usually as exterior walls formed most simply from tamped earth or more expensively from adobe or fired bricks and rough or cut stone, occur commonly, as well. They typically share with wood-frame houses the other elements of the common Chinese domestic architectural tradition described below—siting, orientation, and decoration. The oldest technique of shaping load-bearing walls, "pounding earth into solid walls—the *hangtu* [夯土] method of construction—has been used throughout Chinese history as a building technique suitable in times of scarcity for anyone having access to soil" (Knapp, *Vernacular* 70). Tamped-earth walls appear also in fortifications, city walls, and even the Great Wall itself. Although the use of bricks for load-bearing wall construction antedates the Ming period, advances in brick-making technology at that time made bricks inexpensive enough to be used in housebuilding commonly.

Three distinct traditional forms of wood framing had been developed by the beginning of Eastern Han: *tailiang, chuandou,* and *miliang pingding.* "The *tailiang* and *chuandou* framing systems are sometimes mixed in the same dwelling" (Knapp, *Vernacular* 84). The details of these framing traditions are examined in several sources cited at the end of this text. It is unnecessary to pursue those details here, but it is useful to have a general sense of these three framing traditions, because the aesthetic they reflect and shape is quite distinct from that of Western architectural tradition. Also, since the framing style defines the possibilities for interior space, a sense of how the house is framed will help one understand the way the family lives within it. These three forms of traditional Chinese timber frame construction are thus briefly described below.

A *tailiang* structure employs two rows of paired pillars (columns, or posts) along anterior and posterior sides of the structure. On these pillars rest massive horizontal beams supporting struts that carry shorter and shorter beams which support struts that carry purlins to create a sloping roofline (see figure 8.1):

Walls are curtain walls. Although load-bearing walls are not fundamental to the *tailiang* or either of the other two traditional styles of Chinese timber framing, structures are sometimes enlarged through the use of a pair of wooden frames in conjunction with load-bearing walls, especially in long dwellings. . . . A dwelling can be enlarged longitudinally by positioning a matching frame beyond the exist-

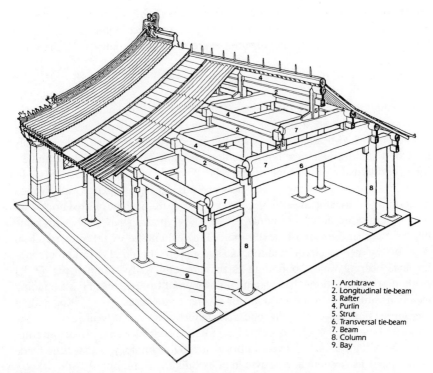

1. Architrave
2. Longitudinal tie-beam
3. Rafter
4. Purlin
5. Strut
6. Transversal tie-beam
7. Beam
8. Column
9. Bay

Figure 8.1 Tailiang construction (Steinhardt, N.S., *Chinese Traditional Architecture.* China Institute Gallery, 1984)

ing structure and adding additional purlins" (Knapp, *House* 41–2). The *tailiang* style is prevalent in central, northern, northwestern, and northeastern China, and it is a style that most Westerners will recognize as identifiably Chinese.

The *chuandou*, or pillar-and-tie, form is common in eastern, southern, and southwestern China. It uses a greater number of pillars than the *tailiang* system and allows for a deeper structure with a more segmented plan. This accommodates the longer summer season and warmer winters of the south.

> Rural houses in southern China are much deeper than those commonly found in north China. With purlins spaced one to one and half meters apart, the depth sometimes reaches ten meters, allowing the interior space to be divided into front and back rooms, a layout rarely encountered in the north. Furthermore, extension beyond the eaves can be added to form a veranda, supported by eaves or peripheral pillars, a common feature of southern dwellings. (Knapp, *House* 42)

The pillars rise successively higher toward the ridgeline, receiving directly the purlins

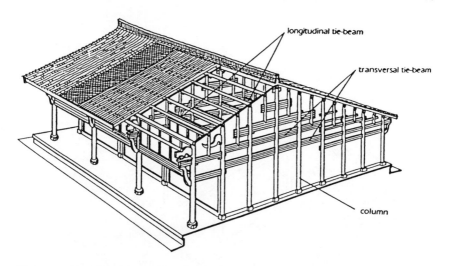

longitudinal tie-beam

transversal tie-beam

column

Figure 8.2 Chuandou construction (Steinhardt, N.S., *Chinese Traditional Architecture.* China Institute Gallery, 1984)

that support the sloping roof. A graduated series of transverse tie beams unites the pillars and steadies the frame. Cladding walls complete the structure (see figure 8.2).

In the *miliang pingding,* or purlin-and-rafter, style, rows of pillars support purlins, which carry horizontal rafters that create a flat roof. Exterior walls support only their own mass. This house style is used commonly in Tibet, Xinjiang, and Inner Mongolia (see figure 8.3).

With its comparatively few pillars and its trait of carrying the structure's weight across two principle axes rather than all four, the *tailiang* method of framing allows greater flexibility for the arrangement of interior space than do the other two systems of pillar and beam construction. But it shares with them a signal feature of all structures that do not depend on load-bearing walls: the interior space may be flexibly apportioned—kept open or divided, at need. As the size of the family, and its proportion of elder and younger, married and single members changes, the spaces housing them can be revised.

Wooden partitions may be added both longitudinally or laterally between columns. The partitioning may assume either "positive" or "negative" modes— "positive," such as sliding screens, folding panels or solid walls that divide the space into parts requiring doors for entry or exit, and "negative," such as *luodizhao* (inverted-U decorative panel), *yuanguangzhao* (moon-door decorative panel) *duobaoge* (open-shelf decorative panel), and *taishibi* (high center screen). The "negative" partitions, being partially closed and requiring no doors, suggest the division of space but allow for free access and some continuity of the line of vision; they thus achieve the effect of "separation" without

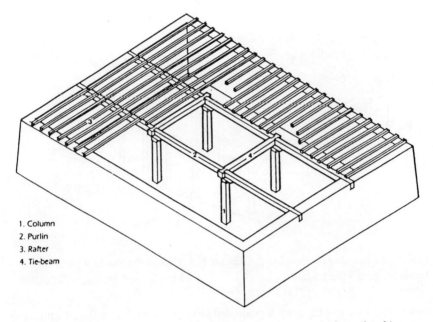

1. Column
2. Purlin
3. Rafter
4. Tie-beam

Figure 8.3 Miliang pinding construction (Steinhardt, N.S., *Chinese Traditional Architecture.* China Institute Gallery, 1984)

"division." In large buildings, the central part may be made into a single floor-to-ceiling story or hall, while the back and two sides may be divided into two stories. Using "positive" and "negative" partitions, it is possible to arrange open and closed interior spaces that are connected and accessible. (Fu 13)

This flexibility, which is aesthetic as well as functional, performs a cohering function not innate to traditional European and North American houses, which are predominantly post-and-beam structures with bearing walls and the functionally specific, patterned division of interior space. The extension and division of the domicile, rather than its interior reshaping, are traditional responses to change in the size and nature of the family in the West. The wing, the "el," and other such additions are built, and eventually separate domiciles are constructed. This is the natural architectural outcome of cultures that celebrate autonomy and individuality, that send the members of the family out to make it on their own. The Chinese architectural tradition reflects other values, values that conserve the connections among members of the family.

Plan and Proportion

Rules of proportion govern the disposition of columns that create the grid for a Chinese timber-frame house. The *jian* 間, or space between columns, is the basic modular unit. This distance, consistent throughout the dwelling, determines its size and proportions, and therefore its overall aesthetic. "No later than Tang (618–907), a modular system with cross-section measurements of each timber, calculated for desired width and depth of the *jian* space, already existed. During Song (960–1279), instructions became even more precise and were recorded in the *Yingzao fashi*, or Building Standards mentioned above" (Fu 13). These *Standards* describe formulae for the length and cross-section of structural elements, with allowable variations that offer the builder some degree of aesthetic freedom.

The smallest dwelling is formed from a single *jian*, or bay, but most houses contain from three to five *jian* linked in a line transverse to the house's principle axis.

> The interdependence of the bay (*jian*) building module and the wooden framework standardizes traditional Chinese architecture to a remarkable degree. As related systems, the bay and wooden framework permit a high degree of flexibility and freedom of design—essential for rural dwellings that normally undergo alteration and expansion as family size and fortune allow. (Knapp, *House* 43)

Jian range in width between three and five meters. The number, width and depth of the *jian* derive from several factors, including regional aesthetics, building function, and the status of the builder: "During the Qing period (1644–1911), imperial sumptuary regulations stipulated that the houses of common people could not exceed three *jian*, houses of officials seven, temples nine, and palaces eleven. . . . Houses with four or six *jian* are rare since they represent inauspicious and asymmetric shapes" (Knapp, *House* 27). Misfortune is implicit in the description of the newlyweds' residence in the 1937 novel *Rickshaw* (Lo-t'o Hsiang Tzu) by Lao She. A two-bay apartment appropriated from space formerly belonging to a family's larger courtyard house, the dwelling has sinister implications for the unhappy couple.

The *jian* allows for various disposition of the interior space, according to the needs of the family dwelling there, but living spaces are disposed by familial tradition, as well. "Chinese folk traditions and the centrality of the family are revealed clearly in the Chinese house. The division and arrangement of space models the family relationships found within the dwelling" (Knapp, *House* 3). The essential plan of the Chinese house combines a common room in the front or center with more private sleeping rooms in the rear or on the sides. "Movement along the axis away from the common room was a passage from public space to private domain. With the courtyard houses of the wealthy, depth along a longitudinal axis represented a similar hierarchical pattern" (53).

In the most basic plan, known as the "one bright, two dark" style, the entry door opens into a single "bright" central common room that is the family's kitchen, storeroom, and ceremonial space. "Dark" sleeping rooms on either side are divided between the elder and younger members of the family. Each features an elevated *kang* 炕, a brick or earthen platform serving as heater and bed. Tradition assigns the eastern sleeping room to the elders, and often the family's best treasures are stored there. This room is also the family's gathering place. The western room usually belongs to the younger generations and often doubles as the storehouse for grain. In each room, the rafters and walls contain hooks, shelves, or poles holding pottery, tools, and other possessions.

Decoration and Furnishings

Chinese folk traditions of symbolic representation are extensive and ancient and affect domestic architectural tradition in a range of ways, from the manner in which a structure is sited and shaped to the way it is adorned. Color, ornament, and furnishings reflect these traditions, as the selective illustrations below indicate. "As with the overall scale of the dwelling, the degree and quality of interior ornamentation reflect the household's wealth and status, though all dwellings share common components" (Knapp, *Vernacular* 117).

Color is integral to architectural design in China, and the Chinese produced some of the most ancient examples of architectural painting. The aesthetics of color in Chinese culture is a complex subject, and only a few features of it will be touched on here. Architectural polychrome painting, or *caihua* 彩畫, is described in writings as early as the Spring and Autumn period (770–476 B.C.E.).

> Since Ming and Qing, red, vermillion, and other warm colors have been widely used in the north on pillars, doors, and windows, while blue, green, and other cool colors, painted in designs similar to those on brocades, are used on *lan'e* or architrave, *duogong*, and other elements that appear in the shadow of the eaves. In southern architecture, except for temples, black and dark brown colors are predominant on exteriors. Northern *caihua* tends to the use of bright colors, while the southern variety is more elegant and subtle; they differ markedly in style. (Fu 13–14)

Red denotes and invites good fortune, particularly in the form of wealth, or *fu* 福, hence its signal use on a house's pillars and portals, and sometimes walls.

> Red has always been a favorite color nationally. With few symbolic restrictions, red (together with its shades of scarlet, crimson, magenta and pink), were fully explored. When opening a store, starting a business, completing a building, and perhaps at a wedding, red firecrackers were exploded from the roof beams. To wedding receptions, guests usually brought two strips of red fabric (silk or cloth) bearing congratulatory poems. (Yau 154)

Similarly, *fu* may be invited to enter a new dwelling by hanging above the lintel a horizontal strip of red paper embossed with the "characters *wu fu lin men* 五福臨門 'the five good fortunes have arrived at the door'" (Knapp, *House* 69).

Other Chinese characters, and the symbols that represent them, commonly ornament a house, appearing on structural elements like carved brackets or posts, beams, cornices, roof tiles, walls, painted gables, or door and window overhangs, or on functional elements like door pulls, ventilation ports, screens, room dividers, paving stones, gates, or shutters. *Shou* 壽 (longevity), for example, may be represented by cranes, evergreen trees, rocks, peaches, tortoises, or deer carved into a lattice panel dividing a room or into the panel of an exterior door. "Within the five good fortunes, aside from longevity only wealth is directly or indirectly depicted in common folk ornamental motifs. . . . Wealth obviously can be represented directly as forms of money, whether round coins with a hole in the centre, cowrie shells, axes, spades, knives, or concave ingots that have served as currency at one time or another in Chinese history" (Knapp, *House* 70–71). Another common symbol for wealth, the carp, represents the achievement of a position of status through long years of scholarship and the passing of the difficult civil service examinations. "The carp is said to metamorphose into a mighty dragon just as a common person can be transformed via the examination route into a successful scholar-official. The depiction of any fish, indeed, is a claim to prosperity understood by all Chinese, because of the homonymic relationship between the characters *yu* [魚 and 餘] representing both fish and abundance" (Knapp, *House* 71).

One common figure in the Chinese house is Zaojun 灶君, the kitchen god, usually represented by a paper image applied within a niche above the stove, an image which is burned at the New Year celebration, and then replaced. Zaojun, introduced to many Western readers by Amy Tan's compelling 1991 novel *The Kitchen God's Wife*, in which he figures malevolently, "serves as a guarantor of household harmony and a symbol of domestic unity" (Knapp, *Vernacular* 144). As Tan depicts him, Zaojun is at best a kind of household spy, whom the family bribe to spread good report at the New Year. Zaojun is courted and appeased during the year by daily lighting incense before his image and, at the New Year, by applying sugar paste to his image's lips just before it is burned to take him on his annual way to the Jade Emperor of Heaven to report on the family members' behavior over the past year (145).

The Baxian 八仙, or Eight Immortals, are also common figures ornamenting a Chinese house, individually, in their common pairings, or as a group. They may appear on any structural or functional element of the house, as well as on forms of fine and decorative arts and crafts, such as in scroll paintings, needlework, shadow puppets, or porcelain. "Singly or in groups, no human figures are more common in the iconography of Chinese homes and temples" (Knapp, *Vernacular* 163). The individual stories of these eight folk heroes, some derived from historical figures, are very well known, although the stories' details vary regionally. The figures are universally recognized through the symbols associated with each story. For example, the most celebrated immortal, Lu Dongbin, always carries a two-edged sword he uses to separate people from their misfortunes and a whip that helps him ride the clouds. The only woman of the group, He Xiangu, who is famed for filial piety and magic, holds either a lotus stem or a kitchen ladle.

Symbolic ornamentation may appear on furnishings, as well as the elements of the house itself. One example common in the Chinese house is the Eight Immortals table:

> Even without an emblematic or pictorial depiction, the Eight Immortals are represented in most Chinese homes by a meter-square table with four long trestle benches. Called *Baxian zhuo* (the Eight Immortals table), this central piece of furniture . . . is a figurative expression of the happiness accompanying the sharing of food and conviviality with family and friends. This table, and not the hearth, is at the core of domestic solidarity in the Chinese home. (Knapp, *Vernacular* 167)

Chinese furniture-building tradition is ancient and employs the same structural principles as architectural tradition. "The earliest wooden timbers yet discovered, from an early Neolithic site at Hemudu south of Hangzhou Bay, exhibit the kinds of mortises and tenons that have always been standard in Chinese furniture and carpentry" (Thorp 61–62). Many excellent studies of Chinese furniture design and building tradition exist, and a few of these are named in this chapter's bibliography.

There is strong, conscious tradition also in the furnishing of the rooms of Chinese houses. "Unlike the Japanese and the Indians, who continued to make more use of the floor, with very low furniture, the Chinese, ever since Tang times if not earlier, have used tables, chairs and bedsteads of similar height to those in Europe" (Boyd 82). A Chinese room usually contains the minimal furniture consonant with its functions. The central *jian* of a simple three-bay house, for example, features a fixed, elevated *kang*, placed either immediately to the left or right of the door, longitudinally, or against the transverse rear wall of the room, and sometimes occupying the whole length of the rear wall. A stove adjacent to the *kang* is connected to it. A small table, a counter for food preparation, a chair or two, a water container, and a wash basin commonly complete the arrangements. Shelves, wall pegs, and ceiling hooks, and sometimes a closet, hold household and personal goods.

The constraints that the loess soil building material places on the dimensions of rooms in an earth-sheltered house make some difference in the furnishings, too, although the traditions described above prevail there, as well. The constrained dimensions,

> impose limits on the type and scale of furniture which can be accommodated within the cave's interior space. Traditionally, furnishings were very simple: a stove for cooking or heating, a heated bed, a small table and chair, a sewing machine and sometimes a closet, a sofa; more recently, radios and even televisions. There are some families with urban-style furniture and others with the simple rural agricultural type. (Golany 104)

The central room of a Chinese house serves ceremonial as well as practical purposes and contains the family's household shrine, which may be as simple as a table or desk displaying the family's most treasured possessions, such as paintings and ancestral objects and documents, and exhibiting photographs and other representations of the ancestors themselves. In more elaborate houses, there is, of course, greater variety and elegance of furnishing, but the aesthetic of Chinese furnishings celebrates utility and visual economy even in these houses.

Two Traditional Chinese Houses

The preceding section explored commonality in Chinese houses, looking at elements they share through China's ancient, highly evolved, consciously articulated domestic architectural tradition. This section investigates difference, looking at two distinct variations in housing design, to give a sense of the architectural variety that is consonant with such shared tradition. Two different vernacular housing types that belong to and derive from a common, ancient courtyard-house tradition are described here, one fundamentally urban, and the other fundamentally rural. They are: the northern courtyard, or Beijing, house and the earth-sheltered dwelling of the loess-soil region of northern China. The discussion of these styles exemplifies the domestic principles and practices discussed earlier and provides a clearer sense of the Chinese family at home. A concluding section treats some of the forces of change in contemporary Chinese architecture and architectural adaptation, focusing on elements of courtyard and earth-sheltered house design that are being consciously employed or reinvented for the purposes of a new, increasingly urban China.

The Northern Courtyard House

A pervasive pattern in northern China, expressed in domestic architecture across a range from the most modest and rural of dwellings to the elegant, extended residences of the urban privileged, the courtyard house is traceable through funerary pottery to the early Han period. In its classic and basic form, the courtyard dwelling is a balanced arrangement of structures, oriented south, gathered by an enclosing wall, and facing a central open space. Sheltered from its surroundings by both the inwardly looking arrangement of the buildings and the presence of an enclosing wall with few or no apertures, the courtyard house classically expresses the Chinese familial ethos of privacy within community and mediates the contact of natural and human natural worlds.

A classic courtyard house combines architectural and decorative effects harmoniously and dynamically, to pleasing effect, a recent Western visitor to a Qing Dynasty house in Luoyang, completed in 1733, observed:

> A walled compound, with four pavilions spaced across three internal courtyards, the building complex had been a merchant's guildhall during the

imperial era. The pavilions were dilapidated, and the wood was unpainted and infested with termites, but their forms were almost perfectly intact, and they were infinitely more elaborate and more beautiful than any of the twentieth-century remakes of ancient buildings that we had seen. The eaves were an explosion of architectural detail, actual works of sculpture in wood, like the flying buttresses of a Gothic cathedral that mutate into gargoyles. The finials were fashioned into writhing serpents or roaring dragons; the latticework was carved, like lace, into a pattern of peonies and birds. The wooden beams on the ceilings were painted in astonishing vermillions, lapis lazulis, and gold leaf—the colors at once more brilliant and more subtle than anything in the Forbidden City. There was a remarkable glazed terracotta emblem of a dragon and a phoenix—simultaneously a painting and a sculpture—which rivaled the ceramic sculptures of the Della Robbia brothers in Renaissance Florence. (Stille 42)

The courtyard house pattern is ancient and flexible, examples display an enormous variety, and the style is not restricted to domestic architecture. Figure 8.4 illustrates a simple expression of the style.

Entering through a door typically situated well off-center along an exterior wall not facing the main street, the visitor steps into a narrow courtyard, a transition space that does not reveal the size or character of the dwelling proper. Often a "spirit wall" defends the house and delineates the reception court from the inner court-

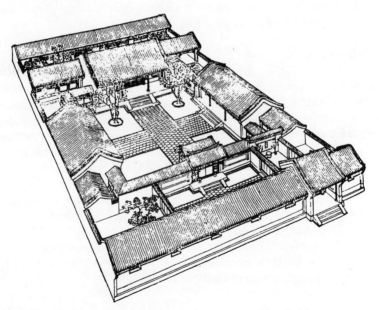

Figure 8.4 A courtyard house

yard. Service rooms, for storage, servants, and perhaps cooking, lie along the external court.

Approaching a usually smaller and often circular, keyhole, or other-shaped opening, the visitor enters the territory of the central court. This is commonly a slightly sunken courtyard, often decoratively paved, containing trees, ornamental gardens, and stone sculptures. Facing south on the inner court and centered on the enclosure's northern wall, the primary dwelling houses the senior members of the family and is typically a three *jian* structure, perhaps with a shallow colonnaded porch. A guest house or house for the family of a married son faces this from the dwelling's opposite wall. Other children's houses and/or storage buildings range along the east and west axes. The cluster contains spaces both public and private, organized centripetally, drawing the outside to the center.

Coming into the courtyard house is an experience of deepening privacy and inclusion, although public and private are not absolute concepts in Chinese culture. They are relative, and thus continually shifting, concepts. What is private in one context is public in another. What is performed or experienced privately may have profound public—social or political or even cosmological—significance. All acts adhere and all inform. Ideally, one's actions express *li* 禮. *Li*, although usually statically defined as "ritual," is dynamic, enactive, and creative. *Li* expresses a cultural ethos, through forms that exist only when filled out, shaped, by the actions they guide. The courtyard house makes a stage for such enactment.

Performed traditionally, the experience of coming within the house derives from and reflects social tradition encoded in the *Liji*, or *Book of Rituals*, compiled in the early Han period, during the second century B.C.E. but most influential through the brief chapter called the *Daxue*, *"The Great Learning."* In the fourteenth century, the *Daxue* was combined with the *Doctrine of the Mean*, the *Analects*, and the *Mencius* to become one of the Four Books, the core curriculum for an educated person, and the textual basis of the Chinese examination system. The contiguous and continuous character of "ritual" experience is expressed in this Confucian passage of the *Daxue*:

> The ancients who wished to illustrate illustrious virtue throughout the kingdom, first ordered well their own States. Wishing to order well their States, they first regulated their families, they first cultivated their persons. Wishing to cultivate their persons, they first rectified their hearts. Wishing to rectify their hearts, they first sought to be sincere in their thoughts. Wishing to be sincere in their thoughts, they first extended to the utmost their knowledge. Such extension of knowledge lay in the investigation of things.
>
> Things being investigated, knowledge became complete. Their knowledge being complete, their thoughts were sincere. Their thoughts being sincere, their hearts were then rectified. Their hearts being rectified, their persons were cultivated. Their persons being cultivated, their families were regulated. Their families being regulated, their States were rightly governed. Their States

being rightly governed, the whole kingdom was made tranquil and happy. (Legge I: 357–59)

The design of the courtyard house makes a stage for the expression, the enactment, of such harmonious, continuous relationship of public and private, inner and outer, the natural (apprehended through what the *Daxue* calls "the investigation of things") and the human natural. The *Liji* sets forth in thoroughgoing detail the behaviors appropriate to entering a house:

> The passing of each gateway is a penetration into new depths of someone's privacy. . . . The honored guest . . . is received with the greatest respect in the hall facing the main courtyard, but the private quarters of the house where the family dwells is beyond, and only intimate guests and relatives may enter there. The dual quality of the house, as a setting for ceremony and as a home, is a most important characteristic of the house as an image of human relationship. (Wu 33–34)

Because the house is "an image of human relationship," traditions of architectural design correspond with "ceremony." "All the components of the building" derive from rules whose purpose is "to allow a large number of people to live together in civilized harmony in a very small space" (Blaser 10). The urban courtyard design accomplishes this end with especial grace and economy. The design appropriates nature to domestic use, conserving it within the built environment. The house is "arranged round a completely secluded centre which is an outdoor space" (9). Where an open vista engages the eye more strongly than other senses, the enclosed garden encourages a wider sensual appreciation, a more deliberate participation. "As the wall blocks only the view, thus creating a visual privacy, it offers a particularly refreshing experience of communication with the outside through the senses of hearing and smell. Chinese literature abounds with examples describing city life through the sounds of the peddlers on the streets and the scent of the flowering trees coming over such a wall" (Wu 32).

The Earth-Sheltered Dwelling

The vast loess-soil regions of the highlands of north and northwest China (through which the Yellow River runs), and the soils of which give it its color and name, have housed Chinese in earth-sheltered dwellings for more than four thousand years. This visually stunning territory, featured in the film *Yellow Earth*, has the highest concentration of Paleolithic and Mesolithic sites in China. Called therefore the cradle of Chinese civilization, it is the region where Chinese earth-sheltered dwellings evolved, a kind of dwelling which today still houses as many as forty million people in China.

The oldest extant Chinese book, the *Yijing*, or *Book of Changes*, dating from the Western Zhou period of the eleventh to eighth centuries B.C.E., refers to earth-sheltered dwellings, and references occur in other ancient Chinese texts spanning the three millennia from that period to our time, such as the *Shijing*, or *Book of Songs* (tenth to seventh centuries B.C.E.) and the *Liji*, or *Book of Rituals*, compiled in the second century B.C.E.. Although these dwellings may have belonged to Bronze Age culture in China, "it is assumed among Chinese researchers that widespread construction of cave dwellings began only during the Han dynasty, that cave-building techniques reached a mature stage in the Sui and Tang dynasties, and that the large-scale proliferation of cave dwellings did not occur until the Ming and Qing periods" (Golany, *Earth-Sheltered* 7). Today, an interesting body of scholarship on this dwelling type is developing as a result of the investigations not only of traditional scholars such as archaeologists, historians, and anthropologists, but also of architects, engineers, urban planners, and others with more practical interest in the technology and aesthetics of earth-sheltered housing.

Commonly but imprecisely called cave dwellings (*yaodong* 窯洞 or *dixia jianzhu* 地下建築), Chinese earth-sheltered houses are part of the courtyard house tradition. They are of two basic types, pit and cliff houses. Although a village may combine these two types, most villages employ one form predominantly or exclusively, and local terrain and soil conditions govern the choice. Chinese cliff houses do not resemble those which characterize indigenous architecture of the American West, such as the Anasazi villages of Mesa Verde in Colorado, which climb seemingly inaccessible vertical cliffs. Not designed with defense in mind, and terraced and ramped, Chinese cliff villages allow ready access to both human and animal inhabitants.

> Cliff type villages typically utilize a site that cannot be used for other purposes, yet leave the soil above for agricultural development. Here, dwellings and other associated built forms in the village are primarily dug into the vertical face of terraced cliffs. The excavated soil is usually spread before each dwelling to create a fronting terrace, which is frequently surrounded by a wall to form a courtyard. (Golany, "Village" 156)

Pit-type dwellings predominate on the loessial plateau, where the land is flat or gently rolling. The number and arrangement of pits in older villages is idiosyncratic, reflecting historical development, but in newer ones, a grid system often governs the villages overall design. From an aerial perspective, the grid resembles a checkerboard with one of its colors punched below the surface.

> Following tradition, extended family dwelling units include from four to eight or more subterranean rooms. Most such dwellings have two rooms on each of the four sides. . . . Pit dwellings satisfy in a unique design the traditional Chinese concept of enclosure and intimacy within the dwelling unit. In some cases, the common vernacular practice of constructing a series of two court-yards is followed, providing a transitional space through an entryway that is formed from a graded stairway constructed partly underground and partly open to the sky. (Golany, "Village" 159)

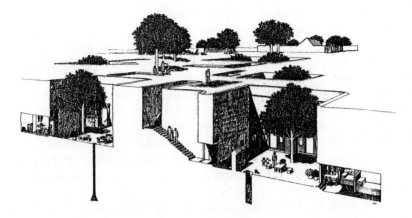

Figure 8.5 A pit-style earth-sheltered dwelling

If the village does not include surface structures, it is invisible to approach from the plateau. The rims of the pits are seldom walled or otherwise demarcated.

Earth-sheltered dwellings have been traditionally identified with rural poverty, although they can be both commodious and comfortable. Cliff dwellers, for example, "enjoy a direct view of the surrounding area, especially the nearby lowlands, and thus are able to overcome the feeling of confinement associated with living in below-ground spaces" (Golany, "Village" 158). Since 1949, the government has taken special interest in subterranean housing, because of its economies of material and construction, and because it offers a tempered environment inexpensive to heat.

In either form, pit dwellings or cliff houses, the living spaces might be either fully subterranean or only partially so. Neolithic Banpo, now a museum site near Xian, the capital of Shaanxi, is one example of a semisubterranean village, built on a flat site. Its dwellings and storehouses, dug into the earth, appear half-sunken. The community is encircled by a moat about six meters deep and wide. Some sites combine above-ground or semisubterranean dwellings at ground level (at the top of a plateau) with sunken courtyards around two or three sides of which are houses dug into the cliffsides. This form is exemplified by the sunken courtyard dwellings in Quian Ling, Henan province, by those in Zhongtou village near Luoyang, Henan, and by others illustrated in sources cited here (Blaser, Boyd, and, most extensively, Golany). A basic illustration of a common type appears in figure 8.5.

For our purposes, the most interesting aspect of the Chinese earth-sheltered dwellings is not their difference from surface housing, but their continuity with it.

> The study of cave dwelling architecture should be viewed within the overall context of Chinese vernacular architecture and the forces that shape it. There is a unity and continuity in the basic principles of Chinese house design, a tradition that has been adhered to in most geographical regions of China.

For example, the roots of the principal cave dwelling design motifs are also to be found in the so-called Beijing house and in the Nanjing round dwelling (*yuanzhai*) typical of Hunan province. All these forms are derived from earlier prototypes of the courtyard house. (Golany, *Earth-Sheltered* 1)

Thus the aesthetic, ritual, and practical features of the northern courtyard house, discussed above, pertain as well to these courtyard habitations, with some physical differences. For obvious example, the dwelling space is necessarily built into the wall enclosing the sunken-courtyard, earth-sheltered dwelling compound, rather than being only embraced by it. Also, chambers are rarely constructed within a southern wall, which is always in shade. Instead, "stairs, a ramp, or both are usually cut into the soil from the south to provide access to the level land above which is used for planting and drying crops" (Knapp, *House* 17).

The traditional orientation and dispensation of living spaces that belong to the northern courtyard house tradition applies as well to the typical pit or cliff earth-sheltered dwelling:

A southern orientation has been applied consistently throughout the history of Chinese urban and house design. The rooms of pit cave dwellings usually surround the patio on all four sides. The rooms on the side facing north are used for storage, for housing livestock, and for the stairway or ramp to the patio. Rooms that face east and west receive less sunlight than those facing south; however, all are used as living areas. Typically, rooms facing south are occupied by senior family members while the children occupy rooms that face east and west. (Golany, *Earth Sheltered* 90)

With some constraints created by local soil and climate conditions, especially precipitation, the earth-sheltered house can be almost as flexible as surface houses with respect to the redesign of living space in response to change in the number or relationship of the family's members, in the family's economic or social status, or in other circumstances affecting the configuration of dwelling space. Distinct regional variations in design exist, and these variations are further focused by village designs that respond directly to the challenges and opportunities of the local terrain.

In addition to having the compositional and social traditions of the courtyard house in common with the northern courtyard house, the earth-sheltered dwelling is, like the other style, importantly contributing to the continuity of Chinese vernacular architectural tradition by exporting some of its key features to the developing contemporary architecture of China, particularly of urban China. As mentioned earlier, earth-sheltered houses are being intently studied precisely because they are considered to have lessons to impart about building ecology and economy, as well as building aesthetic. "These dwellings require the use of very few, if any, building materials, demand only low levels of technology, and are far cheaper to build than equivalent aboveground units. Awareness of environmental design constraints should lead architects and urban designers to improve on these housing settlement forms in order to meet modern needs and standards of living" (Golany 108). This chapter's concluding section, on tradition and change in Chinese domestic architecture, indicates some ways in which that is now happening.

Tradition in Transition: The Contemporary Chinese House

Political, social, and economic change in modern China continues to reshape domestic architectural tradition. Material as well as social incentives, a few of which are sketched here, influence the revision of the practices and forms that have prevailed for millennia. Tradition has survived the changes but is continually under challenge and, to an extensive degree, particularly in urban places, requires reconstruction:

> In this century, governmental attitudes as well as those of educated Chinese have not been kind to tradition. Congeries of social, economic, and political forces, in addition, have buffeted the Chinese people and the Chinese landscape with a corrosive effect on many long-held beliefs and practices. By 1911, the decay of the imperial system and the crumbling of the Confucian precepts which underpinned it was obvious, yet there was nothing substantial to take its place. China's effort to meet this challenge, to regenerate and transform the country into a modern state, often placed "tradition" in an adversarial position. (Knapp, *Vernacular* 175–76)

The Forces of Change

The arts and acts of housebuilding, which have traditionally belonged to craftsmen in China, are increasingly the province of architects and urban planners, in part because the craft tradition deteriorated during the long lapse in housebuilding occasioned by the political and economic phenomena of the twentieth century:

> With the first wave of industrialization, following the Republican Revolution, which overthrew the last emperor, in 1911, the tradition of conserving by rebuilding began to falter, and fell completely out of favor by 1949, when the Communists came to power and condemned most of the imperial art as useless baggage of a feudal society. (Stille 37)

As the economy has improved more recently, "countless unskilled workers, in search of high pay and a trade, are learning on the job or in fewer cases as apprentices to once-skilled building craftsmen" (Knapp, *House* 78). The iconoclasm of the New Culture Movement has not only negatively valued the physical and cultural traditions, but also erased their expressions in the built environment. Household ornamentation provides an interesting example. The folk traditions of decoration discussed earlier, culturally transmitted across both time and place, have suffered seriously, particularly during the Cultural Revolution's deliberate destruction of the emblems of the past. As a result, much of the architectural "text" is gone, and its absence affects both the older and younger generations.[1]

> [Many] aging Chinese have only a vague remembrance of the vestigial calligraphic phrases and historical vignettes adorning old buildings. For many of the young people, the symbols are opaque and obsolete, mere ornamentation without meaning. Many of China's youth are ambiguously insecure about the past with a ready willingness to abandon it and adopt whatever is considered superior because of its foreign or technological origin. (Knapp, *Vernacular* 177)

The construction of communes has radically changed the appearance of the Chinese countryside, not only where new villages have been created but also where traditional ones remain but have been reconfigured. "Communes not only preserved and enhanced collective ownership as the means of production, but also created a hierarchical structure of organization that imprinted the countryside with many patterns and forms that endure to the present" (Knapp and Shen 51). Many older traditional structures were destroyed or made over, large new community facilities were constructed, and, in some areas, nearby villages were organized into cooperatives. The remaking of Dazhai, a Maoist model commune, is an important example. Dazhai "was a small village of eighty-two households farming some 80 hectares of rocky and hilly land in a semiarid area of the Taihang Mountains in Shanxi province of north China. The herculean efforts of the villagers of this vanguard brigade to overcome difficulty were used to inspire other villagers throughout the country in self-reliant rural construction" (56–57). The destruction of most of Dazhai's traditional earth-sheltered pit and surface dwellings in 1963 "led to the complete refashioning of the village itself. Within three years, some two hundred stone-lined caves and more than five hundred dwelling rooms were constructed" (57) in a scheme which replaced traditional patterns with a geometrically regular row-house pattern. In 1964, Chairman Mao made Dazhai a model of socialist development and caused it to be widely emulated.

During the periods of the Great Leap Forward and the Cultural Revolution (1958–1976), political policy directly influenced domestic architecture in other ways. The campaign to resettle urbanites, particularly students, in the countryside caused change in two basic ways. Village families had to absorb large numbers of inexperienced urbanites, with consequent disruption to their traditions of communal living. Also, much new housing had to be constructed to accommodate the migration. This construction "ranged from clearly substandard huts, about which many complaints were issued in the press and in letters home, to substantial brick dormitory-style barracks, which stood in striking contrast to existing village housing stocks" (Knapp and Shen 63). The experience of one young student sent from her home in Chengdu to live in Ningnan, a remote village in Sichuan, is memorably depicted in the 1991 book *Wild Swans,* a family history by Jung Chang. "The village had prepared a residence for us, made of timber and mud and comprising two big rooms—one for the four boys, and one for the four girls. A corridor led to the village hall, where a brick stove had been built for us to cook on" (384).

Since 1949, traditional urban and rural domestic designs have, to some extent, exchanged places. Design that economizes space and preserves privacy—typically urban design and, in China, predominantly courtyard house design—has characterized communal village construction in and since the Maoist era.

> There has been a "townization" of many villages with the creation of geometrically regular settlement forms that echo the spatial structures of Chinese urban places—axial symmetry, an intersecting grid system of paths and roads oriented to the cardinal directions, parallel rows of south-facing dwellings, centrally located administrative offices and services, and sometimes the enclosure of the settlement by a "wall." (Knapp and Shen 47)

Conversely, the advantages of earth-sheltered construction, traditionally a rural domestic technology, have been adapted increasingly in urban environments, for both public works projects and housing, including dormitory construction.

Demographic change resulting from China's one-child policy poses another set of challenges to domestic architectural tradition. It has influenced the increasing construction of single-family dwellings, in a culture where community living has prevailed. "Throughout China, one sees parents continuing to live in their old dwelling, while building and outfitting a new house for their adult children. A concession perhaps for separation is proximity, since parents and married children often live in adjacent dwellings or nearby" (Knapp, *House* 80). Newer construction in the village of Xinxing [Hsin Hsing] in Taiwan exemplifies this trend. Traditionally, village houses "tended to be clustered together in small compounds, reflecting the fact that Hsin Hsing is a multisurname and multilineage (*zu or tsu*) village" (Gallin and Gallin 282). The addition of wings accommodated increase in the family's size. Today, households belonging to the same *zu* 族 continue to live proximately, but "many related families have built houses that are designed like duplex apartments. Families of brothers or patricousins each have their own homes in one of the several narrow buildings that abut each other. Some families have erected free-standing houses in sections of the village distant from the compound where their original apartments stood" (289). Conservative policies regarding land use, particularly in the economic reform period since 1978, have made a counterbalancing influence to the trend for separation of dwellings, however.

Conservative policies regarding land and the use of other resources also influence housing by restricting the employment of traditional materials and methods, especially tamped-earth construction and the use of wood for framing. These policies have power pervasively to change domestic architectural tradition. In adjacent portions of the southern provinces of Fujian and Guangdong since the third or fourth century, for instance, the Hakka, a Han Chinese ethnic subgroup, have established walled villages of communal houses founded in common Chinese architectural tradition but responding to unique cultural imperatives and historical conditions. The plans of Hakka dwellings take a variety of forms, rectangular, circular, and other, but they share basic features. Axial arrangement and symmetry define their plans. The buildings are multistoried and communal, intermixing structures of different heights and purposes. The compound contains both private and public spaces, organized around a central courtyard that contains a hall for guests and for ceremonial use, and usually encloses peripheral courtyards, as well. The compound is ringed by a high wall, built of rammed earth several meters thick. To form lasting load-bearing walls in large structures, the poorer soil predominantly used in tamped earth, or *hangtu*, construction must be mixed with more arable elements, like silt. The construction of Hakka *tulou* 土樓 or earth-buildings, have thus been affected by modern soil-use policies. "Villagers state that none has been built since the 1950s, principally because of strict adherence to policies that forbid the use of the raw material used to construct them" (Laude 166). This distinctive building tradition, whose aesthetic hallmark is the massive fortifying earthen wall, has not adapted by changing building materials. Instead, in "recent decades, only small buildings with limited materials requirements have been built" (166)

New technologies and materials are themselves changing the aesthetic and structural aspects of the domestic architectural tradition. New technologies include active solar designs and reinforced concrete. Nontraditional building materials include prefabricated cement elements such as hollow-core spans, stairs, purlins, or lintels. Structural timber, such as traditional wooden pillars and beams, are increasingly being replaced by reinforced concrete, especially in structures rising more than two stories. Decorative wooden elements, such as lintels and screens, are being replaced by prefabricated concrete. The improving economy has encouraged domestic building since the 1980s. Much of the new construction has been substandard, but the Chinese tendency remains to build as well as one can afford.

Syncretic, innovative building practices, both physical and aesthetic, result from China's increasing interchange with Western cultures and from its own better communication with itself. "In order to go beyond the traditional 'new dwellings in the old style' (*xin fangzi, lao yangzi* [新房子, 老房子]), new design criteria have been drafted by architects and planners throughout the 1980s. A principal impetus has been the need to reduce building lot size, conserve materials, and improve the use of space. Designs have been solicited via provincial and national competitions and popularized in countless plan books and manuals" (Knapp and Shen 66). Since 1981, the government has sponsored national competitions for domestic architectural design. The first prize that year went to a design for duplex housing in south China, a design so traditional it resembles the Han funerary pottery, mentioned above, that is among of the earliest surviving physical evidence of the courtyard house design.

The Strength of Tradition

In addition to ways in which new buildings are being constructed with respect to ancient principles and practices, the continuity of the architectural tradition is demonstrated by the ways in which old buildings are being put to new uses. The Xishi [Hsi-shih] Lane kindergarten in Beijing, for example, was a typical, one-story northern courtyard house of the Qing Dynasty. It has a load-bearing timber frame and brick curtain walls. Before it became a school in 1953, it was (in 1911) the residence of a highly placed military official of the Guomindang. It was "faultlessly renovated and restored" when converted:

> Eight buildings arranged round the court provide play room, recreation rooms, and administrative offices for 200 children and 40 adults, 100 of the children also being accommodated overnight. The kitchen, toilets, and equipment rooms are located in buildings adjoining at the sides. Encircling galleries with gates join two almost square courts. Smaller courts, each of which has an elongated dwelling court at its end, complete the whole. . . . Two square courts, symmetrically patterned, are used as a playground. (Blaser 16)

Another Beijing courtyard house from the Qing period, previously owned by a "high Mandarin politician," was converted to use in 1949 as a government office and, a decade later, became a Szechwan restaurant. "During the renovations the 'spirit wall' near the entrance gate was removed, and lateral buildings and courts for small groups were added to the restaurant" (34).

A study of such conversions inspires both admiration and anxiety. The forces of change affecting China today create real risk for its cultural traditions, even though the traditions are strong, coherent, and ancient. Caution about the risks of change need not, however, promote despair. Aesthetic and functional at once, and intimately bound up with philosophical tradition, the domestic architecture of China helps preserve its history and cultural identity. "As the elementary space in which a family lives and works, the house resonates the tensions between continuity and innovation which characterize China today. . . . There is nonetheless not yet a cascade of innovation of sufficient magnitude to obliterate tradition" (Knapp, *Vernacular* 178). China is fortunate to be experiencing such change during a time when it is possible for both Chinese and those from other cultures to observe, record, and critique change and to see it as challenge and opportunity.

A generation ago, China was essentially a large white space on the world map for most Westerners, undelineated territory with uninscribed margins. Only superficially included in the American secondary school social studies curriculum, for instance, China was studied there in terms of its geographical features, its production and consumption statistics, and its modern history related to Western contact. American students of that generation had only a dim perception of China's antiquity, its interior history, its literature and art, and its cultural traditions. Most American universities had not begun to include Asia in the undergraduate curriculum, either as part of core learning or as individual offerings in the disciplines. Their focus was on the West and on selected aspects of Western culture, studied primarily through a literary canon emerged from Greek and Roman tradition.

The profound political and economic forces of change shaping China and East Asia in this century have conspired to keep closed the doors to better Western understanding of Asian cultures. While the sturdy habit of Western scholarship and exploration of China continued through the dramatic changes that the twentieth century has brought to this immense and variegated land that is home to well over one billion people, China has been only very recently available to the general scholar. It is becoming available rapidly now, in a wealth of ways that could not have been predicted a generation ago. These include: proliferating forms of traditional humanities scholarship, both discipline focused and interdisciplinary; forms of practical scholarship, such as scientific and technological inquiry new to Western study of China; and forms of popular cultural representation of Chinese experience and culture. Chinese films, fictions, and art offer the new student of China particularly appealing ways to begin to see the Chinese family and house. Although it is always unsafe to trust film and fiction to represent a culture with which one is not already deeply familiar, they can be good resources to include. Contemporary Chinese film, which tends to documentary visual representation, offers superior examples, as for instance the films of Zhang Yimou (including *Raise the Red Lantern, Ju Dou,* and *To Live*)[2] and of Chen Kaige (including *Yellow Earth* and *Farewell My Concubine*).

Chinese literature before the modern period is practically devoid of domestic description. Luo Guanzhong's massive fourteenth-century historical novel *Three Kingdoms* is typical in offering none across the broad territory of its thousand pages. Two basic facts help account for this. First, China is so imbued with an ancient, common domestic tradition, as discussed above, that its literature, assuming a Chinese audience, would not need to depict setting to the extent that such depiction is either required or useful in Western literature, with its more independent domestic cultures. Second, Chinese fictional tradition has been, until very recently, almost entirely shaped by men, in a culture which allots to women the management of purely domestic concerns. Chinese literature classically focuses on the domains of men: war and polity. By contrast, the Japanese fictional tradition, developed significantly by women, offers much more domestic information, as exemplified in the eleventh-century *Tale of Genji,* by Murasaki Shikibu. Later Chinese fiction, however, makes up for the absence of domestic detail in earlier works. Of modern Chinese classics, *The Dream of the Red Chamber* is especially rich in domestic description, most of it related to human interaction but some of it architectural, and thus offers a good starting point for the student of Chinese domestic culture. From that point, employing both traditional and novel scholarly resources for understanding the Chinese family—the resources of history, philosophy, anthropology, musicology, archaeology, folklore studies, literary study, and other disciplines—one can explore the Chinese domestic world from within, a place from which the "other" is one's former, uninitiated, uninformed self.

Glossary

Baxian Eight Immortals of Chinese folk tradition; represented individually, in traditional pairs, or in a group, they commonly adorn the Chinese house; in one traditional form, the Eight Immortals table or *Baxian zhuo,* they express familial unity and hospitality.

Beijing house A term commonly used to designate the traditional Chinese urban northern courtyard house.

Book of Songs One of the Confucian classics, sometimes translated as *The Book of Poetry* or *The Book of Odes;* written as *Shijing, Shi Jing,* or *She King.*

Chuandou construction A traditional form of timber-frame construction, common in eastern, southern, and southwestern China; chuandou construction features cladding walls and several rows of pillars successively rising toward a ridgeline and carrying purlins that support a sloping roof.

Dazhai A Maoist model commune in mountainous Shanxi Province in north China; Dazhai's traditional earth-sheltered pit and surface dwellings, destroyed in 1963, were refashioned by this vanguard brigade into about two hundred stone-lined caves.

Fu Good fortune, particularly in the form of wealth; *fu* is associated with the color red, with certain animals or fish such as the carp, with money, and with emblems of items that have historically served as currency, such as cowrie shells, axes, or concave ingots.

Gongbu Gongcheng zuofa zeli An eighteenth-century building code published by the Ministry of Construction of the Qing Dynasty.

Jian The space between columns in a Chinese timber-frame house, ranging between three and five meters in width; the *jian* as the basic modular unit was established by the Tang period, during which a modular system with cross-section measurements of each timber, calculated for desired width and depth of the *jian* space, already existed.

Miliang pinding construction A traditional form of timber-frame construction, common in Tibet, Xinjiang, and Inner Mongolia; *miliang pinding* construction features load-bearing exterior walls and rows of pillars supporting purlins that carry horizontal rafters to create a flat roof.

Purlin A longitudinal member in a roof frame, usually used to support common rafters.

Tailiang construction A traditional form of timber-frame construction, common in central and northern China in both domestic and public architecture; a *tailiang* structure features an anterior and a posterior row of paired pillars, massive horizontal beams, a sloping roofline, and curtain walls.

Yingzao fashi The early-twelfth-century Building Standards for classic Chinese architecture, compiled by Li Jie, a Song Dynasty superintendent of construction at the court of Emperor Huizong.

Zaojun The Chinese "kitchen god," usually represented by a paper image applied in a niche above the stove and burned, then replaced at the New Year's celebration; when burned, the image ascends to report to the Jade Emperor on the family's behavior during the year past.

Notes

1. Stille writes, "The Chinese, for the most part, are surprisingly unsentimental about these changes. 'The Cultural Revolution not only destroyed our monuments; it destroyed people's feelings for them,' said a sensitive young architect. . . . 'It killed off the sense of beauty'" (39).

2. See Bettye Walsh's chapter "Family in the Seventh Art: Modern Chinese Film," for a discussion of *Raise the Red Lantern* and *To Live.*

Works Cited

Ames, Roger T. Presentation on the *Yijing*. NEH Summer Seminar, Chinese Classics in Translation. St. Mary's College, Maryland. 20 June 1996.

Blaser, Werner. *Courtyard House in China: Tradition and Present (Hofhaus in China: Tradition und Gegenwart)*. Basel, Switzerland: Birkhauser Verlag für Architektur, 1979; 2 ed., 1995.

Boyd, Andrew. *Chinese Architecture and Town Planning, 1500 B.C.–A.D. 1911*. Chicago: University of Chicago Press, 1962.

Cartier, Michel. "Nuclear Versus Quasi-Stem Families: The New Chinese Model." *Journal of Family History* 20. 3 (1995): 307–327.

Chang, Jung (Jung Chang). *Wild Swans: Three Daughters of China*. New York: Simon and Schuster, 1991; rpt. Anchor, 1991.

Fu Xinian, "Chinese Architectural Tradition." Trans. Virginia Weng. *Architectural Heritage of the Bronze Age*. Ed. Nancy Shatzman Steinhardt. New York: China House Gallery, April 6–June 10 (1984): 10–33.

Gallin, Rita S., and Bernard Gallin. "Hsin Hsing Village, Taiwan: From Farm to Factory." *Chinese Landscapes: The Village as Place*. Ed. Ronald G. Knapp. Honolulu: University of Hawaii Press, 1992. 279–93.

Glahn, Else. "Unfolding the Chinese Building Standards: Research on the *Yingzao fashi*." *Architectural Heritage of the Bronze Age*. Ed. Nancy Shatzman Steinhardt. New York: China House Gallery, April 6–June 10 (1984): 48–57.

Golany, Gideon S. *Chinese Earth-Sheltered Dwellings: Indigenous Lessons for Modern Urban Design*. Honolulu: University of Hawaii Press, 1992.

———. "Yachuan Village, Gansu, and Shimadao Village, Shaanxi: Subterranean Villages."

Chinese Landscapes: The Village as Place. Ed. Ronald G. Knapp. Honolulu: University of Hawaii Press, 1992. 151–61.

Kirsch, Sandra. "Wind and Water as Business Builder." *Fortune.* 126.3 (1992): 12.

Knapp, Ronald G., ed. *Chinese Landscapes: The Village as Place.* Honolulu: University of Hawaii Press, 1992.

———. *The Chinese House: Craft, Symbol, and Folk Tradition.* Hong Kong: Oxford University Press, 1990.

———. *China's Vernacular Architecture: House Form and Culture.* Honolulu: University of Hawaii Press, 1989.

———. *China's Traditional Rural Architecture: A Cultural Geography of the Common House.* Honolulu: University of Hawaii Press, 1986.

———, and Shen Donqui. "Changing Village Landscapes." *Chinese Landscapes: The Village as Place.* Ed. Ronald G. Knapp. Honolulu: University of Hawaii Press, 1992. 47–72.

Lao She. *Rickshaw* (Lo-t'o Hsiang Tzu). Trans. Jean M. James. Honolulu: University of Hawaii Press, 1979.

Laude, Olivier. "Hekeng Village, Fujian: Unique Habitats." *Chinese Landscapes: The Village as Place.* Ed. Ronald G. Knapp. Honolulu: University of Hawaii Press, 1992. 163–72.

Legge, James, trans. and ed.*The Chinese Classics: Confucian Analects, The Great Learning and The Doctrine of the Mean.* Vol. 2. Hong Kong: Hong Kong University Press, 1960.

Liang Ssu-ch'eng. *A Pictorial History of Chinese Architecture.* Cambridge: MIT Press, 1984.

Stille, Alexander. "Faking It." *The New Yorker.* 15 June. 1988: 36–42.

Thorp, Robert L. "The Architectural Heritage of the Bronze Age." *Architectural Heritage of the Bronze Age.* Ed. Nancy Shatzman Steinhardt. New York: China House Gallery, April 6–June 10 (1984): 60–67.

Wu, Nelson. *Chinese and Indian Architecture: The City of Man, the Mountain of God, and the Realm of the Immortals.* New York: George Braziller, 1963.

Yau, Victoria. "Use of Colour in China." *The British Journal of Aesthetics* 34. 2 (1994): 151–63.

Family in the Seventh Art—
Modern Chinese Film: An Analysis of
Red Sorghum, Raise the Red Lantern,
and *To Live*

Bettye S. Walsh

China, one of the oldest continuous civilizations, has had a long fascination with visual arts. Whether it is the ritual use of bronzes belonging to the house of Shang, the handscrolls of important dynastic families, or the exquisite calligraphy shared among the elite literati, all were created for a spectator waiting, as it were, to be "spoken" to through the visual. Film, the youngest visual "art" in China, is also a powerful medium because it provides another mode of cultural discourse strongly anchored in the cross-cultural orientation toward sight. Not surprisingly, film in China frequently focuses on the Chinese family.

One of the most interesting and often commented on aspects of the Middle Kingdom's culture is the role played by family. For over four thousand years, family has served as a metaphor by which to discuss China's particularity. The dominant relationship—father/son—provides the pattern for both the "ten human relationships" from the *Book of Rites* and the "five human relationships" from the *Mencius.* Even the political nomenclature models family language: the emperor is Son of Heaven.

While the West's concern over what constitutes a legal family (man, woman, and child; single mother and child; single father and child; adult siblings; same-sex partnership) has more to do with exclusion of benefits than with inculcating values, China's definition of family is essentially inclusive, focusing on communal loyalty, respect, responsibility, love, trust, and maintenance of *qi* 氣 (*ch'i*—energy, life essence) through relational living. Family in China, *jia* 家, has a range of meanings, which include the nuclear family but encompass more generations with the possibility of interfamily or intrafamily adoption. Though "five generations under one roof," the Chinese family dream, was more often an ideal than a fact (Such groupings did occur, but only in a small percentage of elite families. By 1982, for example, only 20 percent of all Chinese families contained three or more generations under one roof), the proportion of extended generational families was still seven times greater in China than the proportion in Western countries such as Canada (Zheng 19).

This ideal of the multigenerational inclusive family is often seen in Chinese literature and film. *The Story of the Stone,* sometimes translated as *Dream of the Red Chamber,* a seminal eighteenth-century Chinese novel, captures the notion of the extended family with 425 mothers, sons, son's sons, wives, concubines, cousins, peasant farmers and servants, colliding and conniving in the family compound. Such dynamics are astonishingly complex. While this and other Chinese fiction provides written descriptions of family variances, cinema adds depth to our vision of Chinese culture by providing visual images of family complexities.

Film, the seventh visual art in China, provides a powerful medium through which to examine family. Always popular with the masses, in 1949 more than 47 million Chinese attended movies; and by 1958, 2.8 billion tickets were distributed. In one year, motivated by the Great Leap Forward, film attendance soared to 4.15 billion (Clark 61).

One important potential of film is its ability to focus attention on an issue while entertaining its audience. Since the turn of the century, family melodrama has been dominant in Chinese cinema, partially because of the important social position of the family and the role it plays in social and cultural transformation (Ma Ning 29). According to Yanmei Wei, "films centered around family not only ensure audience involvement; they also enable the director to tackle social problems at the root" (20).

The popularity of film also made it useful for political purposes. Film helped standardize a nationwide language and national dialect, *putonghua* 普通話 (ordinary speech or Mandarin).[1] Further, with the establishment of a national network controlling the production, censorship, distribution, and projection of films, a tremendous political potential developed for regulating thought and ideology.

During the leadership of Mao Zedong, the regime exploited the propaganda potential of the film industry. Mao, like so many charismatic demagogues before him, used film to advance his political agenda. At the now famous Yan'an talks of 1942, Mao stated, "Our aim is to ensure that revolutionary literature and art follow the correct path of development and provide better help to other revolutionary work in facilitating the overthrow of our national enemy" (cited in Denton 458). With this utilitarian purpose, it follows that during certain periods in recent Chinese history, film was heavily censored; only approved topics, carefully edited, were transformed into celluloid. Such controls hampered the development of an internationally competitive film industry. As a result of problems facing the film industry, serious film study was more or less abandoned after the Communists established leadership of China in 1949 (Clark 1).

Chinese films of the sixties were often referred to as "spectacles." Rey Chow notes that these films depicted "the complete and successful overthrow of the past." Further, these films bespoke the "urgency of a new beginning" for China through communism and with it the notion that "this new beginning is primary, unique, henceforth invincible" (37). Essentially, spectacles showed the mobilization of the masses and all its energy toward a cultish "male fatherly figure" in the form of Mao. The rigidity and predictability of this period severely hampered industry development.

The Seventh Art has, however, reestablished itself in China and, with its resurgence, broadened its function in society. Films of the eighties and nineties, "back to nature" films as they are called, focus on the "natural." Desolate and wild landscapes, the harsh reality of rural life, and the many facets of oppression became central images in the hands of creative young Chinese directors. Their work quickly attracted an international audience. Many Chinese films of this period reflect the commodification of rural landscapes, subjugation of women and/or peasants, and the patriarchal system that has come to be associated with the exoticized creation of "old China" (Chow 95). Not only were directors able to capture the exotic otherness of the feudal past, but some dealt with the brutal death and destruction associated with war, bad political decisions, and natural disasters. These "scar films" allow the masses a means of coping with the trauma of China's recent difficulties. One film scholar argues that the nostalgia, the suffering, and sentimentalism of scar films offer an alternative political language:

Suffering is linked ultimately to the injustice of the political administration of social power. In this sense, subjectivity is part of a new political language of the post-Cultural Revolution period. It indicates an aspect of the person beyond that of the citizen. (Browne 53)[2]

In 1991, *Raise the Red Lantern* and its director Zhang Yimou received the Silver Lion Award in Venice and Best Foreign Language Film from the British Academy Awards. *Lantern* was also nominated for an Oscar. *Red Sorghum*, produced by the Xi'an Film Studio, received the Golden Bear Prize at the thirty-eighth West Berlin International Film Festival and was described by European film critics as "one of the best films at international festivals in recent years" (Mujun 172). In 1994 *To Live* received the Special Grand Jury, Best Actor, and Ecumenical Prizes at the Cannes Festival as well as the Best Foreign Language Film from the British Academy. Such prestigious awards support the notion that these are powerful films competitive on the world market.

Further, each film deals with the construct "family" as one of its central concerns. The unique and powerful role of family in China, its metaphorical extension to the larger culture, and the general popularity of the Seventh Art, make film an important medium through which to study representations of the Chinese family. The three titles also represent the development of one of China's most prominent directors, Zhang Yimou, leader of the Fifth Generation (the first group emerging from the Beijing Film Academy after the Cultural Revolution); these directors were not afraid to employ artistic inventiveness, explore China's rich cultural past, and analyze social issues.

Finally, these films comprise the text for this chapter because of their overall filmic, educational, and entertainment quality, their accessibility in the West, and their ability to reflect one director's perspective of the distinctive national character of Chinese cinema.[3]

Raise the Red Lantern

Film in China is considered a "literary" art which privileges the literary source. In fact, cinema is not only called the Seventh Art but also "filmic literature." Notable Chinese films such as *Raise the Red Lantern* debut in print. In this case Su Tong's novella, *Wives and Concubines* (1990), provided the plot but not the title.

International audiences were moved, not always positively, by this powerful story of concubinage set against a patriarchal, hierarchal backdrop. Some critics have suggested that Zhang is merely airing dirty laundry or parodying Western orientalism. Rey Chow, a noted Chinese cinema critic, believes that focusing on topics such as concubinage is a new and complicated kind of orientalism, calling it "an exhibitionist self-display" and "a critique of the voyeurism of . . . orientalism itself (171)."[4]

Social acceptance of concubinage, a practice at least seventeen centuries old in China, was undergirded by law; in the Ming Dynasty (1368–1644), a stringent legal code prescribed who, how many, and at what age concubines could be taken. The law was based on the family's need to have a son; however, this justification was not required in practice. From earliest times Chinese handbooks delineating women's behavior attacked jealousy and competition among the wives. Women were expected to live and work together peaceably as sisters, allowing nothing to disrupt family harmony. One of the most famous of these handbooks reminded women that jealousy was one of the worst violations and that it was one of the seven reasons for divorce (Ming Bao Yue).

While laws of concubinage were implemented locally, and punishment for violations was not the norm, women were never allowed to have more than one husband. Even virgin widows were urged to remain chaste and unmarried. Given these legal and social mores, it is not surprising that a wife's adultery was a serious offense punishable by death. Such draconian, patriarchal laws were not abolished until 1950, several decades after the historical framework of *Raise the Red Lantern*.

The film is set in a province in China in the 1920s, but chronological details are sparse. Songlian, a university student, must quit school after the death of her father. Her stepmother arranges for her to marry the wealthy Chen Zuoqian, but Songlian remarks bitterly to audience and stepmother, "Isn't this [marriage against one's will] women's fate?!" Dressed as a Western school girl, deprived of the traditional bridal palanquin, she begins her journey on foot to join the Chen family, a Confucian family long on ritual, traditions, and image, but short on love. (The Chen family sends a palanquin to carry Songlian but she chooses to walk, a sign of her independence perhaps.) Songlian joins the other wives and concubines as Fourth Wife in the family.

The raucous drum and gong music, a type often used as a prelude to military plays in traditional Chinese opera, lends the opening scene a sense of intensity and doom.[5] When her wedding night is abruptly interrupted by the feigned illness of Meishan, Third Wife and former opera performer, the foreboding music confirms the unhappiness of Songlian's fate. Songlian soon learns that her power and prestige are integrally related to the frequency of Master Chen's visits to her quarters in the claustrophobic, fortresslike mansion. Only then will the line of red lanterns be raised outside her courtyard, only then will she receive the erotic foot massage and the power to set the daily menu. But it is clear that ephemeral powers handed out by the patriarch—a foot massage, favorite dishes, and sexual/financial entitlements—are poor substitutes for real power.

Silverthorne suggests that Songlian plays the game, aware of her limitations but "teased by the mirage of access to phallic power" (87). The raising of the red lanterns signals phallic power that is transferred to Songlian when her husband chooses her for the night. But such power cannot override or negate the family's longstanding tradition and ritual. Transgressors pay. In a scene of ominous foreshadowing, Songlian finds the manacles used to imprison a previous generation's adulterous wife high in the compound tower (Later, Meishan will be killed in the same room, in the same way, when, intoxicated, Songlian inadvertently exposes the affair between Third Wife Meishan and young doctor Gao.)

Given the forced nature of her marriage to Master Chen, it is not surprising she cannot find it in her to love him. In fact, Songlian's own love for men seems limited to her dead father, and to Feipu, Master Chen's son by First Wife, both of whom are metaphorically anchored to her by imagery of the flute. Feipu plays a haunting melody which attracts her attention and makes her recall her father's musical virtuosity. The flute also has certain symbolic connotations in Chinese cultural tradition.

In classical legend the flute is the emblem of Han Xiangzi, one of the Eight Immortals of Daoism. This legendary flute player possessed the power of causing miraculous growth and flowering in plants, and popular legend connects the flute to romance (Yanmei Wei 24). In another legend, Lan Caihe, a female Daoist immortal, warns of the temporal and transitory nature of pleasure, feelings evoked by the melancholy and haunting melody of Feipu's flute. Further, we might view the flute as a phallic symbol and the "act of performing upon it as the displacement of one's erotic desire" (24). Songlian has a keepsake flute, sole memento of her deceased father, among her personal things. It is not coincidental that Chen, master of her physical and emotional life, controls the symbol of her erotic desire. He destroys the flute and sets in motion Songlian's revenge against Yan'er (the jealous, spurned maid who Songlian accuses of the theft) and the ensuing series of catastrophic events.

Throughout *Raise the Red Lantern* traditional Chinese music plays an important role in establishing the film as theater.[6] The military music at the start of a performance in Chinese theater stopped audience chatter and announced genre. In this film, its use hearkens to the older theatrical symbolism. Zhang uses a highly polished female chorus, often singing wordless, melancholy tunes. Yanmei Wei comments that Zhang uses the female chorus to "inter[vene] at every critical moment and mediate between the narrative and the spectator" (25), a technique which, for instance, allows the sorrow in the choral voices on Songlian's wedding night to contrast with the jubilation of lanterns, costumes, and decorations in her quarters, and in general create a powerful ironic tension between the foreboding tone of the chorus and visual images of Songlian. Some poignant moments are marked by rapid, frenetic music, foregrounding discord, confusion, foreshadowing tragedy.

Raise the Red Lantern unfolds on an operaticlike set consisting of a staged area of enclosed houses and courtyards. Even the architecture and landscape of the set's design reinforce the sense of isolation of the players and their slavery to the seemingly choreographed reenactment of Chen family traditions. Frequent long shots taken from above the roofline looking down on the ornate roof profile provide the viewer with a feeling of distance and isolation, while shots of the compound or characters break the filmic flow, but still show Songlian as isolated, as when she sits on her bed, framed by the red glow of lanterns and the bed's curtains as she waits for Master Chen to come to her for the first visit. Later after the master has left, Songlian sits as if in a dream on her bed. Characters seem to move on this stage in a constant enactment of learned lines and behaviors; no one gets to be "real." Survival depends on the ability to play-act. Second Wife has learned to feign friendship; the housekeeper instructs Songlian to kowtow to the family ancestors. Even the master's life seems dictated by tradition. Each plays a role.

Lighting and shot angles also affect the spectator's view of this theatrical production. Angled face shots portray Master Chen as a shadowy stock character. In his entrance to Songlian's bedchamber, he walks to a chair and sits stage right shrouded in almost total darkness. In later scenes, lighting on Chen's face is only slightly increased. In addition, the viewer is deprived of any voyeuristic erotic pleasure since the camera avoids love scenes and sensual body shots. On her wedding night, Master Chen commands Songlian to disrobe, which she does behind the bed drapes in shadows and quickly pulls the cover up to her neck. Close-ups of Songlian yield an implacable and impenetrable face that creates discomfort rather than pleasure in the viewer. In the opening close-up of schoolgirl Songlian's face, there is no joy at the approaching marriage; and the close-up resolves into a tear trickling down her cheek. Her persona seems set, again linking her to the notion of theater vis à vis a fixed operatic mask.

Other traditional theatrical techniques in the film include seasonal changes that establish the environmental setting and passage of time: summer, autumn, and winter divide and order the film's progression. Decorations in Meishan's quarters are replete with theatrical props, and her arias are memorized love songs, which she confesses she sings because they "deceive" her in this loveless, real-life family.

Deception, strongly associated with the stage, is a subtext in this family drama. Meishan deceives her husband with adultery; Songlian deceives the family with feigned pregnancy; Songlian's female servant Yan'er deceives herself into thinking she may become the master's wife (signaled by her placing in her room discarded red lanterns). The family is trapped in its own production. No matter how well they perform their roles, the rules and the script will not change. The players are powerless. The idea of family imprisoned by the theatrical is reinforced when one of the closing camera shots frames Songlian against the master's house. The scene thus created is a visualization of the Chinese character for "prisoner" (Yanmei Wei 27). Thus, the family circumstance, delineated artistically by the contained, claustrophobic *mise en scene* of the closed courtyard, the angles connoting helplessness, and the frenetic, wordless tunes, is imprinted and can be decoded by "reading" the lines within the frame as a Chinese ideograph. Most critics see the work as a "feminine" film whose tone is "burdened and helpless" (27). The film seems to perpetuate gender stereotypes by pronouncing Songlian a prisoner of the mind, a prisoner of patriarchy, a prisoner of the role of femininity, and a prisoner of the family.

Red Sorghum

Red Sorghum is based on Mo Yan's novel *Red Sorghum: A Novel of China* (1993), a suite of interconnected novellas, the first of which informs the film. Critically acclaimed abroad, the film was not well received in China. For a Chinese audience trained to value restraint, refinement, and Confucian ethical and moral sobriety and decorum, the film is controversial. Some detractors criticize its "mindless sensationalism and libidinal impulse for 'the ugly' . . . 'the uncivilized and the savage'"(Wang cited in Berry 81). In Chinese thinking, a film about desire, sex, and human transgression is a filmic transgression in and of itself. The story is set in Gaomi County in Shandong Province, a remote Chinese countryside replete with harsh, cruel, nightmarish, lush, life-giving, and life-taking qualities. The sense of place is palpable, and Zhang with his photographer's eye translates the visual richness of place into the film.

The narrator tells the story of his grandparents, which begins with the arranged marriage of "my grandma," Jiu'er. Her greedy father and heartless mother can benefit by "selling" their beautiful daughter for a mule. The exuberant bridal sedan sequence focuses on the symbolic imprisonment of the sixteen year old transported to another imprisonment, marriage to a leprous husband who is heir to the Shan's sorghum wine distillery. The rough ride is designed to elicit tears, nausea, vomiting, and urine from the young bride. For several minutes the screen is filled with color and action, punctuated with traditional music and lusty, vulgar comments from the sedan carriers like "to rock urine out of the bride" (Yingjin Zhang 31).

The audience meets "my grandpa," Yu Zhan'ao, as the strongest of the bridal bearers. With angled shots from inside the palanquin, his muscular shoulders glisten in sharp contrast to the pathetic husband who awaits his bride's arrival at the distillery. During the ride, Yu proves his strength by overpowering a masked thief masquerading as a famous highwayman who threatens Jiu'er, and the attraction between Jiu'er and Yu Zhan'ao begins. Reluctantly, Yu delivers Jiu'er to the distillery and her future husband. She enters but does not consummate the marriage, protecting herself through the night with sewing scissors.

She fulfills the customary visit to her parents' home three days later, borne on a mule (symbolizing her compliance). During this time, the viewer is led to believe that Yu Zhan'ao, the love-struck bridal carrier, murders Shan in order to free his beloved. On her return along the road, in a moment rich in imagery of the sacred, Yu takes Jiu'er into the natural world of the sorghum field to make love. The shot captures Jiu'er prostrate and Yu kneeling, both viewed from high above, in the middle of a circle. Here Zhang presents this moment in an almost religious fashion through his use of shot, angle, color, and *mise en scene*.

After the seduction scene, the storyline is interrupted with a kidnapping, a mirroring or doubling technique which Zhang uses in his films. The mirrored event is important as a statement of power—who has it and how it is enforced. The would-be bandit of the earlier scene is unmasked and beaten to death as a fake and fraud before he kidnaps Jiu'er. The second sequence is a successful kidnapping by the authentic bandit, strong, passionate, dangerous. Jiu'er is returned safely; and in a bold confrontation, Yu spares the outlaw, who did not violate his lover.

Yu drinks excessively in the film. His first visit to Jiu'er at the distillery is marred by his drunkenness. In another sequence, he is too drunk to protest when the workers toss him into a large wine vat to sober up. After this disgrace, Yu displays his masculinity by acts of physical strength and urinating in a vat of wine (which miraculously gives the wine a deliciously mellow flavor). In an interesting aside, the bride bearers tried to get urine from the bride and failed; it is the male who brings forth urine, another example of Zhang's use of doubling.

Nine years pass. The story moves from the civil war period to the war of resistance. Japanese officers round up villagers to watch the public flaying of Uncle Luohan, the universally respected ex-distillery foreman, an alleged anti-Japanese bandit. The villagers vow revenge for this atrocity. They ambush a Japanese truck but pay heavily with lives including that of Jiu'er. Survivors include the narrator's grandfather and his father as a small boy who ends the film chanting for his dead mother.

This film depicts family as locus of passionate resistance. One critic notes that the film is "basically about the life of the couple and their small community who cherish freedom and resist oppression" (Zhang Jia-Xuan 43). For Chinese sensitivities, the couple is uncharacteristically wild and passionate. Jiu'er uses scissors to avoid consummating her unwanted marriage; Yu, it is elliptically suggested, murders the leper-husband to win the bride; the two make wild love in the sorghum field; Jiu'er takes control of and wins respect from the distillery workers; Yu beats a would-be kidnapper to death and spares a real one; he urinates in a wine vat. These are coarse and unrefined yet defiant acts.

Passion is further suggested through lush setting which, in this film, comes in part from the use of imagery associated with sorghum. Sorghum—title, metaphor, and central visual focus of the film—is a peasant crop, coarse and plentiful, eaten in the absence of white rice, which was usually reserved for the wealthy and elderly. The plants are a deep rusty green and appear to change colors with maturation and light. Fields are thick, almost overpowering, since stalks tower seven to eight feet tall. A sorghum field provides the perfect setting for the unknown: an isolated spot for illicit love/rape, or protection for a hidden enemy/bandit.

Not only does Zhang use the lush fecundity of this crop to underscore sensuality, but he also employs the sumptuous open endedness of the Daoist leitmotif of a road or "way" that divides life's passion into the known and unknown. The *dao* 道 (*tao*) or "way" presented in the film through road imagery, is integral to Daoist philosophy.[7] In this film the road (the known) bisects the vast "unknown" of the sorghum fields on either side. As in life, the characters move from the known to the unknown and back to the known as they follow the *dao*.

The valorization of the primitive and passionate is visible through the use of heavy drinking, raw masculinity, and linkage to a respected outlaw past. Wang Yuejin recalls that historically in China wine drinking acts as a kind of externalization of masculinity as well as a challenge to authority (87). In the Western tradition, Greek drinking bouts were tied to choral presentations during festivals of Dionysus, the god of wine. The choral music that supports this film, though thoroughly Eastern, also supports masculinity. The untrained voices are rough, male, and delivered almost as shouts. Interestingly, Zhang admits that he had been reading Nietzsche's *Birth of Tragedy* and that he admired its "Dionysian spirit" (cited in Yanmei Wei 27).

Furthermore, in *Red Sorghum*, masculinity is clearly linked to outlaws, bandits, and sheer strength: survival of the fittest. While decorum and balance are important in Chinese culture, the male swashbuckler also belongs to the classical tradition. One of the best examples is *Outlaws of the Marsh*, a fourteenthth-century story based on historical fact, that glorifies the bandit, brotherhood, and the sword. Yu not only harkens to this older image of the glorious outlaw but also proclaims its superiority in something of a medical discourse on the healthy male versus the morally, spiritually diseased male. We might also read the image of the swashbuckler-outlaw in terms of a national allegory. The passion and power of the outlaw sensibility is in sharp relief to the national disease of numbness and insensitivity of China in the post-Mao era. Also, masculinity in the film seems to be attached to the natural and innocent; wealthy, educated men are impotent and weak (Yanmei Wei 27). Masculinity, passion, and innocence further underscore *Red Sorghum's* revolutionary message.

Real men suffer silently. Uncle Louhan and the bandit, in a powerful and brutal scene, are tortured but kept alive throughout the ordeal. The flaying spectacle offers a tragic example of the horror of war, but it does not seem to be gratuitous violence. Beyond reinforcing who is really a man, the action is symbolic. Real men being "skinned alive" by Japanese aggressors refers symbolically to the flaying of China as a nation by foreign powers.

This family is a family filled with passion, and the film aspires to a liberation of the human body (Yingjin Zhang 39). Director Zhang says "the fast-moving pace and the celebratory mood in *Red Sorghum* are to awaken and return Chinese people to their lost vitality, thus rejuvenating (the body of) the whole nation" (cited in Yingjin Zhang). Many critics note that while *Lantern* is decidedly feminine and marked by the pain of the traditional subordination of Chinese women, *Sorghum* is decidedly masculine with its tone of joyous optimism (Yanmei Wei 27). Nevertheless, the family is ruptured by the death of Jiu'er, and while the line survives, the story is relinquished to a subsequent generation whose vision is based on memory and hope, not passion and experience.

To Live

This film, thought by many to be Zhang Yimou's finest work to date, is also taken from literature, a recent novella of the same name by the relatively unknown Yu Hua. Zhang shifts not only the medium but also the message when he changes the novella's voice from a first-person narrator to the film's multiple perspectives. Further, he changes the tale from a remembered history of a sole survivor to something unfolding—living—on screen (Chow, "Endure" 1046). Particularly rich in history, the story moves chronologically, allowing an audience unfamiliar with China's tumultuous past to become placed in "time." It encompasses the civil war between Nationalists and Communists (1947–1949), the Communist Liberation (1949), The Great Leap Forward (1958), and the Cultural Revolution (1966–1976). The film depicts the family of Fugui and Jiazhen living through the 1940s, 1950s, 1960s, and some years beyond this.

The ancestral Xu family breaks down early in the film. Master Fugui, the heir and guardian of his family fortune and ancestral estate, gambles heavily while a shadow-puppet troupe performs in the background. With each toss of the dice, Long'er, his gambling partner, gets closer and closer to owning the family's palatial home. Fugui's long-suffering wife, Jiazhen, begs him to give up gambling since she is pregnant again. He promises to stop but returns to the gambling hall the next evening certain that his luck has changed. Jiazhen comes to the gambling parlor and implores Fugui to leave with her.

His wife's presence makes him lose face and this concerns him, but he seems oblivious to the fact that he is on the verge of ruining his life. Jiazhen leaves, Fugui throws the dice, and Long'er wins the family's home. On the day of reckoning, as the accountants go over the son's losses on an abacus, the old patriarch verifies each loss by his son's calligraphy and thumbprint. Enraged and disgusted, he nevertheless says "a gambling debt is a debt and debts must be paid." He signs over the house, but turns on Fugui with murderous intent. The loss is too great for the old man and he dies. Jiazhen, with her daughter, has already returned to her parent's home. Filial piety and wifely submission, long a mainstay of the Confucian family model, have crumbled.

In the following segment of the film, however, Fugui learns the importance of family as he recognizes and accepts responsibility for his destructive actions. He cares for his ill mother in a one-room apartment and ekes out a living as a street vendor. Eventually, Jiazhen returns with their daughter, Fengxia, and newborn son, Youqing, because she hears Fugui has changed. With his family now reunited, Fugui must support them. Humbling himself, he goes to Long'er and asks for a loan to open a business. Long'er refuses, but gives him the wooden trunk full of shadow puppets, a family of sorts, which had played in the background during their gambling bouts. He tells Fugui that as long as he had the puppet troupe he never went hungry. With no other recourse, Fugui accepts the puppets and sets out with a friend, Chunsheng, to entertain in the countryside.

Acting as a symbolic family, the puppets early on say "It's great to be alive." They perform during good and bad times. Fugui and Chunsheng, partners in the troupe, are like a family with Fugui acting as older brother. They perform together, drag heavy artillery together, and almost freeze together when they are forcibly embroiled in the struggle between the Nationalists and the Communists. They survive liberation when thousands do not. Armed with a commendation for service to the liberation forces, Fugui returns with his puppets to his biological family while Chungeng stays with an ideological family, the victorious troops, in order to learn to drive a truck.

Another grouping in *To Live* is family as "the people," which offers a rather controversial view of village life. The dissolute life of the wealthy class, represented early in the film by Fugui and later by Long'er, is repeatedly juxtaposed to the abject poverty of the masses, setting the stage for subsequent social changes. The masses— poor, uneducated, and ready for change—resort to acts of violence. Because Long'er lives in a grand estate, which he won gambling with Fugui, he is deemed a rich landowner and is murdered by his own community while Fugui watches. This collective family condones murder when one of its members is deemed guilty by a set of historically fluctuating definitions.

In what by now strikes the viewer as a seemingly endless ordeal, the various "families" portrayed by Zhang move stoically through the Great Leap Forward, Mao's short-lived, disastrous economic development program. The puppet box (a family within a family), once again becomes a focus when Youqing, Fugui's son, is ordered to give the puppets, assembled with metal pins, up for smelting. Eventually, however, the puppets are saved since they can entertain the masses, motivating them to greater productivity. Fugui's family, again reduced to poverty, endures insults, fear, and hard work, then devastating personal tragedy when Fugui's friend from the puppet troupe, Chunsheng (obsessed with driving, now a Communist official), accidentally runs over Youqing and kills him, an act that irrevocably severs his relationship with Jiazhen and harms his relationship with Fugui. Chunsheng's incompetency behind the wheel may symbolically mirror Mao's mad obsession to collect iron and metal for smelting, his unsuccessful plan for bringing China into world competition, and the resultant disruptive impact of these events on the family in China.

The Cultural Revolution that followed united people by thoughts, age, and training, and the shadow-puppet family made up of emperors, generals, scholars, beauties, and gentry does not survive this period, burned in a frenzy of destruction inspired by Mao. While the Cultural Revolution placed severe stress on the traditional family structure, it also encouraged creation of new affiliations. Red Guards worked, marched, marauded, and in a sense replaced traditional family linkages. Yet, it is during this period that Fengxia, Fugui, and Jiazhen's daughter (deaf from childhood, the only surviving child, and married to Wan Erxi, a Red Guard leader who is also handicapped), dies in labor due to the incompetence of hospital personnel (most of the trained staff have been sent to the countryside), highlighting the senseless destruction of this period.

For all its affirmation of life, death pervades the film. But in the closing moments, the puppet box, empty for some time, is brought out to hold the baby chicks—the new life—of Little Bun, Fengxia's child, Fugui and Jiazhen's grandson who has survived. Fugui, in a moment imbued with positive energy, chants the same children's ditty to Little Bun that he had chanted to Youqing on the day of his death. The next generation of the family lives, perhaps with childlike hope and optimism.

Food imagery, especially toward the end of the film, takes on a prominent role in *To Live*. Families must have food to survive. In China, a country that has known immense famine and starvation, the traditional image is deprivation. *To Live* gives a complex, subtle sense of how food can be an offering, threat, or disabler, as well as sustainer. Major filmic moments are marked by food that is unconsumed or inedible (Chow, "Endure" 1046), perhaps reminding audiences that neither man nor family lives by bread alone. The segment of *To Live* that culminates in Youqing's death is dominated by *jiaozi*, meat dumplings. Run over in a car driven by his father's friend, Youqing dies before sampling the *jiaozi*. The food displayed on Youqing's grave is a family ritual anchored in respect and desire for spiritual well-being. Not surprisingly, the dumplings reappear—cold, unappealing, unconsumed—displayed on Youqing's grave.

The shadow-puppet family is involved in an inedible food scene. Youqing makes a concoction of "tea" for his father and offers it as a token of forgiveness after they have fought; but the drink is repulsive, undrinkable. His father spews the liquid on the shadow-puppet show screen. Family-as-the-people are also touched by negative food imagery. In the communal kitchen, Youqing takes more than a normal portion of noodles and liberally laces it with burning hot sauce. The bowl is inedible. He pours the fiery noodles over the head of a local bully, which sets off tremendous familial pressures. In another scene, the steamed buns eaten by the elderly doctor called to help deliver Fengxia's child are indigestible and he is rendered unconscious; the subsequent tragedy, Fengxia's unnecessary death, is an equally undigestible outcome. The closing scene employs shared food among the enduring traditional family members (Fugui, Jiazhen, and Little Bun), an act that foregrounds the poignancy of the negative food imagery. Beyond food as offering, threat, disabler—the indigestible in life—food can sustain and comfort. Zhang seems to suggest that the multiple and varied family that is China does not live by dumplings, noodles, or tea alone.

Summary

China, in spite of its long emphasis on the ideal multigenerational family, does not produce one picture of family. As these films suggest, the idea of family is not easily reduced to a label with neatly categorized descriptors. The variety and complexity of family in China assure its continued usefulness as a vehicle for studying the culture.

Zhang Yimou's films demonstrate the richness of this metaphor. In *Raise the Red Lantern*, the Chen family, harshly controlled by traditions and ritual, provides the opportunity to view *family as theater*, where the lines, moves, and outcomes are set, where everyone is a prisoner of the script. In *Red Sorghum*, the family of Yu and Jiu'er, constantly in conflict with tradition and oppression, represent the wild fullness of life and love lived on the edge. *Family as lived passion* does not always yield happiness or longevity, but it offers the victory of the struggle and the raw reality of the unpredicted. In *To Live, multiple familylike* groups emerge. Fugui and Jiazhen's family struggle as they are buffeted by a changing world and political forces which complicate issues of life and death and show how vulnerable and yet enduring this social construct is. Metaphorical families such as the puppets or the Red Guards are similarly afflicted. The role of food, normally the source of survival, is strangely reversed. Scenes focusing on the inedible and indigestible, remind us of the complexity of life and the power of a family's determination to live. In his works, Zhang Yimou has demonstrated the richness of the family metaphor as a vehicle for the exploration and understanding of Chinese history and culture.

Glossary

Angle Angle of a shot affects audience interpretation of a visual's meaning. Eye-level shots are routine—the way the real world is regularly viewed—but a bird's-eye view or high-angle shot suggests the opposite meaning of the same scene shot from a low angle. Higher angles suggest entrapment, powerlessness, even fatality while lower angles can speed motion, enhance confusion, or heighten the importance of a character who thus looms over the audience. Oblique angle shots signal tension, transition, or imminent movement; while powerful, they disorient the viewer and are used infrequently.

Color and contrast These terms are important to film because they relate to an object's meaning. The viewer actively decodes lines, but color generates subtle meanings and moods. While specific color symbolism is culturally acquired, implications of colors among cultures are often similar. See the list of colors and moods below. Colors may be used in different ways by different cultures: for example, white is a wedding color in the West and a funeral color in the East; red is the wedding color of the East and the color associated with prostitution in the West. Consider carefully the use of colors and contrasts in the selected films and whether Zhang uses color symbolically to imply the same or different meanings across his films.

Color and mood Colors in film may suggest mood: Tranquility/Blue, Aloofness/Green, Serenity/Violet are considered cool colors. Warm colors and their corresponding moods are Aggressiveness/Red, Violence/Yellow, Stimulation/Orange.

Fifth generation A term applied to the generation of filmmakers who graduated after the end of the Cultural Revolution. Some theorists find the term odd since there is no fourth or sixth generation.

Mise en scène From French theater, it literally means placing on stage. In film it includes the staging and placement of the action and the way action is photographed. Each image is "framed" by the screen but the dramatic action begs the viewer to assemble the frames in sequence not in isolation. Isolating a frame for critical analysis may yield a symbolic meaning determined by directorial placement at center, top, bottom, or edge of frame. In reality, frames are not created for static or fixed visualization.

Notes

1. See Linda Pickle's chapter "Written and Spoken Chinese: Expression of Culture and Heritage."

2. Myriad films of high quality and interesting subject matter emerged during the past two decades, which makes text selection for a chapter such as this demanding and at best only a fragmentary representation. I have decided to focus on three films directed by Zhang Yimou: *Dahong Denglong Gaogao Gua* (*Raise the Red Lantern*, 1991, 125 mins.), *Hong Gaoliang* (*Red Sorghum*, 1987, 91 mins.), and *Huozhe* (*To Live*, 1994, 130 mins.). I might have selected texts representative of certain time periods: films of the thirties and forties such as *The Goddess* or *The Spring River Flows East*; or films of the Hundred Flowers Movement, minority, or revolutionary period such as *Loyal Partners* or *The Red Detachment of Women*. Another approach would have been by type: melodramas by Xie Jin such as *The Legend of Tianyun Mountain* or *Hibiscus Town*, or Zhuangzhuang's focus on marginal cultures in *On the Hunting Ground*. Finally, I could have focused on themes such as Chinese bureaucracy, as seen in Huang Jianxin's first of a trilogy, *The Black Cannon Incident*, or combined several of the above genres.

3. In *Electric Shadow: 45 Years of Chinese Cinema* Tony Rayns discusses the characteristics of Chinese cinema: he argues the following: First, that Chinese cinema is fundamentally

a literary art. Many Chinese films, like *Red Sorghum, Spring Silkworms,* and *Raise the Red Lantern,* are taken from short stories or novels. In itself, this is not uniquely Chinese, since Western cinema often does the same; however, for many reasons, one of which may have been the chaos of the film movement in China and its vulnerability to radical changes, Chinese cinema developed in the wake of literature, not on the crest or even as coequal.

Second, the notion of genre has little place in Chinese film with the exception of the retrospective, the before-and-after-liberation stories, and the melodrama. Critics have established taxonomies in an attempt to group Chinese film. Browne's taxonomy includes melodrama, postsocialist film, and film of the eighties. Semsel's taxonomy classifies Chinese films as the Xie Jin model (melodrama) film, the Fifth Generation film, the entertainment film, and the cultural film.

Third, filmic action spans months, years, even decades. Poetic metaphors are drawn frequently from nature (red sorghum or yellow earth, for example). Characters are rarely fully developed but are portrayed as "types." And disparate materials are often fused into seamless, noncontradictory texts.

Fourth, artistic unity is not a central tenet in Chinese aesthetics; therefore, the film narrative often flows from the realistic to the lyric or from fiction to historical fact, employing an overlapping or interspersing technique that draws attention to the space within the narrative unit. Rayns warns that one should not overstate the point, but he notes the absence of unity of space (and often time), the use of events as discrete units, and the sense of unfettered movement among the intimate, the highly personal, and historically concrete, as well as admixtures of drama, documentary, and lyrical episodes.

Fifth, Chinese cinema points to Chinese theater. The many examples of borrowed stage conventions in film reflect a close attachment to the stage.

Sixth, the power of the written poetic tradition is apparent in the lyrical interludes and visual metaphors of Chinese cinema.

Seventh, some technical strategies reflect cinema's debt to Shanghai, Hollywood, and also Soviet revolutionary aesthetics.

Eighth, a key structuring device in many Chinese films is the doubling/redoubling (where actions appear and then reappear) and contradiction (a dramatic point is made and undercut in the next scene).

Ninth, censorship forced filmmakers to be creative about materials that presented the need for radical social change. Audiences often completed the meaning by responding to calculatedly provocative endings that sounded notes of firm resolution, faint optimism, total despair, and rejoicing. The *divisive* nature of film endings is a shift since the first sixteen years of film in the People's Republic were *unificatory* in spirit with decisive and affirmatory endings.

Finally, Rayns notes that the audience inscribed into Chinese film is Chinese. Contemporary critics, however, are challenging this notion. International competition and the concomitant pressure to attract Western audiences may cause a loss of Chinese distinctiveness or may cause directors to "orientalize" or exoticize the Chineseness that they seek to preserve.

4. "Wives and Concubines" would have been a more revealing title than the film's idiosyncratic symbolism associated with the red lantern ritual. Immediately, the spectator becomes involved with concubinage, an ancient Chinese marriage arrangement. Exactly

where, how, or why, concubinage evolved is difficult to establish. But records suggest that as early as the third century C.E. concubinage was firmly in place in China, and with it, the relational complications within families peculiar to it, including jealousy, lies, bickering, intrigue, deceit, treachery, revenge, even murder. (See Mary Gallagher's chapter "Women and Gender.")

    5. See Kathleen Higgins' chapter "Chinese Music and the Family."

    6. Again, see Higgins.

    7. See Vance Cope-Kasten's chapter "Meeting Chinese Philosophy." For a fuller discussion of Daoism see also Arthur Waley's *The Way and its Power: A Study of the Tao Tê Ching and its Place in Chinese Thought*. New York: Grove Press, 1988.

Works Cited

Berry, Chris., ed. *Perspectives on Chinese Cinema*. London: British Film Institute, 1991.

Browne, Nick et al. *New Chinese Cinemas: Forms, Identities, Politics*. Cambridge: Cambridge University Press, 1994.

Chow, Rey. *Primitive Passions: Visuality, Sexuality, Ethnography, and Contemporary Chinese Cinema*. New York: Columbia University Press, 1995.

———. "We Endure, Therefore We Are: Survival, Governance and Zhang Yimou's *To Live*." *The South Atlantic Quarterly* 95:4 (Fall 1996): 1039–64.

Clark, Paul. *Chinese Cinema: Culture and Politics Since 1949*. New York: Cambridge University Press, 1987.

Denton, Kirk A., ed. *Modern Chinese Literary Thought: Writings on Literature, 1893–1945*. Stanford: Stanford University Press, 1996.

Gabriel, Teshome. *Third Cinema in the Third World: The Aesthetics of Liberation*. Ann Arbor: University of Michigan Press, 1982.

Ma Ning. "Symbolic Representation and Symbolic Violence: Chinese Family Melodrama of the Early 80s." *Melodrama and Asian Cinema*. Cambridge: Cambridge University Press, 1993: 29–58.

Ming Bao Yue. Lecture. February 1997. University of Hawaii.

Mo Yan. *Red Sorghum: A Novel of China*. Trans. Howard Goldblatt. New York: Penguin, 1993.

Mujun Shao. "Notes on *Red Sorghum*." *Chinese Literature*. (Spring 1989):172–180.

Rayns, Tony, and Scott Meek. *Electric Shadow: 45 Years of Chinese Cinema*. London: British Film Institute, 1980.

Semsel, George, Xia Hong, and Hou Jianping. *Chinese Film Theory: A Guide to the New Era*. New York: Praeger, 1990.

Silverthorne, Jeanne. "The Haunted Woman." *Artforum* March 1992: 8+.

Waley, Arthur. *The Way and its Power: A Study of the Tao Tê Ching and its Place in Chinese Thought*. New York: Grove Press, 1988.

Wang Yuejin. "*Red Sorghum*: Mixing Memory and Desire." *Perspectives on Chinese Cinema*. Ed. Chris Berry. London: British Film Institute, 1991.

Yanmei Wei. "Music and Femininity in Zhang Yimou's Family Melodrama." *Cineaction* 42:15 (1997): 18–27.

Yingjin Zhang. "Ideology of the Body in *Red Sorghum*: National Allegory, National Roots, and Third Cinema." *Colonialism and Nationalism in Asian Cinema.* Ed. Wimal Dissanayake. Bloomington: Indiana University Press, 1994.

Zhang Jia-Xuan. "RED SORGHUM." *Film Quarterly* 42.3 (1989): 41–43.

Zhang Yimou (director). *Red Sorghum.* Xi'an Film Studio, 1987.

———. *Raise the Red Lantern.* 1991.

———. *To Live.* 1994.

Zheng Yi. *Family Dynamics in China: A Life Table Analysis.* Madison: University of Wisconsin Press, 1991.

Works Consulted

Barnet, Sylvan. *A Short Guide to Writing about Art.* 4th ed. New York: Harper, 1993.

Jameson, Fredric. "World Literature in an Age of Multinational Capitalism." *The Current in Criticism: Essays on the Present and Future of Literary Theory.* Ed. Clayton Koelb and Virgil Locke. West Lafayette: Purdue University Press, 1987.

"Leftist Chinese Cinema of the Thirties." *Cineaste* 17.3 (1990): 36–37.

Toroptsev, Sergei. "The Space of the Subjective: Pre-Fifth Generation Chinese Cinema." *Cinemaya* (Summer 1992): 14–17.

SELECTED ANNOTATED READINGS

Philosophy and the History of Ideas

Chan, W. T. *A Sourcebook in Chinese Philosophy*. Princeton, N. J.: Princeton University Press, 1969. A valuable source of primary material from ancient to modern times. Chan's short introductions to each set of readings are excellent.

Creel, H. G. *Chinese Thought: From Confucius to Mao Tse-tung*. New York: Mentor, 1953. An old standard, which provides a still quite reliable overview of the entire sweep of Chinese philosophy except for the reemergence of Confucianism in recent decades.

De Bary, Wm. Theodore, Wing Tsit Chan, and Chester Tan. *Sources of Chinese Tradition*. Vol. 2. New York: Columbia Univeristy Press, 1960. Chapter 24: "The New Culture Movement" includes key primary texts on the "Attack on Confucianism" and "The Literary Revolution," which give the cultural context for the May Fourth 1919 movement.

Ebrey, Patricia. *The Inner Quarters: Marriage and the Lives of Chinese Women in the Sung Period*. Berkeley: University of California Press, 1993. The book is a welcome antidote to a field where women authors are few and far between.

Fingarette, Herbert. *Confucius—The Secular as Sacred*. New York: Harper, 1972. A short, readable account of Confucius that makes a clear and compelling case for thinking that the thought of Confucius is still important today.

Graham, A. C. *Disputers of the Tao*. LaSalle, Ill: Open Court, 1989. Rather difficult and sophisticated, but considered by many to be the best overview of the ancient period.

———*Chuang Tzu: The Seven Inner Chapters and Other Writings from the Book "Chuang Tzu."* London: Allen, 1981. A reliable and helpful translation, which is currently out of print.

Hall, David L., and Roger T. Ames. *Thinking through Confucius*. Albany: State University of New York Press, 1987. A sophisticated book, requiring a considerable background in philosophy, but one that has revolutionized much thinking in the West about Confucius.

Lao Tzu. *Tao Te Ching*. Trans. Stephen Addiss and Stanley Lombardo. Indianapolis: Hackett, 1993. And Lao Tzu. *Tao Te Ching*. Trans. D. C. Lau. New York: Penguin, 1963. Two inexpensive and, from a scholarly point of view, reliable editions.

Lau, D. C., trans. *Confucius: The Analects*. New York: Penguin, 1979. A reliable translation with a very informative introduction.

————, trans. *Mencius*. New York: Penguin, 1970. The most developed statement of the Confucian position in ancient times, this work has been the most influential text of the tradition for the last thousand years or so.

Legge, James. *The Chinese Classics*. 5 vols. 1871; Hong Kong: Hong Kong University Press, 1960. Legge is Victorian in some of his moral judgments, but his extensive notes draw on a long Chinese tradition of interpretation extending back to the Han Dynasty. The printed Chinese characters are striking.

Mair, Victor. *Wandering on the Way: Early Taoist Tales and Parables of Chuang Tzu*. New York: Bantam, 1994. A recent and inexpensive translation of the whole book of Zhuangzi, done by someone more interested in it as literature than as philosophy.

Mitchell, Stephen. *Tao Te Ching*. New York: Harper, 1988. This version is a provocative "translation" based on other translations (in English, German, and French).

Munro, Donald. *The Concept of Man in Early China*. Stanford, Calif.: Stanford Univeristy Press, 1969. A ground-breaking introduction that shows the importance of the idea of the family.

Red Pine, trans. *Lao-tzu's Taoteching*. San Francisco: Mercury, 1996. It is interesting and instructive to compare different translations of the key work attributed to Laozi, the *Daodejing* (Tao Te Ching). This is said to be the most widely translated book in the world, after the Bible, and so there are many versions. This translation is highly recommended because it includes Chinese text, a rather literal translation, and selected commentaries from subsequent Chinese thinkers.

Schwartz. Benjamin I. *The World of Thought in Ancient China*. Cambridge, Mass.: Harvard University Press, 1985. A thorough yet readable overview of the ancient period.

Spence, Jonathan D. *The Gate of Heavenly Peace: The Chinese and Their Revolution, 1895–1980*. New York: Viking, 1981. Concentrates on three individuals "whose personal experiences help to define the nature of the times through which they lived."

————. *The Search for Modern China*. New York: W. W. Norton, 1990. A comprehensive history that features a number of minor individuals including Ding Ling.

Tu Wei-ming. *Centrality and Commonality*. Albany: State University of New York Press, 1989. Presented in the form of a commentary on *The Doctrine of the Mean*, this book makes a clear case for the relevance of Confucian outlook for our time.

Waley, Arthur, trans. *The Analects of Confucius*. New York: Vintage, 1989. This is another reliable translation with helful notes.

Watson, Burton. *Early Chinese Literature*. New York: Columbia University Press, 1962. A classic. A general overview of the philosophical and other writings (poetry and history) in China from the beginning to about 100 C.E. Watson notes how early Chinese historians and poets are also "philosophical."

Wilhelm, Hellmut. *The I Ching or Book of Changes*. Trans. C. F. Baynes. 1950; Princeton, N.J.: Princeton Univeristy Press, 1967. The foreword by Carl Jung is only one aspect that makes this version, of many available, fascinating, informative, and beautifully written.

—— and Richard Wilhelm. *Understanding the I Ching*. Princeton, N.J.: Princeton University Press, 1995. A clear set of lectures introducing readers to this ancient classic that has had a great impact on subsequent philosophy. Especially helpful are the first several of Helmut Wilhelm's chapters.

Watson, Burton. *Chuang Tzu: Basic Writings*. New York: Columbia University Press, 1964. A selection of Chuang Tzu's writings with a helpful introduction. This volume is a good place to begin study of this fascinating though at times difficult is thinker.

——, trans. *Basic Writings of Mo Tzu, Hsun Tzu, and Han Fei Tzu*. New York: Columbia University Press, 1963–1964. Mozi's (Mo Tzu) opposition to Confucius begins the record of philosophical debate in China. Xunzi (Hsun Tzu) offers an important alternative to Mencius's Confucianism. Hanfeizi (Han Fei Tzu) was a Legalist Philosopher, a group whose ideas were important in the thinking of the first "modern" empire, the Qin, who effectively ended philosophical debate in ancient China.

History of Art

"China." *Dictionary of Art*. Ed. Jane Shoaf Turner. New York: Grove/Macmillan 1996. The long article on Chinese art, in many sections by many authors, is an excellent summary of recent scholarship. The extensive section on architecture fills a major gap left by all the surveys listed below. This may be the best place to begin a research project.

Clunas, Craig. *Art in China*. Oxford History of Art. New York: Oxford University Press, 1997. Probably the best compact one-volume introduction now available. A fresh rethinking of the whole topic, but not without its idiosyncrasies: the author is interested in art primarily as material culture, so literature and philosophy get little attention here. The arrangement is thematic, by social context, but it is also roughly chronological. Excellent supplemental material and illustrations.

Fong, Wen. C, and James C.Y. Watt, eds. *Possessing the Past: Treasures from the National Palace Museum, Taipei*. New York: Metropolitan Museum of Art/Abrams, 1996. This lavish survey, written around the great National Palace Museum collection, is in fact a magisterial *history* of the arts of China written by leading American scholars. It takes a traditional chronological approach, with ample consideration of ideas and cultural context.

Li Zehou. *The Path of Beauty: A Study of Chinese Aesthetics*. Trans. Song Lizeng. New York: Oxford University Press, 1994. A fascinating chronological history of Chinese aesthetics, emphasizing parallels between literature, philosophy, and the arts. First published in the People's Republic of China in 1981, its views of the past are colored by Communist Party doctrine, but it is no less interesting for that.

Rawson, Jessica., ed. *The British Museum Book of Chinese Art.* New York: Thames and Hudson, 1993. Also thematically arranged, but by medium, with a historical synopsis at the end. Splendid individual essays, particularly Rawson's own on ritual jades and bronzes. The introduction, also by Rawson, would make an excellent one-chapter introduction to the broad topic of Chinese art in society. The beautiful illustrations are mostly drawn from the British Museum's own collection, which may not be ideal for students outside of Britain.

Sullivan, Michael. *The Arts of China.* 3 ed. Berkeley: University of California Press, 1984. A long-time standard introduction, strictly chronological by dynasty with illustrations of all the canonical works, including many in American collections. It is especially useful for its frequent references to classic Chinese literature, including many excerpts. Perhaps a bit dated now in its romanticism and its conservative choice of topics and media to include.

Tregear, Mary. *Chinese Art.* New York: Thames and Hudson, 1985. A compact chronological introduction in the "World of Art" series.

Literature

Barlow, Tani E. Introduction. *I Myself Am a Woman: Selected Writings of Ding Ling.* Ed. Tani E. Barlow and Gary J. Bjorge. Boston: Beacon, 1989

Denton, Kirk A., ed. *Modern Chinese Literary Thought: Writings on Literature, 1893–1945.* Stanford: Stanford University Press, 1996. Includes six essays by Lu Xun, Ding Ling's 1942 essay "We Need the Zawen Essay," and Mao Zedong's "Talks at the Yan'an Forum on Literature and Art," where he quotes and refutes the Zawen essay by Ding Ling.

Ding Ling. *Miss Sophie's Diary and Other Stories.* Trans. W. J. F. Jenner. Beijing: Panda, 1985. Also includes eight "other" stories: "Shanghai in the Spring of 1930," "From Dusk to Dawn," "The Hamlet," "A Certain Night," "Rushing," "The Reunion," "When I was in Xia Village," and "Night."

———. *I Myself Am a Woman: Selected Writings of Ding Ling.* Ed. Tani E. Barlow and Gary J. Bjorge. Boston: Beacon, 1989. Includes: "Miss Sophie's Diary," "A Woman and a Man," "Shanghai, Spring 1930," "Net of Law, Mother," "Affair in East Village," "New Faith," "When I was in Xia Village," "Thoughts on March 8," "People Who Will Live Forever in My Heart," and "Du Wanxiang". The introduction is thorough yet conveys reservations about Ding Ling's life and actions.

Fenollosa, Ernest. *The Chinese Written Character as a Medium for Poetry.* Ed. Ezra Pound. San Francisco: City Lights, 1968. This essay was among Fenollosa's notes when he died in 1908 and left Pound his manuscripts. The influence of Pound's version, published in London in 1920, has been routinely recognized in the history of American literary criticism.

Feuerwerker, Yi-tsi Mei. *Ding Ling's Fiction: Ideology and Narrative in Modern Chinese Literature.* Cambridge, Mass.: Harvard University Press, 1982. A very thorough critical analysis informed by postmodern feminism.

Hsia, C. T. *A History of Modern Chinese Fiction: 1917–1957.* New Haven, Conn.: Yale University Press, 1961. What used to be the standard work on modern Chinese fiction.

Isaacs, Harold R. *Straw Sandals: Chinese Short Stories 1918–1933.* Foreword by Lu Hsun. Cambridge, Mass: MIT University Press, 1971. This collection was put together in 1934, but thought to be unpublishable until 1973 when efforts were renewed. It should be noted that this collection put together with Lu Xun's help, juxtaposes his preface to "Call to Arms," his "Diary of a Madman" and "Miss Sophie's Diary." Also includes Ding Ling's "One Certain Night" about the execution of her husband.

Kalgren, Bernhard. *The Book of Odes: Chinese Text, Transcription and Translation.* Stockholm: Museum of Far Eastern Antiquities, 1950. The Chinese characters are given and then a literal translation with notes. A useful book to have in the library so that students can judge the accuracy of various translations.

Lau, Joseph S. M., and Howard Goldblatt, eds. *The Columbia Anthology of Modern Chinese Literature.* New York: Columbia University Press, 1995. As well as Lu Xun, this includes Ding Ling's "When I was in Xia Village."

Lu Xun. *The Complete Stories of Lu Xun.* Trans. Yang Xianyi and Gladys Yang. Bloomington: Indiana University Press, 1981. Includes stories from "Call to Arms" and "Wandering."

Owen, Stephen, trans. and ed. *An Anthology of Chinese Literature: Beginnings to 1911.* New York: Norton, 1996. An extensive array of poetry, prose, and plays, with ample introductions placing the works in a cultural/historical context. Owen is currently the preeminent American working in this field.

———. *The Great Age of Chinese Poetry: The High T'ang.* New Haven, Conn.: Yale University Press, 1981. A clear and highly respected work that puts Du Fu at the center.

Snow, Edgar. *Living China: Modern Chinese Short Stories.* Westport, Conn.: Hyperion, 1937. When this book was published, Isaacs felt it edged his collection out of possible publication. The introduction gives the flavor of the time when Ding Ling was feared to be dead. Includes "The Flood" and "News"; scorned by Hsia as ill-written Communist propaganda.

Waley, Arthur. *The Book of Songs.* 1937; New York: Grove, 1960. The poetic quality of Waley's translations is unchallenged, but he is not literal. Waley's early translations of Chinese poems in 1918 made them accessible and popular.

Watson, Burton. *The Columbia Book of Chinese Poetry.* New York: Columbia University Press, 1984. This work has only recently been supplanted by Owen's anthology as the definitive collection. Watson's translations are often very beautiful, and his scholarship is impeccable.

CHINESE DYNASTIES

Legendary Emperors (Yao and Shun)	Third millennium B.C.E.
Xia	ca. 2205–1766 B.C.E.
Shang	1766–1122 B.C.E.
Zhou	1122–256 B.C.E.
Western Zhou	1122–770 B.C.E.
Eastern Zhou	770–256 B.C.E.
Spring and Autumn Period	722–481 B.C.E.
Warring States Period	403–221 B.C.E.
Qin	221–206 B.C.E.
Han	206 B.C.E. –220 C.E.
Western Han	206 B.C.E. –9 C.E.
Eastern Han	25–220 C.E.
Three Kingdoms	220–280
Wei	220–265
Shu-han	221–263
Wu	222–280
Jin	265–420
Western Jin	265–316
Eastern Jin	316–420
Southern and Northern Dynasties	420–589
Sui	589–618
Tang	618–907
Five Dynasties and Ten Kingdoms	907–960
Song	960–1279
Northern Song	960–1127
Southern Song	1127–1279
Yuan (Mongol)	1279–1368
Ming	1368–1644
Qing (Manchu)	1644–1911
Republic of China	1911–1949
People's Republic of China	1949–present

PRONUNCIATION SUGGESTIONS

The Pinyin system is used for most Chinese words in this book. Letters with unfamiliar pronunciations appear below. Other letters approximate Standard English sounds.

Vowels

a	as in f*a*ther
ai	as in *ai*sle
ao	as in n*ow*
e	as in b*oo*k
ei	as in sl*eigh*
i	as in h*ea*t
	as in d*i*verse (when preceeded by c, s, z)
	as in h*er* (when preceeded by ch, r, sh, or zh)
ia	as in *ya*rn
ian or yan	as in *yen*
iu	as in tr*io*
ie	as in h*ere*
o	as in f*o*r
ou	as in sm*o*ke
u	as in fl*u*me
	as in p*u*dding (when syllable ends with n)
	as in German umlaut 'ü' (when preceeded by j, q, x, y)
ui	as in s*way*
uo	as in *wa*r

Consonants

c	as in i*ts*
j	as in su*ds*
q	as in *ch*eer
x	as in *sh*e
z	as in su*ds*

Pronunciation Suggestions

zh   as in *ju*mp

Reprinted from *Chinese Folktales* by Howard Giskin, 1997. Used with permission of NTC / Contemporary Publishing Group, Inc.

NOTES ON CONTRIBUTORS

Roger T. Ames is Professor of Philosophy and Director of the Center for Chinese Studies at the University of Hawaii. He is editor of *Philosophy East and West* and *China Review International.* His recent publications include translations of Chinese classics: *Sun-tzu: The Art of Warfare* (1993); *Sun Pin: The Art of Warfare* (1996), and *Tracing Dao to Its Source* (1997) (both with D. C. Lau); and the *Confucian Analects* (with H. Rosemont) (1998). He has also authored many interpretive studies of Chinese philosophy and culture: *Thinking through Confucius* (1987), *Anticipating China: Thinking through the Narratives of Chinese and Western Culture* (1995), *and Thinking from the Han: Self, Truth, and Transcendence in Chinese and Western Culture* (1997) (all with D. L. Hall).

Fay Beauchamp, Professor of English at Community College of Philadelphia, credits the Asian Studies Development Program of the East-West Center/University of Hawaii with transforming her academic career into one centered on international education. She has traveled and studied abroad, including trips to Mexico, Italy, Indonesia, and Japan; the NEH Institute on Chinese Classics in the summer of 1996, directed by Henry Rosemont and Roger Ames, and the 1997 Asian Studies Development Program/East-West Center-sponsored Silk Road Field Trip from Xian to Kashgar led her to continued study of Chinese literature, art, and philosophy. Other activities include an NEH Summer Institute on Japan, sabbatical study at the East-West Center, founding an Asian Studies Regional Center at her college, and helping to design and implement a national workshop "Africa/East Asia: Challenging Cultural Faultlines." Dr. Beauchamp has been Co-Director of two U.S. Department of Education Title VI grants; the first year brought to her campus not only Professors Rosemont and Ames, but also Robert Hymes, Haili Kong, and Paul Rouzer, all of whom she thanks for enabling her to write this chapter.

Lawrence E. Butler is Associate Professor of Art History at George Mason University, where he has been active in interdisciplinary education programs across the humanities. A recipient of Fulbright, Mellon, and Kress Fellowships, he received his Ph.D. in Art History from the University of Pennsylvania in 1989 with concentrations in Byzantine and Islamic art and architecture. More recently he has extended his Medievalist interests to include China and the Silk Road.

Vance Cope-Kasten, though starting a little late, is a happy family man, which is partly why the theme of this book resonates so strongly. A latecomer to Chinese philosophy as well, he spent a sabbatical at the University of Michigan in 1995, receiving advanced beginner guidance from Donald J. Munro. He was awarded the Ph.D. from that same university in 1971 and a B.A. from Lawrence University in 1966. He has spent a year as a Fulbright Fellow at Albert-Ludwigs Universität in Freiburg, Germany, and is currently Professor of Philosophy and Chair of his Department at Ripon College in Wisconsin, where he has taught for three decades and where he harbors an interest in the philosophical significance of the concept of loneliness. The seminar on the Chinese Classics at St. Mary's College of Maryland in the summer of 1996 with Roger Ames and Henry Rosemont, Jr. was his second NEH grant; the first, in 1973, was to study violence at Brandeis University's Lemberg Center.

Mary Gallagher, a professor of Anthropology at Montgomery College in Maryland, manages to combine her scholarly research with her commitment to teaching. She did her undergraduate work at Rice University and earned a Ph.D. from the University of Colorado with a dissertation on the Women's Liberation Movement. She has visited the People's Republic of China several times between 1977 and 1999, and in 1985, she together with her family, taught and lived at Tsinghua University in Beijing for a year. In 1994 she developed and led a travel/study class to China. She has co-authored a text, *Discovering Culture: An Introduction to Anthropology*, and published articles on gender issues and Latin-American cultural change. A long-time teacher in the Montgomery College honors program, she regularly teaches a class on Archaeological and Cultural Field Methods that includes a ten-day stay in St. Croix, U.S. Virgin Islands. Dr. Gallagher is currently chair of her department and manages a grant from the Maryland Historical Trust for archaeology in Montgomery County.

Howard Giskin is Associate Professor of English at Appalachian State University in North Carolina, where he teaches World Literature. He received his Ph.D. in Comparative Literature from the University of Connecticut in 1988, has published in the area of Latin American Literature, and is the editor of *Chinese Folktales* (NTC/Contemporary, 1997). He has taught in Africa, China, Latin America, and Europe, and maintains a long-standing interest and involvement in international education. His interests have also included directing student summer study-abroad programs, as well as sponsoring conferences on World Literature.

Kathleen M. Higgins is Professor of Philosophy at the University of Texas at Austin. She works primarily in the fields of aesthetics and Nineteenth Century German philosophy. She is author of *Nietzsche's Zarathustra* (Temple, 1987), *The Music of Our Lives* (Temple, 1991), and (with Robert C. Solomon) *A Short History of Philosophy* (Oxford, 1996). She has also edited two books on comparative philosophy with Robert C. Solomon, *From Africa to Zen: An Invitation to World Philosophy*

(Rowman and Littlefield, 1993), and *World Philosophy: A Text with Readings* (McGraw-Hill, 1995).

Linda S. Pickle was born in Chicago and raised on a farm in Nebraska. She received the B.A. from the University of Nebraska and the M.A. and Ph.D. in German Language and Literature from the University of Colorado. She has studied and taught as a Fulbright scholar in Germany and as an exchange professor in Xi'an, China. Her teaching has been in the areas of German, Humanities, and Chinese Studies. Her forty-plus publications encompass German literature and pedagogy, German-American history, and women's literature and history. After more than two decades as Professor of German at Westminster College in Missouri, she is now the Head of the Modern Languages and Intercultural Studies Department at Western Kentucky University.

Judy Schaaf, Professor of English and Dean of the College of Arts and Sciences at the University of Massachusetts Dartmouth, has a career-long involvement with programs integrating the disciplines and developing understanding of world cultures. She has worked both within higher education and for public humanities councils to promote and enable such learning. A native Texan educated in New England, she spent a year in Slovenia as Fulbright lecturer. Her interest in Asian studies has been developed in seminars and institutes sponsored by the National Endowment for the Humanities, by a summer's work at the East-West Center, and by other such opportunities for continuing to learn in ways gracious and useful to her as teacher and academic administrator.

Bettye S. Walsh, Professor of English at Piedmont Virginia Community College in Charlottesville discovered that the world is large and complex while exploring South America on a Fulbright in the early nineties. Later, through the support of the Ellen Bayard Weedon Foundation, the National Endowment for Humanities and the East-West Center /University of Hawaii, she turned toward the East for continued professional development. Working and learning in the People's Republic of China, and most recently in Thailand, Cambodia, Myanmar, and Indonesia, confirm her earlier observations of the depth and immensity of other cultures—especially Asian and Southeast Asian. Her scholarly writing reflects interest in both Latin American and Asian literature and she shares her insights with students in a nontraditional world literature course and with colleagues in professional development workshops and conferences. She seeks balance and relatedness on her horse farm in Virginia.

INDEX

omy and, 96; maintenance of independence by, 95; during Mao period, 98–100; marriage and, 91, 94; Marriage Law and, 98, 99; in modern China, 97–102; negative associations with, 93; occupations for, 92; oppression and, 4; orthodox beliefs on, 93–95; pejorative references to, 30; post-Mao period, 100–102; property and, 92, 96; regional effects on, 92; resistance to marriage movement, 96; response to social position, 92–93; responsibilities, 91–92; secret societies of, 95; sisterhoods of, 96, 97; "Speak Bitterness" sessions, 97; subordinate position of, 30; Three Obediences and, 90, 101, 103; traditional lifestyle, 90–97; widow chastity, 94, 95
Women's Association, 98
Wong, Wucius, 35*n5*
Wordsworth, William, 147, 149
World view, 34; calligraphy and, 35*n4;* language and, 27; philosophical, 44–48
Writing. *See* Language, written and spoken
Wu, Fatima, 133
Wu, Hung, 67
Wu, Nelson, 182
Wudi (Emperor), 80
Wu Liang, 68

X

Xia Dynasty: language in, 11; sacrifice in, 63
Xia Gui, 75
Xie He, 71
Xie Jin, 208*n2*
Xie Linyun, 74
Xuan Zong (Emperor), 69
Xunzi, 42, 55, 114, 166

Y

Yan Guei Fei, 69

Yang Xiaoneng, 63
Yanmei Wei, 196, 200
Yau, Victoria, 176
Yeats, W. B., 139
Yellow Earth, 190
Yellow Emperor, 127, 137*n1*
Yijing. See Book of Changes
Yingjin Zhang, 203, 204
Yinyang, 11, 11*fig,* 12, 27; balance of, 70; defining, 56; in music, 110; in philosophy, 47–48
Youzi, 51
Yuan Dynasty: landscape painting in, 75; women artists in, 77
Yu Hua, 204
Yu Tzu, 51

Z

Zhang Jia-Xuan, 202
Zhang Yimou, 190, 198, 200, 202, 203, 204, 208*n2*
Zhao, Qiguang, 126, 127, 128
Zha Siting, 16
Zheng Yi, 196
Zhou Dynasty: ancestor worship in, 61, 64; architecture in, 168–169, 182; burial practice, 61; class rank in, 63; hereditary practice, 61; human sacrifice in, 62; landscape painting in, 73; language in, 13, 14, 15; monster masks in, 64; music in, 112; poetry in, 141; ritual bronzes in, 62, 63
Zhou Fang, 84*n14*
Zhuang Zhou, 54
Zhuangzhuang, 208*n2*
Zhuangzi, 42, 53, 54
Zhu Xi, 71
Zigong, 46
Zilu, 7
Zong Bing, 73